EDUCATION IN A COMPETITIVE AND GLOBALIZING WORLD

ELEMENTARY AND SECONDARY EDUCATION ACT

REFORM, REAUTHORIZATION AND ACCOUNTABILITY CONSIDERATIONS

EDUCATION IN A COMPETITIVE AND GLOBALIZING WORLD

Additional books in this series can be found on Nova's website under the Series tab.

Additional E-books in this series can be found on Nova's website under the E-book tab.

EDUCATION IN A COMPETITIVE AND GLOBALIZING WORLD

ELEMENTARY AND SECONDARY EDUCATION ACT

REFORM, REAUTHORIZATION AND ACCOUNTABILITY CONSIDERATIONS

DANIEL M. BROWN
AND
AUDRIANNA DAVIES
EDITORS

Nova Science Publishers, Inc.
New York

For permission to use material from this book please contact us:
Telephone 631-231-7269; Fax 631-231-8175
Web Site: http://www.novapublishers.com

Additional color graphics may be available in the e-book version of this book.

Library of Congress Cataloging-in-Publication Data

Library of Congress Control Number: 2011946298

ISBN: 978-1-61942-694-8

Published by Nova Science Publishers, Inc. ✝ New York

CONTENTS

PREFACE

The effectiveness of the nation's schools is a concern at all levels of government. It is generally held that all students in elementary and secondary education should have access to quality public schools, providing all students with an opportunity to meet rigorous academic standards. This book examines the federal government's evolving role in supporting state and local accountability for elementary and secondary education and discusses how this role may continue to evolve or change during reauthorization.

Chapter 1 - Federal policies aiming to improve the effectiveness of schools have historically focused largely on inputs, such as supporting teacher professional development, class-size reduction, and compensatory programs or services for disadvantaged students. Over the last two decades, however, interest in developing federal policies that focus on student outcomes has increased. Most recently, the enactment of the No Child Left Behind Act of 2001 (NCLB; P.L. 107-110), which amended and reauthorized the Elementary and Secondary Education Act (ESEA), marked a dramatic expansion of the federal government's role in supporting standards-based instruction and test-based accountability, thereby increasing the federal government's involvement in decisions that directly affect teaching and learning.

As states and local educational agencies (LEAs) have implemented the federal accountability requirements, numerous issues have arisen that may be addressed during ESEA reauthorization. Among these issues are those pertaining to the comparability of data across states and the development of state accountability systems of varying degrees of rigor, the one-size-fits-all set of consequences applied to schools that fail to make adequate yearly progress (AYP), the narrowing of the focus of instruction at the school level, and the evaluation of teachers.

Chapter 2 - Policymaking at the federal level reflects a growing awareness that improving educational outcomes depends greatly upon increasing the quality of classroom instruction. In establishing the student performance standards and accountability provisions in the No Child Left Behind Act of 2001 (NCLB), legislators recognized that the success of these reforms rests largely on improving teachers' knowledge and skills. Thus, in enacting NCLB, Congress amended the Elementary and Secondary Education Act (ESEA) to establish a requirement that all teachers be *highly qualified* and authorized the Title II, Teacher and Principal Training and Recruiting Fund to assist schools' efforts to meet this new requirement.

Chapter 3 - Congress has historically recognized the importance of teacher quality in improving the academic performance of elementary and secondary school students; however, federal policy has only recently begun to address the impact of teacher compensation systems on both quality and performance. Growing concern about the dominant feature of these systems—the single salary schedule—has led to a variety of compensation reform efforts around the country. These efforts include pay-for-performance incentives that attempt to align teacher compensation more closely with student achievement, as well as other reforms that link increased pay to improved teacher competency or to service in hard-to-staff positions.

Congress provided significant support to several existing compensation reform efforts by enacting the Teacher Incentive Fund (TIF) through the Labor-HHS-Education Appropriations Act of 2006 (P.L. 109-149). The concise passage that provides program authority for TIF states that funds are intended to "develop and implement performance-based teacher and principal compensation systems in high-need schools." Little additional guidance has been provided with respect to how these reforms are to be implemented.

Chapter 4 - The primary source of federal aid to K-12 education is the Elementary and Secondary Education Act (ESEA), particularly its Title I, Part A program of Education for the Disadvantaged. The ESEA was initially enacted in 1965 (P.L. 89-10), and was most recently amended and reauthorized by the No Child Left Behind Act of 2001 (NCLB, P.L. 107-110), which authorized virtually all ESEA programs through FY2008. It is widely expected that the 112th Congress will consider whether to amend and extend the ESEA.

The NCLB initiated a major expansion of federal influence upon several aspects of public K-12 education, primarily with the aim of increasing the accountability of public school systems and individual public schools for improving achievement outcomes of all students, especially the disadvantaged. States must implement in all public schools and school districts a variety of standards-based assessments in reading, math and science; make complex annual adequate yearly progress (AYP) determinations for each public school and district; and require virtually all public school teachers and aides to meet a variety of qualification requirements. State AYP policies must incorporate an ultimate goal of all public school students reaching a proficient or higher level of achievement by the end of the 2013-14 school year. Further, participating states must enforce a series of increasingly substantial consequences for most of their schools and almost all school districts that fail to meet the AYP standards for two consecutive years or more. All of these requirements are associated with state participation in the ESEA Title I-A program.

Chapter 5 - This blueprint builds on the significant reforms already made in response to the American Recovery and Reinvestment Act of 2009 around four areas: (1) Improving teacher and principal effectiveness to ensure that every classroom has a great teacher and every school has a great leader; (2) Providing information to families to help them evaluate and improve their children's schools, and to educators to help them improve their students' learning; (3) Implementing college- and career-ready standards and developing improved assessments aligned with those standards; and (4) Improving student learning and achievement in America's lowest-performing schools by providing intensive support and effective interventions.

Incorporating and extending this framework, this blueprint for a re-envisioned federal role builds on these key priorities.

In: Elementary and Secondary Education Act
Editors: D. M. Brown and A. Davies
ISBN: 978-1-61942-694-8

Chapter 1

Accountability Issues and Reauthorization of the Elementary and Secondary Education Act

Rebecca R. Skinner and Erin D. Lomax

Summary

Federal policies aiming to improve the effectiveness of schools have historically focused largely on inputs, such as supporting teacher professional development, class-size reduction, and compensatory programs or services for disadvantaged students. Over the last two decades, however, interest in developing federal policies that focus on student outcomes has increased. Most recently, the enactment of the No Child Left Behind Act of 2001 (NCLB; P.L. 107-110), which amended and reauthorized the Elementary and Secondary Education Act (ESEA), marked a dramatic expansion of the federal government's role in supporting standards-based instruction and test-based accountability, thereby increasing the federal government's involvement in decisions that directly affect teaching and learning.

As states and local educational agencies (LEAs) have implemented the federal accountability requirements, numerous issues have arisen that may be addressed during ESEA reauthorization. Among these issues are those pertaining to the comparability of data across states and the development of state accountability systems of varying degrees of rigor, the one-size-fits-all set of consequences applied to schools that fail to make adequate yearly progress (AYP), the narrowing of the focus of instruction at the school level, and the evaluation of teachers.

- Commonality versus flexibility: States have had the flexibility to select their own content and performance standards, as well as the assessments aligned with these standards. This has resulted in a different accountability system in each state, making it difficult to sum up where students are in terms of skills and knowledge and to gauge the net effect of the NCLB.

- Absolute versus differentiated consequences: Schools simply do or do not meet AYP standards, and there is generally no distinction between those that fail to meet only one or two required performance or participation thresholds to a marginal degree versus those that fail to meet numerous thresholds to a substantial extent.
- Incentives to focus on proficiency: Schools and LEAs are held accountable for the achievement of all student subgroups. They are not, however, held accountable for students at all levels of achievement. Because the goal of the current system is for 100% of students to become "proficient" by school year 2013-2014, schools and teachers may target instructional time and resources towards students who are nearing proficiency rather than distributing resources equally across students at all achievement levels.
- Assessment and the narrowing of the curricular focus: Because assessments are aligned with state content standards, there may be a risk that "teaching to the standards" becomes "teaching to the test." The practice of "teaching to the test"—whether intentional or unintentional—may narrow the curriculum.
- Teacher evaluation and accountability: The NCLB added a requirement that all teachers be highly qualified. Over time, however, the requirement has come to be seen by many as a minimum standard for entry into the profession and a growing body of research has revealed its underlying emphasis on teachers' credentials to be weakly correlated with student achievement. As such, the Administration has moved toward measuring teacher effectiveness based on student achievement, and promoted a focus on output-based accountability for teachers.

INTRODUCTION

The effectiveness of the nation's schools is a concern at all levels of government. It is generally held that all students in elementary and secondary education should have access to quality public schools, providing all students with an opportunity to meet rigorous academic standards. Examining whether students are being held to well-defined academic standards and achievement at desired levels has become one of the primary foci of federal education policy in elementary and secondary schools.

Federal policies aiming to improve the effectiveness of schools have historically focused largely on inputs, such as supporting teacher professional development, class-size reduction, and compensatory programs or services for disadvantaged students. Over the last two decades, however, interest in developing federal policies that focus on student outcomes has increased. Most recently, the enactment of the No Child Left Behind Act of 2001 (NCLB; P.L. 107-110), which amended and reauthorized the Elementary and Secondary Education Act (ESEA), marked a dramatic expansion of the federal government's role in supporting standards-based instruction and test-based accountability, thereby increasing the federal government's involvement in decisions that directly affect teaching and learning.

The 112th Congress may act to reauthorize the ESEA. In approaching this task, Congress may grapple with several substantial issues related to the current accountability requirements included in the ESEA and how, or if, those requirements should be altered. For example, the following issues may receive attention: exploring ways to enhance consistency across state standards and assessments while ensuring sufficient flexibility for states with respect to these decisions, modifying consequences for failure to meet academic targets, incorporating outcomes-based accountability in teacher evaluations and compensation systems, and examining the role of the federal government in improving public elementary and secondary education.

The first part of this report examines the federal government's evolving role in supporting state and local accountability for elementary and secondary education and discusses how this role may continue to evolve or change during reauthorization. The discussion begins with the emergence of this role from the standards-based reform movement that gained traction in the 1980s and the resulting changes made to the ESEA during the 1994 reauthorization. This is followed by a detailed examination of the accountability requirements included in the NCLB. The discussion also examines the authority of the Secretary of Education (hereafter referred to as the Secretary) to make changes to the ESEA that some may view as effectively reauthorizing at least a portion of the ESEA. The second part of the report focuses on broad NCLB implementation issues that have arisen and how the federal role in elementary and secondary education may evolve or change in response during ESEA reauthorization.

EVOLVING ROLE OF THE FEDERAL GOVERNMENT IN EDUCATION-RELATED ACCOUNTABILITY

Historically, education has been the domain of state and local governments. Since the initial enactment of the Elementary and Secondary Education Act in 1965 (P.L. 89-10), federal education policy has focused on equity. For example, since its inception the ESEA has focused on serving disadvantaged students and on meeting their academic needs to close the achievement gap that exists between disadvantaged students and their more advantaged peers. Other federal education policies that were enacted after ESEA, such as the Individuals with Disabilities Education Act and Title IX, have also focused on providing equity. That is, federal education efforts in recent decades have been geared at pushing states and LEAs to provide equal educational opportunities for all students. The role of the federal government with respect to elementary and secondary education, however, began to change substantially in the early 1990s, as a focus on standards and assessments for all students was added to the traditional focus on equity. This section examines the evolution of this changing role beginning with the standards- based reform movement through the Improving America's Schools Act (IASA; P.L. 103-3 82), which reauthorized the ESEA in 1994. Subsequent sections of the report provide an in-depth analysis of the requirements of the NCLB and associated issues.

Standards-Based Reform Movement

During the 1980s, waves of education reform swept across the nation. The first wave included activities that were mostly characterized as "top-down" reforms, meaning that they were imposed on schools primarily from the state level.[1] These included, among other activities, increased requirements for high school graduation, attempts to lengthen the school day or year, increased testing of students' basic skills, and establishment of higher standards for entry or continuation in teaching. Generally, this initial wave of reform is considered to have had little positive effect on student achievement.[2]

Prompted in part by the limited success of the initial wave of the 1980s reforms, policymakers pursued other approaches to reform. The second wave of reform focused on empowerment, variation, and "bottom-up" decision making where policymakers sought to achieve the conditions necessary for educational success in individual schools. Some of these efforts focused on schools as the unit of change, calling for such action as greater school-site autonomy, increased competition among schools, and a greater role for parents in making educational decisions for their children.

In several states (e.g., Kentucky), a third approach that melded elements of top-down and bottom- up strategies was initiated. This course of action was premised on the need for system-wide reform, addressing the needs and problems at all levels of the system in a coherent and integrated fashion. At the heart of this reform was the premise that relevant reform action should be guided by educational goals and standards at each level of educational governance—particularly, state and local—and that reform action should occur simultaneously at these levels.

According to the Consortium for Policy Research in Education (CPRE), "[m]ore state activity aimed at improving public education took place in the 1980s than ever before."[3] This observation was based on the number of education-related bills that were introduced at the state level, increased state aid for education, and the number of state-level education-related task forces and commissions. This increase in state activity may be attributable, in part, to improved state policymaking capacities and growing state tax bases, as well as the publication of *A Nation At Risk*, which decried the condition of education in the nation.[4]

Not only were many states actively engaged in the standards-based reform movement, an event held in 1989 that brought together President George H. W. Bush and state governors, including then-Governor Bill Clinton of Arkansas, would mark a turning point in the federal government's involvement in the standards-based reform movement. At the first national education summit conference in the country's history, President Bush and the nation's governors endorsed the establishment of National Education Goals that would provide a framework for restructuring the federal role in elementary and secondary education. In the following year, they announced six goals. These policymakers agreed that setting goals would be an empty gesture unless progress toward the goals was measured and reported to the nation. To that end, they concluded that there should be standards defining what students need to know in each subject area, standards for performance in those subjects, and assessments to measure student performance. They also created the National Education Goals Panel (NEGP) to monitor national and state progress toward the goals.

Goals 2000

The groundwork laid at the first national education summit coalesced in the enactment of the Goals 2000: Educate America Act (P.L. 103-227)[5] in 1994. Goals 2000 represented a new, structured federal role in the education reform movement that was occurring at the state and local levels. The first three titles of P.L. 103-227 codified eight National Education Goals to be achieved by 2000 (Title I), created a National Education Goals Panel to monitor progress toward the goals (Title II), and authorized a standards-based reform state grant program (Title III). Title I of Goals 2000 enacted into law the six goals originally adopted by President Bush and the governors in 1990 and added two additional goals (the fourth and eighth goals listed below). These goals provided that by the year 2000,

1. all children will start school ready to learn;
2. the high school graduation rate will be at least 90%;
3. students will master a challenging curriculum at grades 4, 8, and 12;
4. teachers will have access to professional development opportunities;
5. U.S. students will be the first in the world in science and math achievement;
6. all adults will be literate;
7. schools will be free of drugs, violence, and firearms; and
8. every school will promote parental involvement in education.

Three kinds of education standards were addressed initially by Goals 2000—curriculum content standards, student performance standards, and Opportunity-to-Learn standards.[6]

To provide national oversight and direction of the standards effort, Title II authorized the establishment of two entities—NEGP (which was created prior to the enactment of Goals 2000) and the National Education Standards and Improvement Council (NESIC). While NESIC was never established,[7] NEGP was charged with reporting annually on state and local progress toward the National Education Goals, reporting on promising or effective measures taken to achieve the goals, and assisting in the creation of a national consensus around the reforms needed to achieve the goals.

Title III authorized a formula grant program to support state standards-based reform by financing the development of state reform plans addressing such elements as teaching, learning, assessments, parental and community support for reform, and education management. Goals 2000 required that a state plan include processes for developing content and performance standards, developing state assessments, aligning curricula and assessments with state content and performance standards, and providing teachers with information about the state standards.

Also authorized by Title III were two waiver authorities. The first permitted the Secretary to waive various regulations of several major U.S. Department of Education (ED) programs for periods not to exceed four years, if requested by individual states or LEAs. To receive a waiver, states or LEAs had to be receiving systemic reform funds or be undertaking comparable reform activities. Under the second waiver authority, the Education Flexibility Partnership Demonstration Act (Ed-Flex), not more than six states[8] could receive authority to determine, on their own, which statutory and regulatory requirements to waive in relation to several major ED programs.[9]

The Goals 2000 legislation triggered widespread controversy at the state and local level. The primary concerns arose over the proper federal role in education. Traditional federal education programs focused on special populations of students, particularly those that states and localities would not, or could not, adequately serve. In contrast, Goals 2000 targeted federal funds and support on some of the central functions of state and local educational systems (e.g., standards for curriculum and student performance) and to the needs of the entire student population. Debate on these issues centered largely on whether the legislation was part of a federal effort to centralize and standardize education.

The Improving America's Schools Act

Following directly on the heels of Goals 2000 was reauthorization of the ESEA. In reauthorizing the ESEA in 1994 through the Improving America's Schools Act (IASA; P.L. 103-382), Congress continued the federal focus on standards-based reform by inserting provisions related to standards and assessments in Title I-A. Title I-A authorizes federal grants to LEAs to provide supplementary educational and related services to low-achieving children attending schools with concentrations of students from low-income families. Title I-A is currently the largest federal elementary and secondary education program; it is funded at $14 billion and accounts for over half of the $25 billion appropriated for ESEA overall.

The IASA attempted to raise the instructional standards of Title I programs, and the academic expectations for participating students, by tying Title I instruction to state-selected content and performance standards. Further, IASA attempted to make Title I tests and evaluations more meaningful and less time consuming by using state-developed or state-adopted assessments, tied to the content standard, for determining the effectiveness of Title I programs. This measure of effectiveness was based on whether schools and LEAs were making "adequate yearly progress" (AYP) toward meeting the content and performance standards. The results on these assessments were also to become the basis for implementing program improvement requirements, including financial rewards to "distinguished" schools and LEAs and corrective actions for "unsuccessful" ones.

As a condition of the receipt of Title I-A funds, states were required to develop or adopt content and performance standards, as well as assessments aligned with the standards. If a state had standards and assessments that were applicable to all LEAs and students statewide, then these standards and assessments had to be used for Title I programs and students.[10] However, the Title I statutory requirements did not require states to have standards and assessments that were applicable to all students statewide.[11] Thus, in discussions of "state systems of standards and assessments" in reference to IASA, it should be kept in mind that the standards and assessments were not necessarily uniform for all students statewide.

Under IASA, states were required to adopt standards and assessments in the subjects of reading/language arts (hereafter referred to as reading) and mathematics at three grade levels—at least once in each of the grade ranges of 3-5, 6-9, and 10-12. More specifically, in order to receive Title I-A funds, states were required to develop or adopt curriculum content standards, as well as academic achievement standards and assessments tied to the standards. The performance standards were required to establish three performance levels for all students—advanced, proficient, and partially proficient. States were also required to develop assessment systems that included all students in the grades being assessed who had attended schools in the LEA for at least one year. Limited English proficient (LEP) students were to be assessed, to the extent practicable, in the language and form most likely to yield accurate and reliable information on what they know and can do. "Reasonable" adaptations and accommodations had to be provided for students with "diverse learning needs," including LEP students and students with disabilities, where such adaptations and accommodations were necessary to measure the achievement of those students relative to state standards. The assessment system had to be capable of producing results for each state, LEA, and school that could be disaggregated by gender, major racial and ethnic groups, English proficiency status, migrant status, disability status, and economically disadvantaged status. These data were to be included in annual school profiles.

Several statutory constraints were placed on the authority of the Secretary in enforcing the standards and assessment requirements. For example, state standards did not have to be linked to national standards that might be developed by any organization or entity. No state could be required to submit its content or performance standards or assessments to the U.S. Department of Education (ED). ED was prohibited from disapproving a state plan on the basis of specific content or performance standards or assessments. In addition, nothing in the act authorized ED to "mandate, direct, or control" a state's, LEA's, or school's standards, curricula, assessments, or program of instruction as a condition for receipt of Title I funds.

States were given several years to meet the IASA requirements, in part because states were at widely varying stages of the process of developing instructional goals, curriculum frameworks, and assessment systems that were aligned with these goals and frameworks. States were given until the beginning of the 1997-1998 school year to develop or adopt content and performance standards for reading and mathematics. Assessments that were aligned with these standards had to be developed or adopted by the start of the 2000-2001 school year.[12] The full system of standards and assessments was not required to be in place until the 2000-2001 school year. Under IASA, state standards developed under Title III of Goals 2000 were considered to meet the Title I-A standards requirements under IASA.

Despite the increased federal emphasis on the development and implementation of state standards and assessments for all students, about half of the states failed to meet the 1997-1998 school year deadline included in Title I-A for the development of content standards. By March 2000, however, all but two states had adopted the required content standards, but only about half of the states had approved performance standards.

It is important to note that IASA did not mark the beginning of federal efforts to hold states and LEAs accountable for student performance under Title I-A. Since enactment of the ESEA in 1965, the ESEA has included requirements that states and LEAs report on the academic progress of students being served under Title I-A. Subsequent evaluations of Title I found that LEAs were not effectively implementing testing systems, were using tests to draw inferences that were inappropriate based on the tests, and were measuring only basic skills.[13] That is, LEAs essentially had low expectations for disadvantaged students, rather than high expectations for all students. The standards and assessment provisions enacted through IASA addressed three long-standing and widely shared concerns about Title I programs. In addition to believing that Title I programs had not been sufficiently challenging academically, perpetuating low expectations for the achievement of participating students, many analysts also felt that Title I programs had not been well integrated with the "regular" instructional programs of participants and had required extensive student testing that was of little instructional or diagnostic value and was not linked to the curriculum to which the students were exposed.

THE NO CHILD LEFT BEHIND ACT

Many of the underpinnings of the accountability requirements included in Title I-A of the No Child Left Behind Act of 2001 (NCLB; P.L. 107-110) are evident in the accountability requirements included in the IASA; in some cases, the requirements were substantially expanded. For example, in addition to the IASA's requirement for states to implement standards and assessments in reading and mathematics at three grade levels, the NCLB required states participating in ESEA Title I-A to

- develop and adopt standards and assessments in the subjects of mathematics and reading in *each* of grades 3-8 by the end of the 2005-2006 school year, assuming certain minimum levels of annual federal funding were provided for state assessment grants;
- adopt standards in science (at three grade levels—grades 3-5, 6-9, and 10-12) by the end of the 2005-2006 school year; and
- adopt assessments in science (at three grade levels) by the end of the 2007-2008 school year. [14]

The academic achievement standards must include at least three levels of performance: partially proficient (basic), proficient, and advanced. The same academic content and achievement standards must apply to all students.[15] The assessments must be aligned with the state's academic content and achievement standards.

State accountability systems must be based on the academic standards and assessments required above, be the same accountability system for all public schools (except that public schools and LEAs that do not receive Title I-A funds are not subject to outcome accountability requirements), and incorporate rewards and sanctions based on student performance. To the extent practicable, LEP students are to be assessed in the language and form most likely to yield accurate and reliable information on what they know and can do in academic content areas (in subjects other than English itself). However, students who have attended schools in the United States (excluding Puerto Rico) for three or more consecutive school years are to be assessed in English.[16] In addition, "reasonable" adaptations and accommodations are to be provided for students with disabilities, consistent with the provisions of the IDEA.[17]

Similar to IASA, several statutory constraints have been placed on the authority of the Secretary to enforce these standard and assessment requirements. First, the ESEA states that nothing in Title I shall be construed to authorize any federal official or agency to "mandate, direct, or control a State, local educational agency, or school's specific instructional content, academic achievement standards and assessments, curriculum, or program of instruction." Second, states may not be required to submit their standards to the Secretary or to have their content or achievement standards approved or certified by the federal government in order to receive funds under the ESEA, other than the (limited) review necessary in order to determine whether the state meets the Title I-A technical requirements. Finally, no state plan may be disapproved by ED on the basis of specific content or achievement standards, or assessment items or instruments.

Adequate Yearly Progress

A key concept embodied in the outcome accountability requirements of the NCLB—that of AYP for schools, LEAs, and (with much less emphasis) states overall[18]—expands on earlier provisions included in the IASA. The primary purpose of AYP requirements is to serve as the basis for identifying schools and LEAs where performance is inadequate, so that these inadequacies may be addressed, first through provision of increased support and opportunities for families to exercise choice to transfer to another school or obtain supplemental educational services (SES), and ultimately through a series of more substantial consequences (described in a later section of this report, "Performance-Based Accountability"). These actions are to be taken with respect to schools or LEAs that fail to meet AYP for two consecutive years or more.

AYP standards under the NCLB must be applied to *all* public schools, LEAs, and to states overall, if a state chooses to receive Title I-A grants.[19] However, consequences for failing to meet AYP standards for two consecutive years or more need only be applied to schools and LEAs participating in Title I-A,[20] and there are no sanctions for states overall beyond potential identification and the provision of technical assistance.

AYP is determined based on three components: student academic achievement on the required state reading and mathematics assessments, with a focus on the percentage of students scoring at the proficient level or higher;[21] 95% student participation rates in assessments by all students and for any subgroup for which data are disaggregated; and performance on another academic indicator, which must be graduation rates for high schools.[22] Schools or LEAs meet AYP standards only if they meet the required threshold levels of performance on all three indicators for the all-students group and any subgroup for which data are disaggregated. AYP calculations based on assessment scores must be disaggregated; that is, they must be determined separately and specifically not only for all students but also for several demographic groups of students within each school, LEA, and state. The specified demographic groups (often referred to as subgroups) are economically disadvantaged students, LEP students, students with disabilities, and students in major racial and ethnic groups.[23]

It is generally acknowledged that one of the most positive contributions of the NCLB requirements has been the reporting of data by student subgroups, thereby making it possible to see how disadvantaged students are performing relative to other students. The results highlight substantial achievement gaps between minority students and white students, LEP students and non-LEP students, students with and without disabilities, and economically disadvantaged students and their more economically advantaged peers. Having these results echoed nationwide has spurred and may continue to spur attention at the state and local levels on meeting the academic needs of underserved students, which has been a primary goal of ESEA since its inception. Changes to the ESEA over the past two decades have also helped to ensure that all students are held to the same academically challenging standards rather than having lower academic expectations for students served by the Title I-A program. What is unclear, however, is whether the law has actually improved student achievement for the majority of disadvantaged students and whether the federal government has employed policy levers that can bring about this change through the ESEA.

Annual Measurable Objectives

States must develop annual measurable objectives (AMOs) that are established separately for reading and mathematics assessments, are the same for all schools and LEAs, identify a single minimum percentage of students who must meet or exceed the proficient level on the assessments that applies to the all students group and each subgroup for which data are disaggregated, and must ensure that all students will meet or exceed the state's proficient level of achievement on the assessments based on a timeline established by the state. The timeline must incorporate concrete movement toward meeting an ultimate goal of all students reaching a proficient or higher level of achievement by the end of the 2013-2014 school year. This was adopted in response to pre-NCLB AYP requirements in most states that required little or no net improvement in student performance over time.

While NCLB substantially increased federal involvement in student assessment and learning, an argument could be made that this involvement stems from the traditional federal education policy on equity. By requiring each state to ensure that all students make progress toward the ultimate goal of proficiency, that all students are held to the same content and performance standards, and that results are disaggregated and publicly reported for historically disadvantaged student groups, the federal requirements have pressured states into developing one set of expectations for all students and forced them to acknowledge when specific groups of students are not meeting those expectations. Without this federal involvement, it is impossible to know whether states would have taken similar actions. However, as discussed in a subsequent section, the expectations for students across states are anything but consistent.

Performance-Based Accountability: Consequences and Rewards

The NCLB requires states to identify LEAs, and LEAs to identify schools, that fail to meet state AYP standards for two consecutive years for program improvement, and to take a variety of further actions with respect to schools or LEAs that fail to meet AYP standards for additional years after being identified for improvement.[24] Although states are encouraged to establish unitary accountability systems affecting all public schools, and some states do so to varying degrees, the Title I-A statute only requires them to apply performance-based accountability measures to schools and LEAs that receive Title I-A funds, not all schools and LEAs.[25] The "accountability stages" are depicted in Table 1.

School Improvement, Corrective Action, and Restructuring

Title I-A schools that fail to meet AYP standards for two consecutive years must be identified for program improvement. When Title I-A schools do not make AYP for two or more consecutive years, they become subject to a range of increasingly severe performance-based accountability requirements, which are coupled with technical assistance provided by the LEA.

Table 1. ESEA Title I-A Performance-Based Accountability Stages for Schools and LEAs

Cumulative Years Not Making AYP	Accountability Stage	
	School	LEA
1	N/A	N/A
2	School improvement	LEA improvement[a]
3	Second year of school improvement[b]	LEA improvement[a]
4	Corrective action[b]	Corrective action[b]
5	Plan for restructuring[b]	Corrective action[b]
6	Implement restructuring[b]	Corrective action[b]

Source: Table prepared by CRS based on analysis of the requirements of ESEA, Section 1116.

Note: N/A—Not Applicable.

[a] State educational agencies (SEAs) may implement corrective action for an LEA identified for LEA improvement.

[b] Accountability requirements associated with the second year of school improvement, corrective action, and restructuring may be delayed for up to one year for a school or LEA if it makes AYP for one year, or if its failure to make AYP is due to a natural disaster or a significant decline in financial resources.

School Improvement

After not making AYP for two consecutive years, a Title I-A school is identified for school improvement. Being designated for school improvement carries with it the requirement to develop or revise a school plan designed to result in the improvement of the school. LEAs are required to provide schools within their jurisdictions with technical assistance in the design and implementation of school improvement plans. Schools identified for improvement must use at least 10% of their Title I-A funding for professional development.

All students attending Title I-A schools identified for school improvement must be offered public school choice—the opportunity to transfer to another public school within the same LEA.[26] Under public school choice, students must be afforded the opportunity to choose from among two or more schools, located within the same LEA, that have not been identified for school improvement, corrective action, or restructuring, and that also have not been identified as persistently dangerous schools.[27] LEAs are required to provide students who transfer to different schools with transportation and must give priority in choosing schools to the lowest-achieving children from low-income families. LEAs may not use lack of capacity as a reason for denying students the opportunity to transfer to a school of choice.[28] In instances where there are no eligible schools in the student's LEA, LEAs are encouraged to enter into cooperative agreements with surrounding LEAs to enable students to transfer to an eligible public school.

If a school does not make AYP for another year after being identified for an initial year of school improvement, it must be identified for a second year of school improvement. All students attending a school identified for a second year of school improvement must continue to be offered the option of attending another eligible public school within the same LEA. In addition, students from low-income families who continue to attend the school must be offered the opportunity to receive supplemental educational services (SES).[29] SES are educational activities, such as tutoring, that are provided outside of normal school hours and which are designed to augment or enhance the educational services provided during regular periods of instruction. Supplemental educational services may be provided by a non-profit entity, a for-profit entity, or the LEA, unless such services are determined by the state educational agency (SEA) to be unavailable in the local area.[30] The SEA is required to maintain a list of approved SES providers (including those offering services through distance learning) from which parents can select. LEAs may be required to expend up to an amount equal to 20% of their Title I-A grants on transportation for public school choice and supplemental educational services combined.[31]

Corrective Action

If a school fails to make AYP for a total of two years after being identified for school improvement, it must be identified for corrective action by the end of the school year. For schools identified for corrective action, LEAs must continue to provide technical assistance, offer public school choice and supplemental educational services, and implement one of the following corrective actions: replacing school staff relevant to the school not making AYP, implementing a new curriculum, limiting management authority at the school level, appointing an expert advisor to assist in implementing the school improvement plan, extending the school year or the school day, or restructuring the school's internal organization.

Restructuring

If a school does not make AYP for a third year after being identified for school improvement, by the end of the school year the LEA must begin to plan for restructuring while continuing to implement the requirements of corrective action. Restructuring of the school must involve implementation of some form of alternative governance structure, such as reopening the school as a charter school, replacing all or most of the school staff, contracting with an education management organization to operate the school, or turning the school over to the SEA. If an additional year passes without the school making AYP, the LEA must implement restructuring of the school.

Any of the sanctions described above may be delayed for up to one year if the school makes AYP for a single year, or if the school's failure to make AYP is due to unforeseen circumstances, such as a natural disaster or a significant decline in financial resources of the LEA or school. Schools that make AYP for two consecutive years may no longer be identified for school improvement nor be subject to the sanctions associated with school improvement, corrective action, or restructuring.

In addition, in 2008 ED announced a pilot program under which the Secretary would grant waivers to up to 10 states proposing to implement alternative performance-based accountability policies incorporating differentiated consequences.[32] Under these policies, states could distinguish among schools identified for improvement, focusing resources upon, and applying the most significant consequences to, schools with the lowest performance levels. Among the nine states initially approved for the pilot program,[33] the state accountability plans have three characteristics in common: (1) placement of schools identified for improvement into two or more categories, particularly a highest-priority group on which the most substantial consequences and improvement resources would be focused; (2) some adjustment of the order and/or severity of consequences for schools placed into different improvement categories, particularly with respect to school choice and SES; and (3) in many cases, narrowing of certain consequences or actions to focus more specifically on pupil groups with the lowest levels of performance.[34]

As the 2013-2014 deadline for all students to be proficient in reading/language arts and mathematics approaches, the number of schools that fail to make AYP will almost certainly increase as the percentage of students required to be at the proficient level increases. As the number of schools failing to make AYP grows, states and LEAs may become increasingly taxed with respect to their ability to help all of the schools.

LEA Improvement and Corrective Actions

Procedures analogous to those for schools apply to LEAs that receive Title I-A grants and fail to meet AYP requirements. While states are encouraged to implement unitary accountability systems applicable to all students and schools, states may choose to base decisions regarding LEA status and corrective actions only on the Title I-A schools in each LEA. Further, as noted earlier, identification as needing improvement and corrective actions need only be taken with respect to LEAs that receive Title I-A grants, although this includes over 90% of all LEAs nationwide.

LEAs that fail to meet state AYP standards for two consecutive years are to be identified as needing improvement. Technical assistance, "based on scientifically based research," is to be provided to the LEA by the SEA, and parents of students served by the LEA are to be notified that it has been identified as needing improvement.

SEAs are to take corrective action with respect to LEAs that fail to meet state standards for a fourth year (two years of failing to meet AYP standards after having been identified for improvement without, in the meantime, meeting AYP standards for two consecutive years). Such corrective action is to include at least one of the following (at SEA discretion): reducing administrative funds or deferring program funds, implementing a new curriculum, replacing relevant LEA staff, removing specific schools from the jurisdiction of the LEA, appointing a receiver or trustee to administer the LEA, abolishing or restructuring the LEA, or authorizing students to transfer to higher-performing schools in another LEA (and providing transportation) in conjunction with at least one of these actions.

Rewards Based on Performance

Each state participating in ESEA Title I-A is required to establish an Academic Achievement Awards Program for purposes of making academic achievement awards to schools that have either significantly closed academic achievement gaps between student subgroups or exceeded their AYP requirements for two or more consecutive years. States may also give awards to LEAs that have exceeded their AYP requirements for two or more consecutive years. Under Academic Achievement Awards Programs, states may recognize and provide financial awards to teachers or principals in schools that have significantly closed the academic achievement gap or that have made AYP for two consecutive years. States may fund Academic Achievement Awards for schools and LEAs by reserving up to 5% of any Title I-A funding that is in excess of the state's previous-year allocation.[35]

Recent AYP Results for Schools and LEAs

Nationwide, 33.7% of all public schools and 36.3% of all LEAs failed to make AYP based on AYP determinations for the 2008-2009 school year.[36] Table 1 provides data on the percentage of schools and LEAs failing to make adequately yearly progress, on the basis of 2008-2009 assessment results, as reported by ED, based on Consolidated State Performance Reports.[37] These data are based on all public schools and LEAs in each state, not just those participating in Title I- A.[38] Overall, 48 states, including the District of Columbia and Puerto Rico, had at least 10% of their public schools fail to make AYP based on AYP determinations for the 2008-2009 school year (Table 2). Ten states, however, had over 50% of their public schools fail to make AYP. At the LEA level, 38 states had at least 10% of their LEAs fail to make AYP, while 19 states had at least half of their LEAs fail to make AYP.[39] The percentage of public schools failing to make adequate yearly progress for 2008-2009 varied widely among the states, from 5% for Texas to 76.6% for Florida (Table A-1).[40] Among the states, there was even greater variation with respect to the percentage of LEAs making AYP. Two states—Maine and Wisconsin—reported that just under 1% of their LEAs failed to make adequate yearly progress, while 94.5% of the LEAs in West Virginia failed to meet AYP standards.

Recent Performance-Based Accountability Results for Schools

As shown in Table 3, most states, including the District of Columbia and Puerto Rico, had at least 10% of their Title I-A schools in some form of performance-based accountability sanction during the 2009-2010 school year, and over half of the states have at least 20% of their Title I-A schools in improvement, corrective action, or restructuring.[41] Overall, about 28% of Title I-A schools in the nation have been identified for improvement (Table A-2). However, the percentage of schools identified varies widely by state, ranging from about 3% of Title I-A schools in Oklahoma to about 85% of Title I-A schools in Georgia.

Table 2. Number of States with Various Percentages of Public Schools and LEAs that Failed to Make Adequate Yearly Progress Based on AYP Determinations from the 2008-200 9 School Year

Entity	Number of States Where More Than 10% of Public Schools or LEAs Failed to Make AYP	Number of States Where More Than 25% of Public Schools or LEAs Failed to Make AYP	Number of States Where More Than 50% of Public Schools or LEAs Failed to Make AYP
Public schools	48	35	10
LEAs	38	28	19

Source: Table prepared by CRS, November 24, 2010, based on data available from the U.S. Department of Education, Education Data Express System. The original source of the data is the EDFacts/Consolidated State Performance Report, 2008-09, available online at http://www2.ed.gov/ admins/lead/account/consolidated/ index.html.

Notes: Not all states reported data for all types of performance-based accountability sanctions. Therefore, due to missing values, national level data may not accurately represent national trends. The District of Columbia and Puerto Rico have been included as "states."

While the percentages of schools identified for some type of improvement vary across the states, so too does the percentage of students taking advantage of the public school choice and SES options.[42] For example, during the 2008-2009 school year 2.7% of all students eligible for public school choice took advantage of this option.[43] However, the participation rate by state varied from less than 0.1% (e.g., District of Columbia) to nearly 80% in South Dakota. In addition, 15.6% of eligible students took advantage of the availability of SES.[44] As with the school choice option, the participation rate varied substantially by state, ranging from less than 1% in Montana to over 97% in the District of Columbia and 40.2% in Maryland.

Table 3. Number of States with Various Percentages of Title I-A Schools in Improvement, Corrective Action, or Restructuring During the 2009-2010 School Year Based on Adequate Yearly Progress Determinations from the 2008-2009 School Year

Performance-Based Accountability Sanction	Number of States with More than 10% of Their Title I-A Schools Subject to the Sanction	Number of States with More than 20% of Their Title I-A Schools Subject to the Sanction
School in improvement, year one	19	3
School in improvement, year two	9	0
Corrective action	4	0
Planning for restructuring	5	1
Implementing restructuring	14	5
School subject to any of the performance-based accountability sanctions (i.e., improvement, corrective action, or restructuring)	42	29

Source: Table prepared by CRS, November 22, 2010, based on data available from the U.S. Department of Education, Education Data Express System. The original source of the data is the EDFacts/Consolidated State Performance Report, 2008-09, available online at http://www2.ed.gov/admins/lead/account/consolidated/ index.html.

Notes: A Title I-A school is a school that received federal funds through the Title I-A program authorized by the Elementary and Secondary Education Act (ESEA). States are only required to apply the performance-based outcome accountability requirements to Title I-A schools that fail to make adequate yearly progress. The District of Columbia and Puerto Rico have been included as "states." There are no data for Indiana because the state developed new improvement statuses under a differentiated accountability pilot that do not correspond with the existing improvement statuses. Not all states reported data for all types of performance-based accountability sanctions. Therefore, due to missing values national-level data may not accurately represent national trends.

Ability of ED to Affect Current Accountability Requirements

ED has the ability through regulatory and waiver authority to alter the current requirements of the ESEA. As part of its role, the Secretary has the authority to issue regulations that affect program implementation. Both Section 410 of the General Education Provisions Act (GEPA) and Section 9535 of the ESEA provide the Secretary with the authority to promulgate regulations related to programs administered by the Secretary. In addition to regulatory authority, Section 9401 grants the Secretary the authority to grant waivers of any statutory or regulatory requirement of the ESEA[45] for a SEA, LEA, Indian tribe, or school. Entities requesting waivers must meet specific requirements, such as describing for each school year the "specific, measurable education goals" in accordance with the Title I-A accountability requirements for the SEA (if applicable) and for each LEA, Indian tribe, or school that would be affected by the waiver and the methods that would be used to measure annual progress toward meeting such goals and outcomes.

Since the reauthorization of the ESEA in 2002, and particularly as Congress has worked toward reauthorizing the ESEA, the Secretary has used regulatory authority to make substantive changes to ESEA program requirements. For example, former Secretary of Education Spellings took the opportunity to expand federal regulation of ESEA programs as well as allow selected, substantial forms of flexibility through the use of waiver authority provided under Section 9401. New regulations published in October 2008 substantially expanded ESEA Title I-A requirements dealing with high school graduation rates, as used in AYP determinations, as well as school choice and supplemental educational services for students in schools identified for improvement.[46] At the same time, these regulations codify a previously initiated waiver program allowing use of growth models of AYP, and a new waiver pilot allowing a limited number of states to implement differentiated consequences for schools that fail to make AYP.

With respect to the use of waiver authority, ED is required to publish an annual accounting of all waivers granted under Section 9401. The most recent announcement covers waivers granted during calendar year 2009.[47] During calendar year 2009, the Secretary issued 351 waivers. Over half of the waivers granted (196) were provided to LEAs and schools with respect to the treatment of their Title I-A funds granted under the American Recovery and Reinvestment Act (ARRA; P.L. 111-5).[48] The majority of the remaining waivers addressed ESEA-specific issues (as opposed to issues resulting from ARRA enactment) such as the "growth model" pilot and the "differentiated accountability" pilot.[49]

Collectively, these actions reflect a trend toward influence over design elements of accountability requirements by Administration initiatives, as opposed to statutes. Using waiver authority, in particular, it is possible that the Secretary could act to expand upon the specific provisions for which he would be willing to grant waivers; thereby, further changing the accountability requirements included in Title I-A, regardless of whether Congress acts to reauthorize the ESEA. Given that a large percentage of schools and LEAs are already failing to make AYP, and a good deal more are expected to join those ranks as 100% proficiency is required by the end of the 2013-2014 school year, it has been suggested that the Secretary could act to make some adjustments to the NCLB accountability requirements through waiver authority if Congress does not act to reauthorize the ESEA.

Issues Related to Implementation and Reauthorization

The standards-based movement and accompanying test-based accountability movement were initiated at the state and local levels. It does not appear likely that states would abandon efforts to develop rigorous content standards and implement measures to determine whether students have learned the material included in these standards. Federal involvement in public

K-12 education, however, is significantly more extensive than in the past, while the aggregate federal contribution to public K-12 education revenues remains relatively small (approximately 9%). In considering the ESEA for reauthorization, Congress may decide whether to continue this active federal strategy, perhaps expanding it further through increased assessment or other requirements, or alternatively decide to place tighter limits on the scope of federal involvement in state and local K-12 education systems. A hybrid approach might involve continued or expanded federal requirements regarding student outcomes combined with fewer requirements regarding the purposes for which federal grant funds can be used. Examples of the latter might include program consolidation, an expansion of current authority to transfer funds among ESEA programs, or policies offering increased flexibility in return for reaching specified levels of performance. It is also unclear what role common standards and assessments (discussed below) might play in an ESEA reauthorization effort. It is possible that a tradeoff could be made in this area as well. For example, states that adopt the common standards and assessments could receive increased flexibility in the consequences applied to schools and LEAs that fail to make AYP.

The remainder of the report highlights and examines several broad issues related to the implementation of the NCLB and possible issues to consider during the reauthorization of the ESEA. Several policy-related issues have arisen as NCLB requirements have been implemented. These include issues pertaining to the comparability of data across states and the development of state accountability systems of varying degrees of rigor, the one-size-fits all set of consequences applied to schools that fail to make AYP, the narrowing of the focus of instruction at the school level, and the evaluation of teachers

Commonality versus Flexibility

The accountability requirements included in the NCLB represented unprecedented federal involvement in school- and LEA-level accountability for student performance; however, the requirements are still broad enough that states were able to select their own content standards, and determine how those standards would be assessed (i.e., which tests would be used), and what would constitute a proficient level of performance on the tests. Thus, a byproduct (perhaps unintended) of NCLB enactment has been the creation of more than 50 different accountability systems across the nation. As state accountability systems differ so substantially, one of the tradeoffs in this approach is the lack of comparable data on student performance across states. Because states are using different standards and assessments, it is difficult to determine where students are in terms of skills and knowledge and to gauge the net effect of the NCLB. In addition, as noted by the Center on Education Policy (CEP), it is seemingly not possible to determine whether any gains observed in student achievement are directly attributable to the NCLB, as states and LEAs have implemented policies and programs of their own initiative and in response to the NCLB.[50] It is also not possible to determine what would have happened with respect to student achievement in the absence of the NCLB, as its provisions have probably affected every public school student in the nation.

A related issue is whether states have implemented challenging accountability systems. That is, questions have been raised about whether some states have implemented systems in which attaining proficiency is relatively easy, providing the appearance that the state is doing an excellent job educating students, while other states have implemented more rigorous accountability systems and results demonstrate that fewer students are succeeding academically. While the United States does not have a national test that examines what students know in a given subject area, all states that accept Title I-A funds are obligated to participate in the National Assessment of Educational Progress (NAEP), also referred to as the Nation's Report Card. While states have not written their content standards to be aligned with the NAEP standards, a comparison of NAEP test results for 4th and 8th grades in reading and mathematics has consistently shown that state accountability systems label substantially more students as being proficient than the results from the NAEP assessments would indicate. A recent study involving NAEP performance standards and state performance standards found that no state's reading performance standards were as high as the NAEP proficiency standards. In mathematics, Massachusetts (grades 4 and 8) and South Carolina (grade 8) were the only states where the state standards for proficiency were in the same range as the NAEP standards for proficiency.[51]

Researchers have developed a method for mapping each state's standard for proficiency in reading and mathematics onto the NAEP proficiency scale to permit a comparison of proficiency performance standards across states.[52] Researchers found that the differences from state to state in the percentage of students scoring at the proficient level or higher could be explained by the variation in the degree of difficulty of performance standards for proficiency. States with higher performance standards based on the NAEP scale had fewer students scoring at the proficient level on the reading and mathematics assessments. This indicates that students of similar academic skill levels, but living in different states, are being evaluated against different performance standards. Similar results were found when another group of researchers compared state proficiency standards with benchmarks for two international assessments.[53] For example, researchers compared the performance standards in Massachusetts with those of the states with the lowest standards. They found that in the latter states, the 8th grade performance standards were equivalent to the 4th grade performance standards in Massachusetts.

Thus, it is clear that "proficient" does not carry the same meaning across states. In addition, in order to comply with the requirement that all students are proficient (however the state defines "proficient") in reading and mathematics by the end of the 2013-2014 school year, states can continue to exercise the flexibility they are granted by the NCLB to select performance standards that make it easier for more students to meet the proficiency bar.

Common Standards and Assessments

Concerns about the diversity of accountability systems across the nation have spurred a grassroots movement led by the National Governors Association (NGA) and the Council of Chief State School Officers (CCSSO) to develop common standards for reading and mathematics in grades K-12 (referred to as the common core standards) and upon which common assessments could be created to test student knowledge of the standards. Adoption and implementation of the standards and assessments is optional. Currently, 43 states and the District of Columbia have adopted the standards.[54] It remains to be seen how many of these states will ultimately implement the standards and implement the standards as they were developed. In addition, 44 states and the District of Columbia have joined at least one of two groups currently working on developing common assessments for use by the 2014-2015 school year.[55] A decision to participate in the development process, however, does not necessarily translate into eventual adoption and use of the assessments.

The movement toward common standards and common assessments is not a federally led effort, per se. However, the movement clearly has the support of the Obama Administration. In its blueprint for the reauthorization of the ESEA,[56] the Administration proposes requiring states to adopt and implement common standards, presumably the aforementioned standards, or to have their standards vetted by a local university system. In addition, the Administration provided additional points to states competing for Race to the Top (RTTT) grants authorized by the ARRA if they adopted the common standards by a certain date. This incentive may have resulted in many more states agreeing to adopt the standards than would have otherwise occurred. Now that RTTT grants have been awarded to 11 states and the District of Columbia, however, it is possible that some states that failed to secure a grant may reconsider their adoption of the standards. With respect to support for common assessments, the Administration used a portion of the funds available for RTTT to run a $350 million competitive grant program to support the development of common assessments based on common standards by non-federally affiliated groups.[57]

Despite these grassroots efforts and actions by the Obama Administration to support the efforts, the end result will not yield a single set of national standards in reading and mathematics nor a single set of assessments in these subject areas. For example, states that adopt the common core standards are permitted to add additional standards of their own choosing to the common core standards.[58] Thus, each state adopting and implementing the common core standards could continue to have a unique set of state standards that share common elements with other adopting states. As a result of the RTTT common assessment competition, there will be at least two different assessments linked to the common core standards. It is unclear how the common assessments would accommodate any additional standards that states choose to add to the common core standards. Presumably, if states added additional standards to the common core standards, they would also want to determine how well students are mastering those standards. In addition, it is possible that multiple states could choose to use the same assessments to measure student performance but select different levels of performance on the assessments as indicating proficiency (e.g., one state could say that students must get 75% of the questions correct on the common assessment to be considered proficient, while another state could set the bar at 50%).

It is important to note that neither the common core standards movement nor the assessments movement is proposing a common curriculum. Decisions regarding how standards are taught to students and how students are prepared for assessments would remain a state and local decision. However, if enough states that adopted the common core standards actually implement the standards, it is possible that states could work together to develop, or textbook publishers and other organizations that develop materials for classroom use may develop, materials that are clearly aligned with the common core standards; thus, these entities would possibly contribute to a de facto national curriculum.

In the long term, however, if the push for more commonality gains momentum, there are several issues that remain unresolved regarding the common core standards. For example, who is responsible for maintaining and updating the standards? Who pays for this? How often should changes be made to the standards, as changes to the standards would require concomitant changes to assessments, teacher training, and curricula? If the common core standards are included in the ESEA, would there be a federal role in maintaining or updating the standards? Similar questions may apply to any common assessments that are developed, particularly with respect to the responsibility for maintaining and updating the assessments if the standards to which they are aligned change.

If ESEA reauthorization includes common standards or common assessments as part of a revised accountability system, this may increase the number of states that actually implement the standards and ultimately use the assessments. This may be particularly appealing if the adoption of common standards and assessments involves some sort of tradeoff, such as increasing state and local flexibility with respect to the consequences applied to schools and LEAs that fail to meet AYP (or some other required performance target). Alternatively, Congress could choose not to incorporate common standards or common assessments into a revised ESEA, leaving the common standards and assessments movements at the grassroots level. Under this scenario, Congress could allow the common standards and assessments to be used to meet whatever accountability requirements continue to apply without actually addressing the issues of the common standards or assessments in statutory language.

Absolute versus Differentiated Consequences

Under the NCLB, LEAs and states simply do or do not meet AYP standards. There is generally no distinction between those that fail to meet only one or two required performance or participation thresholds to a marginal degree versus those that fail to meet numerous thresholds to a substantial extent. Several analysts have suggested that a more nuanced grading scale be allowed (e.g., a division of schools or LEAs failing to make AYP into higher versus lower priority categories, or grades ranging from A to F), as is used in several state accountability systems. A major complication associated with such an approach is determining at what point on such a scale the current automatic consequences (e.g., school choice or SES) are invoked. An additional consideration under the NCLB 's current performance-based accountability system is that the same set of consequences applies to all schools regardless of whether they failed to make AYP for one subgroup or all students. That is, there is generally no distinction between those that fail to meet only one or two required performance thresholds to a marginal degree versus those that fail to meet numerous thresholds to a substantial extent.

Further, studies have determined that when otherwise-similar public schools are compared, those with a wider variety of demographic groups are substantially less likely to meet AYP standards.[59] However, without specific requirements for achievement gains by each of the major student groups, it is possible that insufficient attention would be paid to the performance of the disadvantaged student groups among whom improvements are most needed, and for whose benefit the Title I-A program was established.

As more schools fail to make AYP and are identified for improvement, the funds that LEAs must reserve for public school choice and SES may not be sufficient to help all eligible students. In addition, the public school transfer option may become a moot point, as few LEAs may have enough schools making AYP into which students can transfer. Two studies examined the availability of school choice options during the 2004-2005 school year. The first study[60] found that 39% of LEAs that were required to offer choice failed to do so. Among LEAs required to offer choice, 20% reported that they had no non-identified schools within the LEA to which students could transfer either because they only had one school per grade level or all schools in the LEA had been identified for improvement. Other LEAs noted that a lack of space in non- identified schools or an inability to arrange inter-district transfers were major challenges to implementing the choice provision. A second study[61] echoed these findings and noted that finding physical space and adhering to class size requirements in non-identified schools made it difficult to comply with the choice requirements. Given that more schools have been identified for improvement since the 2004-2005 school year, it is likely that it has only become more difficult for LEAs to comply with the public school choice requirements included in Title I-A.

A related issue is the capacity of states and LEAs to provide assistance to schools and LEAs that fail to make AYP for two consecutive years or more. As more schools and LEAs are subject to performance-based accountability consequences, the ability of states and LEAs to provide assistance may be diminished. It has been suggested that the consequences need to be better differentiated based on the reasons for failure and that assistance may need to be focused on the lowest-performing schools.

Finally, the focus of the current performance-based accountability system has been on consequences for failing to meet required levels of performance. While performance-based rewards are authorized under the NCLB, they are apparently little used, and the current focus is on a variety of performance-based sanctions. The Obama Administration's blueprint for reauthorization would place a greater emphasis on incentivizing improved performance through the use of rewards. Congress could choose to alter its approach to obtaining compliance with ESEA requirements to focus on positive incentives rather than performance-based sanctions or, perhaps, it could achieve a more equitable balance between the two approaches.

Proficiency for All Students

Without an ultimate goal of having all students reach a proficient or higher level of achievement by a specific date, states might establish relative goals that require little or no net improvement over time. A demanding goal might maximize efforts toward improvement by state public school systems, even if the goal is not met. Nevertheless, a goal of having all students at a proficient or higher level of achievement, within any specified period of time, may be criticized as being unrealistic, if one assumes that proficiency has been set at a challenging level. It is very likely that many states, schools, and LEAs will not meet the NCLB's 2014 AYP goal, unless state standards of proficient performance are significantly lowered or states are allowed by ED to aggressively pursue the use of statistical techniques such as setting high minimum group sizes and confidence intervals.

The assessment data that have been collected since the enactment of the NCLB could possibly now be used to develop new goals for student performance that are grounded in empirical evidence of what levels of growth may be achievable. For example, in reauthorizing the ESEA, Congress could rely on empirically developed thresholds for student performance. Alternatively, required progress could be benchmarked against a school or LEA that is already considered to be effective. Regardless of the strategy used to develop academic achievement goals for students, the strategy may need to recognize that as the percentage of students who are required to be proficient increases, it will be harder to realize large gains in the percentage of students who are proficient.

Incentives to Focus on Proficiency

A potentially positive outcome of the NCLB performance-based accountability system has been an increased focus on the proficiency of *all students*, including previously underserved groups such as disadvantaged students, students with disabilities, and LEP students. By disaggregating assessment results by subgroup, the achievement of various student groups is transparent and schools are held accountable for the achievement of these previously underserved groups.

Although schools and LEAs are held accountable for the achievement of students in various student groups, they are not held accountable for students at all levels of achievement. Under the NCLB performance-based accountability system, states set targets for the percentage of students achieving proficiency in reading and mathematics. States are not currently required to set targets for the percentage of students achieving other levels of achievement, such as "basic" or "advanced." The accountability system, therefore, does not reward schools or LEAs for increasing the percentage of students moving from achievement levels that are far below basic to the "basic" level of achievement. Likewise, the system does not reward schools or LEAs for increasing the percentage of students moving from "proficient" to "advanced" levels of achievement.

Because the goal of the current system is for 100% of students to become proficient by school year 2013-2014, schools and teachers may target instructional time and resources toward students who are nearing proficiency rather than distributing resources equally across students at all achievement levels. Congress could choose to alter the requirements of the current performance-based accountability system to provide a more balanced approach in rewarding gains in student achievement. For example, a performance-based accountability system could be designed to reward schools for increasing student growth in achievement, even if the ultimate level of achievement does not reach the cut-off score for proficiency. Schools and LEAs could similarly be rewarded for increasing student growth above the level of proficiency.

There has been an increasing interest in implementing state accountability systems that incorporate measures of student growth rather than one end-of-year assessment that determines proficiency. Currently, a limited number of states use growth models for accountability purposes;[62] however, ED's requirements for growth models are considered to be relatively restrictive. [63] The current Administration has also expressed an interest in assessing student growth rather than static achievement.[64] To date, the current Administration has not provided details on how new measures of student growth would differ from the previous Administration's growth model requirements. As such, it is difficult to gauge how this renewed interest in growth models would change current policy. If Congress chooses to expand the use of growth models in state accountability systems, the assessment requirements for the growth model must be considered. Some growth models require assessing students more than once per year; some growth models require assessments to be aligned across multiple grade levels. If states are granted the flexibility to use less restrictive growth models,

Congress may want to consider implementing a review procedure that ensures that the states have the appropriate assessments in place to inform their growth model.

Assessment and the Narrowing of the Curricular Focus[65]

The NCLB placed student assessment at the heart of federal education policy. One potentially positive outcome of using student assessments has been an increased focus on state content standards and teaching to those standards. There is some evidence that using content standards and assessments can help teachers focus their instruction and obtain feedback on the effectiveness of instruction.[66] On the other hand, the use of assessments in test-based accountability systems may be affecting the curriculum in less desirable ways. Because assessments are aligned with state content standards, there may be a risk that "teaching to the standards" becomes "teaching to the test." The practice of "teaching to the test"—whether intentional or unintentional—may narrow the curriculum in several ways. For example, teachers may reallocate instructional time towards tested subjects and away from non-tested subjects. Surveys of teachers have consistently reported that their instruction emphasizes reading and mathematics over other subjects like history, foreign language, and arts.[67] "Teaching to the test" can also lead to a narrowing of the curriculum within tested subjects. If teachers are aware that the assessments measure certain skills *within* the reading and mathematics standards, it is more likely that these skills would be taught— possibly at the expense of other, non-tested skills that are more difficult to measure. For example, if teachers know that a mathematics assessment typically assesses basic facts, it is less likely that higher-order skills, such as problem solving, would be adequately emphasized in the curriculum. A typical multiple-choice test that consists of 40 to 50 items per content area translates into roughly one or two test items per standard, leaving many curricular objectives within the standard untested—particularly those that are difficult to measure.[68]

A related concern is the potential for score inflation. Score inflation is a phenomenon in which scores on high-stakes assessments, such as state assessments used in accountability systems, increase at faster rates than scores on low-stakes assessments.[69] If teachers are, in fact, "teaching to the test" (i.e., the state assessment), it is likely that scores will increase faster on the state assessment than on other tests of student achievement. Studying the prevalence of score inflation is difficult because schools and LEAs may be reluctant to give researchers access to test scores for the purpose of investigating possible inflation. Nevertheless, several studies have documented the problem of score inflation by comparing gains on state assessments (high stakes) to those made on the NAEP (low stakes).[70] Studies have consistently reported discrepancies in the overall level of student achievement, the size of student achievement gains, and the size of the achievement gap. The discrepancies indicate that student scores on state assessments may be inflated and that these inflated scores may not represent true achievement gains.[71]

One possible way to reduce the problem of score inflation is to consistently use a low-stakes audit assessment, such as NAEP, to corroborate gains on state assessments.[72] If gains on state assessments generalize to another audit assessment, it increases the likelihood that gains are due to true achievement gains. This type of corroboration may help policymakers separate the policies that lead to true student achievement from those that lead to score inflation.

It can be argued that the assessment requirements of the NCLB accountability system have become burdensome and that more assessment decisions should be made at the state and local levels. Alternatively, it can be argued that the assessment requirements of the NCLB have the potential to drive curriculum, and that Congress should consider expanding the requirements to include subjects like writing, history, civics, and the arts. If the requirements are expanded to include additional subjects, these requirements may provide an incentive to states and LEAs to broaden school curricula. Even if the federal assessment requirements were expanded to include additional subjects, however, it is unclear whether scores from these new assessments would be included in the NCLB accountability system. For example, states are currently required to assess science, but the science score is not counted in AYP determinations. If scores from additional assessments are not counted in AYP determinations, it is unclear whether an assessment without consequences would broaden the curriculum.

It can be argued that the current assessments should be redesigned to measure more higher-order thinking skills. States currently administer standardized, multiple-choice assessments, largely due to the ease of administration, scoring, and reporting; however, this practice is sometimes considered undesirable because it may not adequately measure important higher-order thinking and skills. As such, supporters of innovative assessments may argue that the federal government should support other types of assessments that are more likely to assess higher-order thinking skills, such as extended constructed response and performance-based assessments.[73] Others may argue that the federal government should require the use of multiple measures.[74] That is, in addition to a state assessment score, AYP determinations could include data from a portfolio of student work, a performance assessment, or observations of student behavior and achievement in the classroom.

Technical Quality of Assessments[75]

Using student assessments in performance-based accountability systems provides a method of determining whether students are meeting certain academic targets. It highlights areas of excellence and areas of need within schools, LEAs, and states. Without the use of assessments, states would not have a baseline measurement of academic achievement to gauge whether certain instructional, curricular, or policy changes led to improved student outcomes. Nevertheless, the use of assessments in performance-based accountability systems is not without limitations. For example, most states currently use one, end-of-year assessment score in reading and mathematics
to inform the accountability system.[76] Because of the emphasis placed on a single assessment score, the appropriate interpretation of that score is critical. If assessments are not used and interpreted accurately, changes in student achievement scores may be used inappropriately to support or dismiss certain school reform efforts.

Given the emphasis placed on the results of these assessments, it is important that teachers, administrators, and policymakers understand the limitations of the assessment. Educational assessments can be limited by issues of technical quality, such as validity, reliability, and fairness.

Validity. Validity is arguably the most important concept to understand when evaluating educational assessment; it is not a property of the assessment itself, but rather a property of the interpretation of the result of the assessment. Validity refers to the degree to which a certain interpretation of an assessment score is appropriate and meaningful. That is, from a single assessment score, one could make a valid or an invalid interpretation. For example, state assessment results from a school are a representation of what students in the school know and can do relative to the state academic content standards. Suppose a group of students in School A scored well on these assessments and a group of students in School B scored poorly. One possible valid inference from this result is that students from School A were more likely to demonstrate proficiency in the academic content than students from School B. There are, however, many possible inferences that may be less valid. For example, one could infer that School A had a better academic curriculum than School B. Or, one could infer that School A had better teachers than School B. Neither of these inferences may be valid because state assessments were designed for the purpose of determining students' mastery of the content standards of the state, not for the purposes of evaluating teachers or curriculum. The validity of an inference, therefore, is tied inextricably to the purpose for which the test was created.

Reliability. Reliability refers to the consistency of measurement of an assessment. It describes the precision with which assessment results are reported and is a measure of the certainty that the results are accurate. The concept of reliability presumes that each student has a true score for any given assessment. The score on the assessment, or the observed score, is simply an approximation of a student's true score. The higher the reliability of the assessment, the more likely it is that a student's observed score reflects the true score. That is, the higher the reliability of the assessment, the more likely it is that an assessment score reflects student achievement.

Fairness. Fairness is a term that has no technical meaning in assessment procedures, and the concept has multiple interpretations. In general, fairness refers to the concept of equal treatment for all students who participate in an educational assessment. For example, the assessment process may lack fairness if it is biased against certain individuals. In a reading test, unnecessarily complex vocabulary can potentially bias a test against LEP students (e.g., using the word "parakeet" where "bird" would suffice). Or, the assessment process may lack fairness if certain individuals have been provided more test preparation opportunities. Some schools may emphasize test-taking skills and expose the students to items from previous state assessments to familiarize them with the general form and content. Other schools, however, may not emphasize test-taking skills, opting instead to use the time to deliver more instruction. The extent to which test preparation boosts scores on state assessments is unknown; however, if one school conducted extensive test preparation and another did not, comparisons between the two schools may not be "fair."[77]

The results of state assessments are a major component of the NCLB performance-based accountability system. Consequences for schools and LEAs are based primarily on the results of state assessments. As such, test users have a responsibility to examine the validity, reliability, and fairness of an assessment to draw defensible conclusions about student achievement. If a subgroup of students does not make AYP based on an assessment that lacked adequate evidence of reliability or fairness, schools and LEAs would still be subjected to the increasingly severe consequences of the performance-based accountability system. If the consequences applied to schools and LEAs are based on assessment scores that are invalid, it can be argued that current school reform efforts are not targeted appropriately. Some schools or LEAs that provide relatively sound educational opportunities for students may be required to implement a series of reform efforts because the assessments used within the accountability system did not accurately and fairly measure the achievement of all students, while other schools and LEAs may fail to be identified as needing to improve their educational offerings.

Teacher Evaluation and Accountability[78]

One of the goals of the NCLB is to improve educational outcomes for all students. Policymaking at the federal level reflects a growing awareness that improving educational outcomes depends greatly upon increasing the quality of classroom instruction. In establishing the student performance standards and accountability provisions in the NCLB, Congress recognized that the success of these reforms rests largely on teachers' knowledge and skills. Thus, in enacting the NCLB, Congress amended the ESEA to establish a requirement that all teachers be *highly qualified*. Furthermore, Congress required that states establish a plan for the equitable distribution of highly qualified teachers across classrooms and schools. The equitable distribution of highly qualified teachers was intended, "to ensure that poor and minority children are not taught at higher rates than other children by inexperienced, unqualified, or out-of-field teachers."[79]

The NCLB highly qualified teacher requirement has been the cornerstone of federal teacher policy for nearly a decade. In that time, the requirement has come to be seen by many as a minimum standard for entry into the profession (rather than a goal to which teachers might aspire) and a growing body of research has revealed its underlying emphasis on teachers' credentials to be weakly correlated with student achievement.

Meanwhile, federal interest has begun to shift from a focus on teacher input (i.e., quality) to teacher output (i.e., effectiveness). The most recent congressional action in this area came with the passage of the American Recovery and Reinvestment Act and, in particular, enactment of the RTTT program. Within the RTTT program, ED provided the first federal definition of "effective teacher" and required applicants of this program to measure a teacher's effectiveness based on student growth in achievement. In addition, applicants of this program were to use the measurement of teacher effectiveness within an overall teacher evaluation system that would inform rewards for and recruitment, development, and retention of teachers.

ED provided RTTT applicants with an incentive to become more systematic about using student data to inform teacher instruction and to measure teacher effectiveness. One specific method that is used by some school districts (and at least one state)[80] to measure teacher effectiveness based on student achievement data is value-added modeling (VAM). VAM is a set of statistical approaches that seek to isolate a teacher's effect on student achievement. This method of modeling is seen as promising because it has the potential to promote education reform and to create a more equitable accountability system that holds teachers and schools accountable for the aspects of student learning that are attributable to effective teaching while not holding teachers and schools accountable for factors outside of their control (e.g., the potential impact of socioeconomic status on student learning). Although there are other methods for assessing the effectiveness of teachers, VAM has garnered increasing attention in education research and policy, and many states proposed VAM systems in RTTT applications.[81]

To date, the shift from input-based accountability (i.e., teacher quality) to output-based accountability (i.e., teacher effectiveness) has been an initiative led by the Administration. Congress has not enacted similar provisions, although this may receive attention during ESEA reauthorization. During reauthorization, Congress may choose to maintain the highly qualified teacher requirements as they are, replace or supplement these requirements, or include these requirements as part of a new, more comprehensive set of quality/performance requirements. In addition, Congress may revisit the requirement for the equitable distribution of highly qualified teachers to ensure that it is functioning as intended to ensure that poor and minority children are not taught by inexperienced or unqualified teachers at higher rates than other children.[82]

On the other hand, if Congress chooses to move toward outcome-based accountability, it may consider whether to codify ED 's definition of "effective teacher" or whether to consider alternate definitions. If ED's definition is adopted, reauthorization legislation has the opportunity to clarify the weight that student growth in achievement should have in the definition of an effective teacher. Furthermore, if Congress chooses to adopt any definition of an effective teacher, the equitable distribution of "highly qualified teachers" may need to be revised to reflect the change to an emphasis on "effective teachers."

Finally, Congress may consider whether the federal government will have a sustained role in incentivizing states to develop new teacher evaluation systems that would inform rewards for and recruitment, development, and retention of teachers. Through the Teacher Incentive Fund (TIF), Congress currently provides grants to support compensation reforms for teachers.[83] TIF grants must consider gains in student achievement, classroom evaluations conducted multiple times during each school year, and other factors that provide educators with incentives to take on additional responsibilities and leadership roles. Through RTTT, ED required that grantees of this program go beyond TIF requirements and use evaluations to inform high-stakes decisions such as granting tenure, awarding full certification, and removing ineffective teachers. In practice, some school districts are using teacher evaluation systems based on VAM for these high-stakes decisions. Some have cautioned against using VAM for tenure, certification, and removal decisions because the measurement of teacher effectiveness may not be precise enough to support these decisions without additional corroborating evidence.[84] If the measurement of teacher effectiveness lacks precision, Congress may consider the appropriate weight given to teacher effectiveness in an overall teacher accountability system.

APPENDIX. RELATED TABLES

Table A-1. Percent of All Public Schools and LEAs that Did Not Make AYP: 2008-2009 School Year

State	Percentage of All Public Schools That Did Not Make AYP	Percentage of All LEAs That Did Not Make AYP
Alabama	13.3%	2.3%
Alaska	43.8%	–
Arizona	25.6%	39.2%
Arkansas	45.7%	9.6%

Table A-1. (Continued)

State	Percentage of All Public Schools That Did Not Make AYP	Percentage of All LEAs That Did Not Make AYP
California	49.9%	64.0%
Colorado	43.9%	53.8%
Connecticut	41.1%	32.0%
Delaware	33.8%	36.8%
District of Columbia	74.7%	85.7%
Florida	76.6%	–
Georgia	14.0%	60.2%
Hawaii	64.4%	–
Idaho	33.7%	55.0%
Illinois	40.8%	49.4%
Indiana	49.9%	16.8%
Iowa	30.2%	9.7%
Kansas	12.2%	11.5%
Kentucky	38.4%	57.5%
Louisiana	9.2%	56.1%
Maine	35.3%	0.9%
Maryland	23.0%	84.0%
Massachusetts	62.2%	79.0%
Michigan	9.2%	36.3%
Minnesota	53.7%	61.1%
Mississippi	35.4%	88.8%
Missouri	62.6%	72.9%
Montana	26.4%	32.1%
Nebraska	11.7%	19.3%
Nevada	42.8%	35.3%
New Hampshire	54.0%	48.2%
New Jersey	35.1%	16.5%
New Mexico	68.2%	52.7%
New York	11.7%	4.9%
North Carolina	28.9%	89.6%
North Dakota	25.2%	23.0%
Ohio	39.4%	51.8%
Oklahoma	10.6%	11.6%
Oregon	29.9%	52.6%
Pennsylvania	21.5%	7.2%
Puerto Rico	93.5%	–
Rhode Island	18.9%	22.5%
South Carolina	49.8%	–
South Dakota	20.7%	5.7%
Tennessee	20.3%	16.9%
Texas	5.0%	17.3%
Utah	16.8%	13.1%
Vermont	29.0%	26.9%
Virginia	28.1%	54.9%
Washington	58.2%	69.3%

State	Percentage of All Public Schools That Did Not Make AYP	Percentage of All LEAs That Did Not Make AYP
West Virginia	19.7%	94.5%
Wisconsin	6.7%	0.9%
Wyoming	27.4%	8.3%
National average	33.7%	36.3%

Source: Table prepared by CRS, November 24, 2010, based on data available from the U.S. Department of Education, Education Data Express System. The original source of the data is the EDFacts/ Consolidated State Performance Report, 2008-09, available online at http://www2.ed.gov/admins/ lead/account/consolidated /index.html.

Notes: Due to missing values, national-level data may not accurately represent national trends. States with missing data are not included in the national average calculation.

A dash (–) indicates that the data are not available.

Table A-2. Number of Title I-A Schools in Improvement, Corrective Action, or Restructuring During the 2009-2010 School Year Based on Adequate Yearly Progress Determinations from the 2008-2009 School Year

State	Number of Title I-ASchools: 2008-2009 School Year	Number of Title I-A Schools in Improvement, Year 1	Number of Title I-A Schools in Improvement, Year 2	Number of Title I-A Schools in Corrective Action	Number of Title I-A Schools Planning for Restructuring	Number of Title I-A Schools Implementing Restructuring	Total Number ofTitle I-A Schools in Restructuring	Total Numberof Title I-A Schools in Need of Improvement	Percentage of Title I-A Schools in Need of Improvement
Alabama	855	9	5	9	11	4	15	38	4.4%
Alaska	282	26	8	10	13	61	74	118	41.8%
Arizona	1,176	49	66	55	36	40	76	246	20.9%
Arkansas	812	101	86	66	50	100	150	404	49.8%
California	6,013	748	309	323	328	1,075	1,403	2,783	46.3%
Colorado	603	81	17	21	8	37	45	164	27.2%
Connecticut	507	64	48	31	14	80	94	237	46.7%
Delaware	106	4	6	1	-	3	3	14	13.2%
District of Columbia	189	19	26	25	22	37	59	129	68.3%
Florida	1,361	120	97	96	145	541	686	999	73.4%
Georgia	1,292	-	-	-	-	-	-	-	-
Hawaii	180	16	3	13	8	65	73	107	59.4%
Idaho	375	55	39	35	27	8	35	164	43.7%
Illinois	2,272	209	92	48	36	336	372	721	31.7%
Indiana	843	-	-	-	-	-	-	258	30.6%
Iowa	648	100	7	5	7	1	8	120	18.5%
Kansas	659	11	10	4	3	4	7	32	4.9%
Kentucky	820	29	21	19	7	30	37	106	12.9%
Louisiana	1,059	32	26	1	1	15	16	75	7.1%
Maine	421	37	9	4	1	4	5	55	13.1%
Maryland	358	10	10	7	6	38	44	71	19.8%
Massachusetts	985	146	111	102	100	188	288	647	65.7%
Michigan	1,922	-	106	18	-	84	84	208	10.8%
Minnesota	862	132	83	36	19	13	32	283	32.8%

Table A-2. (Continued)

State	Number of Title I-ASchools: 2008-2009 School Year	Number of Title I-A Schools in Improvement, Year 1	Number of Title I-A Schools in Improvement, Year 2	Number of Title I-A Schools in Corrective Action	Number of Title I-A Schools Planning for Restructuring	Number of Title I-A Schools Implementing Restructuring	Total Number ofTitle I-A Schools in Restructuring	Total Numberof Title I-A Schools in Need of Improvement	Percentage of Title I-A Schools in Need of Improvement
Mississippi	707	37	25	5	4	3	7	74	10.5%
Missouri	1,125	212	101	65	24	56	80	458	40.7%
Montana	630	71	13	7	4	40	44	135	21.4%
Nebraska	466	14	1	1	-	-	-	16	3.4%
Nevada	154	32	15	23	41	20	61	131	85.1%
New Hampshire	238	57	32	24	17	2	19	132	55.5%
New Jersey	1,370	130	69	37	31	73	104	340	24.8%
New Mexico	570	93	60	54	69	118	187	394	69.1%
New York	3,262	100	69	47	36	175	211	427	13.1%
North Carolina	1,133	160	149	110	54	48	102	521	46.0%
North Dakota	305	5	7	2	-	14	14	28	9.2%
Ohio	2,133	186	176	191	99	123	222	775	36.3%
Oklahoma	1,122	20	5	3	5	2	7	35	3.1%
Oregon	574	47	8	-	7	10	17	72	12.5%
Pennsylvania	1,821	122	64	47	28	130	158	391	21.5%
Puerto Rico	1,487	224	65	86	137	430	567	942	63.3%
Rhode Island	154	13	6	5	8	12	20	44	28.6%
South Carolina	491	67	51	29	30	88	118	265	54.0%
South Dakota	344	16	4	11	2	21	23	54	15.7%
Tennessee	982	57	22	8	9	11	20	107	10.9%
Texas	5,093	159	66	58	39	30	69	352	6.9%
Utah	246	9	3	-	-	-	-	12	4.9%
Vermont	223	35	4	15	2	7	9	63	28.3%
Virginia	711	58	26	6	7	6	13	103	14.5%
Washington	923	237	142	14	35	40	75	468	50.7%
West Virginia	356	6	6	1	3	7	10	23	6.5%
Wisconsin	1,152	41	20	9	4	5	9	79	6.9%
Wyoming	179	15	2	1	3	1	4	22	12.3%
Total	52,551	4,221	2,396	1,788	1,540	4,236	5,776	14,561	27.7%

Source: Table prepared by CRS, November 22, 2010, based on data available from the U.S. Department of Education, Education Data Express System. The original source of the data is the EDFacts/Consolidated State Performance Report, 2008-09, available online at http://www2.ed.gov/admins/lead/account/consolidated/index.html.

Notes: A Title I-A school is a school that received federal funds through the Title I-A program authorized by the Elementary and Secondary Education Act (ESEA). States are only required to apply the performance-based outcome accountability requirements to Title I-A schools that fail to make adequate yearly progress. There are no data for Indiana because the state developed new improvement statuses under a differentiated accountability pilot that do not correspond with the existing improvement statuses. Due to missing values, national-level data may not accurately represent national trends.

End Notes

[1] Consortium for Policy Research in Education, *Putting the Pieces Together: Systemic School Reform*, RB-06-4/91, 1991, http://www.cpre.org/images

[2] See, for example, *Education Reform in the '90s*, ed. Chester E. Finn, Jr. and Theodor Rebarber (1992), p. xi.

[3] Center for Policy Research in Education, *State Education Reform in the 1980s*, RB-03-1 1/89, 1989, http://www.cpre.org/images

[4] National Commission on Excellence in Education, *A Nation at Risk: The Imperative for Educational Reform*, April 1983, http://www2.ed.gov/pubs/NatAtRisk/index.html.

[5] Goals 2000 includes all titles of P.L. 103-227 except Titles V and IX.

[6] Opportunity-to-Learn (OTL) standards describe the resources needed to give all students an opportunity to acquire the knowledge and skills included in the content standards. The Omnibus Consolidated Rescissions and Appropriations Act of 1996 (P.L. 104-134) eliminated the requirement that states develop OTL standards or strategies as a condition of receiving Goals 2000 funds. It also repealed grant programs to develop national OTL standards and state assessments.

[7] P.L. 104-134 repealed the authority to establish the NESIC. If it had been funded, NESIC would have certified voluntary national standards for curriculum content, pupil performance, and OTL, as well as voluntarily submitted state standards.

[8] Participation was originally limited to six states, but P.L. 104-134 increased the participation limit to 12 states.

[9] P.L. 106-25, the Education Flexibility Partnership Act, authorized Ed-Flex independent of the Goals 2000 legislation and allowed any state to participate. Currently 10 states have Ed-Flex authority: Colorado, Delaware, Kansas, Massachusetts, Maryland, North Carolina, Oregon, Pennsylvania, Texas, and Vermont. For more information, see CRS Report RL3 1583, *K-12 Education: Special Forms of Flexibility in the Administration of Federal Aid Programs*, by Rebecca R. Skinner.

[10] If a state had developed content and performance standards under Title III of Goals 2000, or under a similar procedure, then those standards had to be used for Title I programs. The authorization for Title III of Goals 2000 expired at the end of FY2000.

[11] If a state did not have such statewide standards or assessments (as was the case for Iowa and Nebraska), then one of two alternative strategies could be adopted: (1) statewide standards applicable only to Title I students and programs, or (2) a mix of state and local, or local only, standards and assessments that were subject to state guidelines to ensure that they would meet the requirements of Title I.

[12] The Secretary was authorized to provide a one-year extension of the deadline for assessments for the correction of problems identified in the field testing of assessments.

[13] Paul Manna, *Collision Course: Federal Education Policy Meets State and Local Realities* (Washington, DC: CQ Press, 2010).

[14] As with IASA, if no agency or entity in a state has authority to establish statewide standards or assessments (as is generally assumed to be the case for Iowa and Nebraska), then the state may adopt either (1) statewide standards and assessments applicable only to Title I-A students and programs, or (2) a policy providing that each LEA receiving Title I-A grants will adopt standards and assessments that meet the requirements of Title I-A and are applicable to all students served by each such LEA.

[15] One exception to this provision involves students with disabilities. For more information, see CRS Report R40701, *Alternate Assessments for Students with Disabilities*, by Erin D. Lomax.

[16] LEAs may continue to administer assessments to pupils in non-English languages for up to a total of five years if, on a case-by-case basis, they determine that this would likely yield more accurate information on what the students know and can do.

[17] For further information on this and related topics, see CRS Report RL32913, *The Individuals with Disabilities Education Act (IDEA): Interactions with Selected Provisions of the No Child Left Behind Act (NCLB)*, by Ann Lordeman and Nancy Lee Jones.

[18] For more information on this topic, see CRS Report RL32495, Adequate Yearly Progress (AYP): Implementation of the No Child Left Behind Act, by Rebecca R. Skinner; and CRS Report RL3373 1, Education for the Disadvantaged: Reauthorization Issues for ESEA Title I-A Under the No Child Left Behind Act, by Rebecca R. Skinner.

[19] Currently, all states receive Title I-A funds.

[20] States are encouraged to apply these consequences to all public schools and LEAs, but are not required to do so. State practices vary on this point.

[21] Results from the science assessments do not have to be included in the AYP calculation.

[22] States select the other academic indicator for elementary and middle schools. Generally, states choose to use attendance rates.

[23] Several constraints apply to the consideration of these student groups in AYP calculations. First, student groups need not be considered in cases where their number is so relatively small that achievement results would not be statistically significant or the identity of individual pupils might be divulged. The selection of the minimum

number ("n") of students in a group for the group to be considered in AYP determinations has been left largely to state discretion. Since the same minimum group size policies are applied to schools and to LEAs overall, groups that are too small to be separately considered for individual schools often meet the minimum group size threshold at the LEA level. Second, it has been left to the states to define the "major racial and ethnic groups" on the basis of which AYP must be calculated. And third, pupils who have not attended the same school for a full year need not be considered in determining AYP at the school level, although they are still to be included in LEA and state AYP determinations, if they attended schools in the same LEA or state for the full academic year. A number of special rules, which have evolved over time, apply to two of the disaggregated pupil groups: LEP pupils and pupils with disabilities. For a detailed discussion of these, see CRS Report RL32495, *Adequate Yearly Progress (AYP): Implementation of the No Child Left Behind Act*, by Rebecca R. Skinner; and CRS Report RL32913, *The Individuals with Disabilities Education Act (IDEA): Interactions with Selected Provisions of the No Child Left Behind Act (NCLB)*, by Ann Lordeman and Nancy Lee Jones.

[24] ED is required to establish a peer review process to evaluate whether states overall have met their statewide AYP goals, beginning after the third year of implementation of the NCLB. States that fail to meet their goals are to be listed in an annual report to Congress, and technical assistance is to be provided to states that fail to meet their goals for two consecutive years or more. For further information on this topic, see CRS Report RL33371, *K-12 Education: Implementation Status of the No Child Left Behind Act of 2001 (P.L. 107-110)*, coordinated by Gail McCallion.

[25] Over 90% of all LEAs, and approximately three-fifths of all public schools, participate in the Title I-A program.

[26] For further information on public school choice, see CRS Report RL33506, *School Choice Under the ESEA: Programs and Requirements*, by David P. Smole.

[27] For more information on persistently dangerous schools, see CRS Report RL33371, *K-12 Education: Implementation Status of the No Child Left Behind Act of 2001 (P.L. 107-110)*, coordinated by Gail McCallion.

[28] 34 CFR 200.44(d).

[29] For further information on supplemental educational services, see CRS Report RL3 1329, *Supplemental Educational Services for Children from Low-Income Families Under ESEA Title I-A*, by David P. Smole.

[30] Schools identified for improvement, corrective action, or restructuring, and LEAs identified for improvement or corrective action, lose their eligibility to supplemental educational services providers.

[31] More specifically, LEAs are to use an amount equal to 5% of their Title I-A grant for public school choice and transportation costs, 5% for SES, and up to an additional 10% for either, to the extent needed. These funds may be taken from the LEA's Title I-A grant or from other sources.

[32] See http://www.ed.gov/news/pressreleases/2008/03/03182008.html.

[33] The nine states are Arkansas, Florida, Georgia, Illinois, Indiana, Louisiana, Maryland, New York, and Ohio.

[34] The state plans may be found at http://www.ed.gov/admins/lead

[35] States may fund teacher and principal awards by reserving such sums as necessary from the amount received under ESEA Title II-A-1—Teacher and Principal Training and Recruiting Fund, Grants to States. Guidance on procedures for reserving funds for State Academic Achievement Awards Programs is available in U.S. Department of Education, Office of Elementary and Secondary Education, *Guidance: State Educational Agency Procedures for Adjusting Basic, Concentration, Targeted, and Education Finance Incentive Grant Allocations Determined by the U.S. Department of Education*, May 23, 2003, pp. 32-34.

[36] U.S. Department of Education, Education Data Express System. The original source of the data is the EDFacts/Consolidated State Performance Report, 2008-09, available online at http://www2.ed.gov/admins/lead/ account/consolidated/index.html.

[37] See http://www.ed.gov/admins/lead

[38] Data are also available on Title I-A-recipient schools and LEAs that fail to make adequate yearly progress. However, in the aggregate, the results are quite similar. For 2008-2009, 35% of all public schools and 36% of all Title I-A schools were reported as failing to make AYP. For LEAs, 35% of all LEAs and 38% of all Title I-A LEAs failed to make AYP.

[39] It should be noted that neither Hawaii nor Puerto Rico reported LEA-level data. Both states have only one LEA. In both cases, the single LEA failed to make AYP based on determinations for the 2008-2009 school year. Therefore, 21 states had at least half of their LEAs fail to make AYP.

[40] In Puerto Rico, 93.5% of public schools failed to make AYP.

[41] Data were not readily available for LEAs.

[42] For more information on reasons why students may not be taking advantage of public school choice and SES options, see U.S. Department of Education, Office of Planning, Evaluation and Policy Development, Policy and Program Studies Service, *State and Local Implementation of the* No Child Left Behind Act*: Volume VII—Title I School Choice and Supplemental Educational Services: Final Report*, Washington, DC, 2009, http://www.ed.gov/rschstat/eval/choice/ nclb-choice-ses-final/choice-ses-final.pdf.

[43] Data obtained by CRS from the U.S. Department of Education, ED Data Express System, November 22, 2010.

[44] Data obtained by CRS from the U.S. Department of Education, ED Data System, November 22, 2010.

[45] There are some limits placed on the Secretary's ability to grant waivers of ESEA provisions. For example, requirements related to fiscal accountability, civil rights, parental participation, and the equitable participation of private school students may not be waived.

[46] The October 2008 regulations are available online at http://www2.ed.gov/legislation 102908a.html.

[47] U.S. Department of Education, "Notice of Waivers Granted Under Section 9401 of the Elementary and Secondary Education Act of 1965, as Amended," 75 *Federal Register* 56833-56856, September 16, 2010.

[48] For example, LEAs received waivers to exclude the amount Title I-A funds received under ARRA when calculating their obligation to spend their funds for public school choice and professional development and when calculating the per-pupil amount for SES, and to waive the carryover limitation more than once every three years. For more information, see U.S. Department of Education, "Notice of Waivers Granted Under Section 9401 of the Elementary and Secondary Education Act of 1965, as Amended," 75 *Federal Register* 56833-56856, September 16, 2010.

[49] Under growth models, the achievement of the same pupils is tracked from year-to-year. This type of model is not explicitly mentioned in the NCLB statute; however, it is authorized in regulations promulgated by ED. Using waiver authority available to the Secretary under Section 9401, the Secretary is able to approve a state's use of growth models. To date, 15 states (Alaska, Arizona, Arkansas, Colorado, Delaware, Florida, Iowa, Michigan, Minnesota, Missouri, North Carolina, Ohio, Pennsylvania, Tennessee, and Texas) have been approved to use growth models.

[50] Center on Education Policy, *Has Student Achievement Increased Since 2002? State Test Score Trends Through 2006-07*, Washington, DC, February 2008, http://www.cep-dc.org/document/docWindow.cfm?fuseaction= document.viewDocument&documentid=24 1 &documentFormatId=4309.

[51] U.S. Department of Education, National Center for Education Statistics, *Mapping State Proficiency Standards Onto NAEP Scales: 2005-2007*, NCES 2010-456, Washington, DC, October 2010, http://nces.ed.gov/ nationsreportcard/pdf/ studies/2010456.pdf.

[52] U.S. Department of Education, National Center for Education Statistics, *Mapping State Proficiency Standards Onto NAEP Scales: 2005-2007*, NCES 2010-456, Washington, DC, October 2010, http://nces.ed.gov/ nationsreportcard/pdf/ studies/2010456.pdf.

[53] The two international tests used in the study were the Trends in International Mathematics and Science Study (TIMSS) and Progress in International Reading Literacy Study (PIRLS). For more information, see Gary W. Phillips, *International Benchmarking: State Education Performance Standards*, American Institutes for Research, Washington, DC, October 2010, http://www.air.org/files/AIR_Int_Benchmarking_State_Ed __Perf_Standards.pdf.

[54] The following states have not adopted the common standards: Alaska, Maine, Montana, Nebraska, North Dakota, Texas, and Virginia. Minnesota only adopted the common standards for reading/language arts. For more information, see http://www.corestandards.org/in-the-states.

[55] The following states did not join one of the two groups working on common assessments: Alaska, Minnesota, Nebraska, Texas, Virginia, and Wyoming. For more information, see U.S. Department of Education, "U.S. Secretary of Education Duncan Announces Winners of Competition to Improve Student Assessments," press release, September 2, 2010, http://www.ed.gov/news/press-releases/us-secretary-education-

[56] U.S. Department of Education, *A Blueprint for Reform: Reauthorization of the Elementary and Secondary Education Act*, March 2010, http://www2.ed.gov/policy

[57] For more information, see U.S. Department of Education, "U.S. Secretary of Education Duncan Announces Winners of Competition to Improve Student Assessments," press release, September 2, 2010, http://www.ed.gov/news/pressreleases/us-secretary-education

[58] States adopting the common core standards are required to adopt all of the standards but may add an additional 15% of its own materials to the standards. For more information, see PowerPoint presentation dated March 2010, available online at http://www.corestandards.org/about-the-standards.

[59] See, for example, U.S. Department of Education, *State and Local Implementation of the No Child Left Behind Act Volume IX—Accountability under NCLB: Final Report*, 2010, pp. 55-57, http://www2.ed.gov/rschstat/eval/disadv/nclbaccountability/nclb-accountability-final. pdf.

[60] U.S. Department of Education, Institute of Education Sciences, *National Assessment of Title I: Interim Report, Volume I: Implementation*, February 2003, p. 65, http://www2.ed.gov/ rschstat/eval/disadv/title1interimreport/ vol1.pdf.

[61] Center on Education Policy, *From the Capital to the Classroom: Year 3 of the No Child Left Behind Act*, 2005, http://www.cep-dc.org/_data/n_0001/resources/live/Supplemental %20Education%20Services%20and% 20Choice.pdf.

[62] States with currently approved growth models include Alaska, Arizona, Arkansas, Colorado, Delaware, Florida, Iowa, Michigan, Minnesota, Missouri, North Carolina, Ohio, Pennsylvania, Tennessee, and Texas. For more information, see http://www2.ed.gov/news /pressreleases/2009/01/01082009a.html.

[63] The growth model requirements were outlined by Secretary Spellings under the previous Administration.

[64] U.S. Department of Education, *A Blueprint for Reform: Reauthorization of the Elementary and Secondary Education Act*, March 2010, http://www2.ed.gov/policy

[65] For general information on assessment in elementary and secondary education, see CRS Report R40514, *Assessment in Elementary and Secondary Education: A Primer*, by Erin D. Lomax.

[66] L. Mabry, J. Poole, and L. Redmond, et al., "Local Impact of State Testing in Southwest Washington," *Education Policy Analysis Archives*, vol. 11, no. 22 (July 18, 2003), http://epaa.asu.edu/epaa/v11n22/.

[67] Laura Hamilton, "Assessment as a Policy Tool," *Review of Research in Education*, vol. 27 (2003), pp. 25-68; Laura S. Hamilton and Mark Berends, *Instructional Practices Related to Standards and Assessment*, RAND, WR-374-EDU, Washington, DC, April 2006, http://www.rand.org/pubs/working_papers/2006/RAND_ WR374.pdf; Patricia Velde Pederson, "What is Measured Is Treasured: The Impact of the No Child Left Behind Act on Nonassessed Subjects," *Clearing House: A Journal of Educational Strategies, Issues and Ideas*, vol. 80, no. 6 (July/August 2007), pp. 287-291; Jennifer McMurrer, *Choices, Changes, and Challenges: Curriculum and Instruction in the NCLB Era*, Center on Education Policy, December 2007, http://www.cep-dc.org/_data/n_0001/resources/ 1%2007.pdf.

[68] Henry May, Irma Perez-Johnson, and Joshua Haimson, et al., *Using State Tests in Education Experiments: A Discussion of the Issues*, U.S. Department of Education, NCEE 2009-013, Washington, DC, November 2009, pp. A-8, http://ies.ed.gov/ncee/pdf/2009013.pdf.

[69] An assessment is considered to be high stakes if there are consequences for individuals, schools, LEAs, or states based on the outcome of the assessment. State assessments for AYP and state exit exams are examples of high-stakes assessments. An assessment is considered to be low-stakes if there are no consequences for the outcome of the assessment. NAEP and various international assessments are examples of low-stakes assessments.

[70] NAEP is administered in grades 4, 8, and 12. Studies comparing student performance on state assessments to the NAEP make comparisons only at grades 4 and 8. B. Fuller, K. Gesicki, and E. Kang, et al., *Is the No Child Left Behind Act Working? The Reliability of How States Track Achievement*, University of California, Berkeley PACE, Working Paper 06-1, Berkeley, CA, 2006; S.P. Klein, Linda S. Hamilton, and Daniel F. McCaffrey, et al., *What Do Test Scores in Texas Tell Us?*, RAND, Santa Monica, CA, 2000; Daniel Koretz and S. I. Barron, *The Validity of Gains on the Kentucky Instructional Results Information System (KIRIS)*, RAND, MR-792-PCT/FF, Santa Monica, CA, 1998; Robert L. Linn and C. Haug, "Stability of School-building Accountability Scores and Gains," *Educational Evaluation and Policy Analysis*, vol. 24, no. 1 (2002), pp. 29-36.

[71] Critics of the audit approach may argue that NAEP and state assessments measure reading and mathematics much differently, and a gain on one assessment would not necessarily be reflected on the other assessment. That is, the two types of assessments measure achievement against different content and performance standards, and a gain on the state assessment may reflect the specific content that is emphasized by the state standards. Others, however, may argue that it is unlikely that the assessments are different to the extent that a gain on one assessment would not likely coincide with a gain on the other assessment. That is, it is unlikely that true achievement gains would be demonstrated on only one assessment.

[72] Daniel Koretz, *Measuring Up: What Educational Testing Really Tells Us* (Cambridge, MA: Harvard University Press, 2008), pp. 247-248.

[73] See, for example, George H, Wood, Linda Darling-Hammond, Monty Neil, et al., *Refocusing Accountability: Using Local Performance Assessments to Enhance Teaching and Learning for Higher Order Skills*, The Forum for Education and Democracy, May 2007, http://www.forumforeducation.org/node/368. An assessment with *extended constructed response* may require a student to write and essay or design an experiment. A *performance-based assessment* may require a student to demonstrate skills and knowledge in an "on-demand" setting, such as a debate or a laboratory experiment. There are many different examples of extended constructed response and performance-based assessments that are not mentioned herein.

[74] Congressman Miller and Congressman McKeon proposed the use of multiple indicators or multiple measures in the 2007 discussion draft to reauthorize the NCLB.

[75] For a guide to the technical validity of educational assessments, see AERA, APA, and NCME, *Standards for Educational and Psychological Testing* (Washington, DC: American Psychological Association, 1999).

[76] States are required to use at least one other academic indicator in their accountability system (e.g., high school graduation rate, attendance, etc.). Some states use growth models in their accountability system. In some growth models, students are tested twice per year to determine growth. In other models, students are tested once per year and the prior year's score is used with the current year's score to determine growth.

[77] For more information on fairness in assessment, see footnote 65.

[78] This section of the report draws on work done by Jeff Kuenzi, Specialist in Education Policy. For more information on teacher policy, see CRS Report RL33333, *A Highly Qualified Teacher in Every Classroom: Implementation of the No Child Left Behind Act and Reauthorization Issues for the 112th Congress*, by Jeffrey J. Kuenzi; and CRS Report R41267, *Elementary and Secondary School Teachers: Policy Context, Federal Programs, and ESEA Reauthorization Issues*, by Jeffrey J. Kuenzi.

[79] ESEA, Section 111 1(b)(8)(C).

[80] Several large school districts – including Chicago, Denver, and the District of Columbia – use value-added systems for teacher evaluations. Tennessee uses a statewide value-added system for teacher evaluations.

[81] For more information on VAM, see CRS Report R41051, *Value-Added Modeling for Teacher Effectiveness*, by Erin D. Lomax and Jeffrey J. Kuenzi.

[82] Although some claim that high-poverty schools are less likely to have highly qualified teachers, given that nearly all teachers are considered highly qualified, it is not clear whether this requirement has proven useful. According to the most recent figures, from the 2007-2008 school year, 95% of all core academic classes are taught by highly qualified teachers; the figure is 99% in more than a dozen states. U.S. Department of Education, *A Summary of Highly Qualified Teacher Data*, Washington, DC, May 2009, http://www2.ed.gov/programs/teacherqual/data2009.doc.

[83] TIF was authorized by P.L. 109-149.

[84] For more information on VAM, see CRS Report R41051, *Value-Added Modeling for Teacher Effectiveness*, by Erin D. Lomax and Jeffrey J. Kuenzi; and Steven Glazerman, Susanna Loeb, and Dan Goldhaber, et al., *Evaluating Teachers: The Important Role of Value-Added*, Brown Center on Education Policy at Brookings, Washington, DC, November 17, 2010, http://www.brookings.edu/~/media/Files/rc/reports/2010/1117_evaluating_teachers/ 11 17_evaluating_teachers.pdf.

In: Elementary and Secondary Education Act
Editors: D. M. Brown and A. Davies

ISBN: 978-1-61942-694-8

Chapter 2

ELEMENTARY AND SECONDARY SCHOOL TEACHERS: POLICY CONTEXT, FEDERAL PROGRAMS, AND ESEA REAUTHORIZATION ISSUES

Jeffrey J. Kuenzi

SUMMARY

Policymaking at the federal level reflects a growing awareness that improving educational outcomes depends greatly upon increasing the quality of classroom instruction. In establishing the student performance standards and accountability provisions in the No Child Left Behind Act of 2001 (NCLB), legislators recognized that the success of these reforms rests largely on improving teachers' knowledge and skills. Thus, in enacting NCLB, Congress amended the Elementary and Secondary Education Act (ESEA) to establish a requirement that all teachers be *highly qualified* and authorized the Title II, Teacher and Principal Training and Recruiting Fund to assist schools' efforts to meet this new requirement.

The NCLB highly qualified teacher requirement has now been the cornerstone of federal teacher policy for nearly a decade. In that time, the requirement has come to be seen by many as a minimum standard for entry into the profession (rather than a goal to which teachers might aspire) and a growing body of research has revealed its underlying credentials to be weakly correlated with student achievement. Meanwhile, congressional interest has begun to shift from a focus on teacher input (i.e., quality) to teacher output (i.e., effectiveness). Most recently, Congress passed provisions in the American Recovery and Reinvestment Act of 2009 which required states applying for State Fiscal Stabilization Funds to provide assurances that they will take actions to improve teacher effectiveness. Further, policymakers at all levels are considering how such issues as teacher compensation, licensure or certification, and tenure may relate to teacher performance in the classroom.

The authorization for ESEA programs expired at the end of FY2008, and the 112th Congress is expected to consider whether to amend and extend the ESEA. This report provides background information for the legislative debates likely to occur as this process unfolds. The report gives a brief overview of the context in which federal teacher policy is situated, describes the evolving federal role in this area and the major federal programs designed to support the quality and effectiveness of teachers, and discuses policy issues that may arise as Congress considers ESEA reauthorization.

INTRODUCTION

Policymaking at the federal level reflects a growing awareness that improving educational outcomes depends greatly upon increasing the quality of classroom instruction. In establishing the student performance standards and accountability provisions in the No Child Left Behind Act of 2001 (NCLB, P.L. 107-110), legislators recognized that the success of these reforms rests largely on improving teachers' knowledge and skills. Thus, in enacting NCLB, Congress amended the Elementary and Secondary Education Act (ESEA) to establish a requirement that all teachers be *highly qualified* and authorized the Title II, Teacher and Principal Training and Recruiting Fund to assist schools' efforts to meet this new requirement.[1] More recently, Congress enacted additional programs to improve the teacher workforce including the Teacher Incentive Fund (TIF), Teacher Education Assistance for College and Higher Education (TEACH) Grants, and amendments to the Higher Education Act (HEA).

The NCLB highly qualified teacher requirement has now been the cornerstone of federal teacher policy for nearly a decade. In that time, the requirement has come to be seen by many as a minimum standard for entry into the profession (rather than a goal to which teachers might aspire) and a growing body of research has revealed its underlying credentials to be weakly correlated with student achievement. Meanwhile, congressional interest has begun to shift from a focus on teacher input (i.e., quality) to teacher output (i.e., effectiveness).[2] Most recently, Congress passed provisions in the American Recovery and Reinvestment Act of 2009 (ARRA, P.L. 111-5) which required states applying for State Fiscal Stabilization Funds to provide assurances that they will take actions to improve teacher effectiveness. The Secretary of Education used ARRA authority to encourage states to better link student achievement and teacher effectiveness.[3] Further, policymakers at all levels are considering how such issues as teacher compensation, licensure or certification, and tenure may relate to teacher performance in the classroom.[4]

The authorization for ESEA programs expired at the end of FY2008, and the 112th Congress is expected to consider whether to amend and extend the ESEA. This report provides background information for the legislative debates likely to occur as Congress considers these programs and issues. The first part of this report gives a brief overview of the context in which federal teacher policy is situated, including such issues as the demographics of the teaching workforce, supply and demand, attrition and retention, compensation systems, certification/licensure policies, tenure rules, and unionization. The second part of this report describes the evolving federal role in teacher policy. Part three describes the major federal programs designed to support the quality and effectiveness of teachers, including Title II of the ESEA, TIF, TEACH Grants, and Title II of the HEA. The final part of this report discusses policy changes and ESEA reauthorization issues that might be considered by the 112th Congress.

TEACHER POLICY CONTEXT

The organization and size of the public K-12 educational enterprise pose a significant challenge to formulating federal teacher policy. Nationwide, nearly four million teachers are employed in almost 100,000 public schools located in about 14,000 school districts.[5] This is a decentralized system; states and localities have legal and administrative responsibility for K-12 education. School districts control most of the major aspects of this system, including the recruitment, hiring, evaluation, professional development, compensation, and retention of teachers. Some aspects of the system—like certification procedures and tenure rules—are dictated at the state level. Pre-service teacher preparation and in-service training often take place at higher education institutions. Teacher assignments and evaluations are often the domain of schools. This section discusses how these factors shape the teacher policy context.

Characteristics of the Teaching Workforce

Demographics

The elementary and secondary teaching force is large.[6] There are just under 3.9 million public school teachers in the United States. Of these teachers, 2.4 million are elementary school teachers, 1.2 million are secondary school teachers, and the remaining teachers (slightly more than 358,000) teach in settings that are a combination of the two. The teaching workforce is split about evenly between urban schools (1.1 million teachers), suburban schools (1.4 million), and rural or small town schools (1.4 million).

Over three-fourths (7 6%) of K-12 teachers are female.[7] For teachers whose main field of assignment is in kindergarten or general elementary education, nearly nine out of 10 are female; compared to six out of 10 in secondary schools. The large majority (84%) of the teaching force is white, while 7% of teachers are black, 7% are Hispanic, slightly more than 1% are Asian or Pacific Islander, and less than 1% are American Indian, Alaskan Native, Native Hawaiian, or other Pacific Islander.[8]

The teaching workforce is aging. The average age of school teachers is 43. This is an increase of three years from 1987-1988 when the average age was 40. One-third (33%) of teachers are age 50 or older; compared to 25% in 1993-1994 and 18% in 1987-1988. On average, school teachers have 13 years of teaching experience; over a third (37%) have 15 or more years of experience and 20% have taught 15 or more years in their current school.[9] Nearly two-fifths (19%) have less than four years of teaching experience and over a third (36%) have been in their current school less than four years. The impending retirement of Baby Boom generation teachers who made lifelong commitments to education may pose both challenges and opportunities for teacher policy.[10]

Supply and Demand

There are those who warn of a potential shortage of teachers in the coming years, precipitated by projected increases in student enrollment and an anticipated rise in teacher retirements due to an aging workforce. Public school enrollment increased 12% between 1993 and 2006 and is expected to continue to grow, at a slightly lower rate, to be about 8% larger by 2018.[11] Further, the average age of public school teachers has risen and more teachers will be eligible to retire. As a result, it is anticipated that the attrition rate from teaching will rise. It already grew somewhat between the late 1980s and mid-1990s—between 1987-1988 and 1988-1989, 5.6% of public school teachers left teaching; between 1993-1994 and 1994-1995, 6.6% left. Some data suggest that the nation may lose as much as half of its teachers to retirement over the next decade. [12]

Others question the possibility or existence of an overall teacher shortage. One of the primary reasons is that the supply side of the equation is particularly difficult to quantify. In 2003-2004, over 238,000 teachers were either newly hired or were returning to teaching that year (that is, they were not teaching in the prior year). Of these teachers, roughly 87,000 (37%) had just completed their schooling in the prior year. Of the remaining 151,000, two-thirds (66%) were former teachers returning to the classroom after taking some time (at least one year) away from teaching and one-third (34%) were delayed entrants (that is, they had prepared to teach at some earlier point but did not enter teaching directly). [13] It is very difficult to estimate the size of this latter group, the so-called *reserve pool* of teachers who either delay entry or return after a time away. Roughly two-out-of-five (41%) teachers are delayed entrants (i.e., they started teaching between one and four years after receiving their bachelor's degree).[14] Annually, about 100,000 bachelor's degrees in education are awarded.[15] Research suggests that about half of these graduates do not teach their first year out of school.[16]

Attrition and Retention

Another reason why the notion of a systemic teacher shortage may be misguided is that much of the demand for teachers results from teacher turnover; especially at so-called *hard-to-staff* schools. This turnover has more to do with failure to retain newly hired teachers as opposed to retirements. Some schools have such low teacher retention that, "most of the demand and hiring is simply to replace teachers recently departed from their positions; moreover, most of this teacher turnover has little to do with the 'graying work force'."[17] While it is true that teacher retirements are increasing, the overall volume of turnover due to retirement is relatively minor when compared with that resulting from other causes, such as teacher job dissatisfaction and teachers seeking to pursue better jobs or other careers. At the end of the 2003-2004 school year, roughly 621,000 (roughly 20% of all) teachers left the school where they had been teaching; about 289,000 transferred to a different school, about 246,000 left teaching, and about 87,000 retired.[18]

Features of the Teaching Workplace

Certification and Licensure

Teacher certification or licensure is a state function.[19] A license to teach typically means that the holder has met at least minimal standards set by the state and is, thereby, permitted to teach. The educational, experiential, testing, and other requirements for licensure vary from state to state. Often, the licensing process in a state includes a provisional license good for a limited number of years and granted to an individual who has completed an approved teacher education program and attained passing scores on an examination given to teacher candidates. This license is usually succeeded by a longer term license awarded, perhaps, for successful completion of the initial entry period of teaching and attainment of additional education. In addition to these regular licenses, many states grant "intern" and "limited" licenses in order to fill vacancies quickly.[20] These temporary licenses may be granted with an expectation that the holder will make progress to full certification through so-called *alternative routes*. Initiatives such as Teach for America, Inc. and IBM's Transition to Teaching program[21] are designed to provide an optional means for bringing non-traditional teaching candidates (e.g., recently graduated, non-education majors and individuals seeking to change careers) into teaching in a structured fashion. [22]

Hiring and School Assignment

The hiring process for teachers is usually handled by districts' human resources department, although some districts give schools a greater role in the process than others. Most districts conduct the entire hiring and placement process. Less often, but perhaps increasingly, human resource departments may simply review applicants' background and credentials and leave the rest up to schools. That is, once applicants clear the initial district screening process, a school- based hiring committee may conduct interviews and choose candidates to offer employment.[23] In general, research has shown that, "most new teachers actually have limited interactions with school-based personnel during the hiring process."[24]

School assignment is typically subject to district staffing rules concerning teacher seniority, often instituted through collective bargaining.[25] Under these rules, tenured teachers with the most seniority are typically given priority in staffing decisions. Research has shown that teachers use "their seniority to move to schools with higher test scores, lower poverty rates, and fewer black and Hispanic students. As a result, high-poverty, low-performing schools had the highest rates of turnover, and inexperienced teachers who [lack] the seniority to request transfers, or teachers who [lack] full certification, were typically assigned to fill vacancies in them."[26] Research suggests that this uneven distribution of teachers by experience also leads to "hidden" funding inequities across schools in a district.[27] Teacher seniority systems "can sharply curtail school principals' control over staff hiring, transfer, and firing decisions"[28] and even prompt some principals to hide their vacancies until late summer to avoid the possibility of being forced to accept unwanted transfers.[29]

Evaluation and Effectiveness

Responsibility for teacher evaluation is generally given to school administration.[30] The process of evaluation is often laid out in collective bargaining agreements in states that have teacher unions or associations; however, these policies often lack detail on local approaches to evaluation. For example, a study of evaluation policies in Midwestern states found that "policy documents were more apt to specify the processes involved in teacher evaluation (who conducts the evaluation, when, and how often) than they were to provide guidance for the content of the evaluation, the standards by which the evaluation would be conducted, or the use of the evaluation results."[31] Typically, provisional, nontenured teachers are evaluated at least once each year, while tenured teachers are evaluated less often. In general, principals and vice-principals perform these evaluations using personnel files and conducting classroom observations (either announced or unannounced), sometimes with pre- or post-observation conferences. Most teachers are simply asked to sign off on a summative evaluation form and many see the process as "a bureaucratic necessity of little use to improving" their instructional capabilities.[32]

Though they may be intended to gauge teachers' job performance, evaluations typically reveal little about their effectiveness in the classroom. A recent study by the New Teacher Project concluded that evaluation systems fail to distinguish between various degrees of effectiveness.[33] Nearly half of the districts in the study used a binary rating for performance (e.g., either "satisfactory" or "unsatisfactory") and virtually all teachers (99%) in these districts receive a satisfactory rating. Differentiation improves when multiple ratings are available; however, often fewer than 10% of teachers receive a rating less than satisfactory. Some argue that evaluation policies must be reformed to require that evaluations use objective measures of classroom effectiveness, such as student achievement. Sixteen states now require that student learning be factored into teacher evaluations and four require that it be the preponderant criterion.[34] Others point out limitations in using student assessments to estimate teacher performance; for example, only about half of the nation's teachers teach subjects that are tested.[35] In a limited number of settings, so-called *value-added models* have been used to estimate teachers' effectiveness using student assessment results.[36]

Tenure and Dismissal

State law typically provides teachers job protection in the form of tenure.[37] These state statutes specify how teachers gain tenure and how they can be dismissed. These laws outline the due process that must be provided teachers facing dismissal. Every state has a law addressing these issues that is specifically targeted to elementary and secondary school teachers. Often a tenure law will identify a period of time during which a new teacher is under probation and being considered for tenure. In nearly every state, that probationary period is specified—the range is between two years and five years, the most common period is three years. Typically, during this probationary period, a teacher is employed under a yearly contract and can be dismissed by the district's board of education for any reason as long as that reason is not constitutionally impermissible. Generally, the law provides for a specified date by which the probationary teacher must be notified that the contract will not be renewed. Once awarded tenure, teachers are assured they will continue to be employed unless dismissed for cause and only under the procedures specified in the law. The grounds for dismissal most frequently cited are incompetency, neglect of duty, insubordination, and immorality. The procedure always includes the opportunity for a hearing, which is typically conducted by the school board. Tenure laws may also specify an appeals process.

Unions and Collective Bargaining Agreements

Over three-quarters (7 8%) of all public school teachers are members of teachers' unions or employee associations that function like unions.[38] Teachers' unions have been criticized as barriers to educational improvement and reform. Critics have argued that the major teachers' unions—National Education Association and American Federation of Teachers—have historically been more interested in job protection and higher salaries than in improving the instruction of students. Others argue that, in recent years, union leaders have been rethinking the role of unions in the current reform environment where traditional relationships among all parties in the educational process are being reconsidered and refashioned.

Two recent studies of provisions in teacher collective bargaining agreements (CBAs) concluded that the most salient feature of CBAs with regard to their impact on school reform is their ambiguity. However, the researchers disagree about whether this impact is positive or negative. On the positive side, this ambiguity could "allow for greater latitude for an aggressive principal who is looking for more flexibility and willing to push the envelope, while serving to limit a more cautious or timid principal who looks to the CBA for explicit authority or permission first before acting."[39] On the negative side, "while leaders in some industries would interpret these ambiguities as green lights, in the bureaucratic halls of public education—where risk-averse principals, central office administrators, school boards, and superintendents are rewarded for loyalty and encouraged by the community to avoid unseemly conflict—regulatory obscurity usually equals inaction."[40]

Compensation Systems

Teacher pay levels are typically set by local school districts, usually within a schedule established statewide that permits local districts to exceed the schedule's salary levels. Most teachers are currently paid under a single salary schedule which provides increases in pay for completion of additional college credits or degrees, as well as for completion of additional years of service. According to the Department of Education, "The average salary for public school teachers in 2006–2007 was $50,816, about 3% higher than in 1996–97, after adjustment for inflation. The salaries of public school teachers have generally maintained pace with inflation since 1990–91."[41]

There is much debate over whether teachers are adequately compensated. Complicating this debate are complex methodological issues concerning how to calculate the number of days per year or hours per week teachers actually work as well as how to factor non-monetary benefits like sick leave, health care, and pensions into total compensation. Research comparing teachers' salaries to those earned by individuals with similar skill sets or similar jobs produce a range of estimates. On the low end of this range is research by the Economic Policy Institute[42] which shows that teachers earned 12% less per week in 2002 compared to accountants, reporters, registered nurses, computer programmers, clergy, personnel officers, and vocational counselors and inspectors. On the other end, according to a Manhattan Institute study of 2005 teacher salaries,[43] public school teachers at that time were paid 11% more than the average professional worker in a similar list of occupations.

Recent efforts to reform teacher compensation attempt to differentiate pay according to how difficult certain positions are to fill, such as schools with low retention rates and subjects in which the supply of teachers is limited. Another focus of teacher compensation reform has been the introduction of performance measures into this equation.[44]

THE FEDERAL ROLE IN K-12 TEACHING

The previous section explained that much of the teacher policy context is dictated at the local level. The systems for preparing, recruiting, certifying, compensating, granting tenure, and structuring the working conditions of elementary and secondary school teachers is primarily the responsibility of states and school districts. These areas have historically been viewed as largely outside the reach of the federal government. However, beginning with the 105th Congress, the federal role in K-12 teaching has greatly expanded. In FY1998, the total amount appropriated for all teacher programs under the U.S. Department of Education (ED) was $498 million.[45] Since that time, funding for this purpose has increased roughly fivefold.[46]

Along with this growth, Congress has redefined the nature of the federal role in this area. This section briefly discusses how this role has evolved and expanded in the last decade.

In-service Training and Professional Development

Federal support for K-12 teaching prior to the 105th Congress largely focused on in-service training and professional development. In FY1998, the largest federal teacher program was the Eisenhower Professional Development program (authorized under Title II of the ESEA, as amended by Improving America's Schools Act of 1994, P.L. 103-382). The Eisenhower program (appropriated $335 million for FY1998) allocated funds to state educational agencies (SEAs), local educational agencies (LEAs), and institutions of higher education (IHEs) to improve the quality of classroom teaching through professional development in core academic subjects.

Five other programs accounted for the remainder ($163 million) of ED's FY1998 funding to support K-12 teaching. Virtually all of these funds were appropriated for programs to support in- service training. Most of this funding ($117 million) supported training for teachers of students with disabilities under the Individuals with Disabilities Education Act (IDEA). Much of the rest ($25 million) supported training of teachers working with limited English proficient students under the ESEA. A smaller amount ($19 million) was appropriated to support advanced certification for current teachers through the National Board for Professional Teaching Standards. Finally, a small portion ($2 million) of federal funding to improve K-12 teaching was appropriated to hire teachers through the Minority Teacher Recruitment program under Title V of the HEA.[47]

Pre-service Training and Class Size Reduction

The 105th Congress began a change in the focus of federal teacher policy through two measures: (1) amending the HEA to include a new Teacher Quality Enhancement program, and (2) appropriating funds for a new Class Size Reduction program under broad authority provided in Title VI of the ESEA. Title II, Part A of the HEA (as amended by the Higher Education Amendments of 1998, P.L. 105-244) authorized three types of competitively awarded grants— state grants, partnership grants, and recruitment grants—with the annual appropriation allocated 45%, 45%, and 10% respectively. State and partnership grant funds were to be used for activities including teacher preparation and holding preparation programs accountable for the quality of their graduates, reforming teacher certification requirements, and professional development.

Recruitment grant funds were to be used for the recruitment of highly qualified teachers. In its first year of funding, FY1999, this program was appropriated $77 million.

Significantly, these amendments also had broad-based accountability requirements for teacher education programs. Funded states and their IHEs were required to report publicly on teacher preparation, including the pass rates of graduates on certification assessments. States also had to identify low-performing teacher preparation programs. If low-performing programs lost state approval or financing, their institutions could not receive professional development funding from ED and could not accept or enroll any HEA-aided student in the teacher education program.

The 105th Congress also established the Class Size Reduction program through the FY1999 omnibus appropriations legislation (P.L. 105-277) and appropriated $1.2 billion for the program. Funds were awarded through formula grants distributed among the states according to either (1) the state's share of ESEA, Title I-A funding (based primarily on numbers of children 5-17 years old living in poverty and levels of state per pupil expenditure), or (2) the state's share of ESEA Title II funding (based on school aged population and the distribution of Title I-A funding, with an overall state minimum of 0.5% of total state grants), whichever share would provide the state with a larger amount. States then awarded subgrants by formula to LEAs—80% on the basis of the distribution of children aged 5-17 living in poverty and 20% on the basis of total enrollment of children aged 5-17. Funds were appropriated for ESEA Title VI but were to be spent in accordance with provisions included in the appropriations statute which specified their use for the general hiring of new teachers to reduce class size. The program broke new ground with its explicit and primary focus on federal support for the hiring of teachers.

Teacher Quality

The 106th Congress continued the redefinition of the federal role in K-12 teaching. For FY2001, Congress specified that appropriated amounts for the Eisenhower program above the FY2000 level ($335 million) were to be spent on such activities as reducing the percentage of teachers without certification or with emergency or provisional certification, the percentage teaching out of field, or the percentage lacking requisite content knowledge. These excess funds could also be directed to such other activities as mentoring for new teachers, multi-week institutes providing professional development, and retention efforts for teachers with a record of increasing low- income students' academic achievement. Among other new money for teachers approved in the FY200 1 appropriations for ED was $3 million for the Troops-to-Teachers program (supporting entry of former military personnel into teaching) and $31 million for the Transition to Teaching program (targeting recruitment of mid-career professionals in other occupations and highly qualified recent college graduates with BAs in fields other than education).

Requirement that All Teachers be Highly Qualified

The 107th Congress further expanded the federal role concerning issues of teacher quality. On January 8, 2002, the No Child Left Behind Act (NCLB) was signed into law (P.L. 107-110). This legislation continued to authorize federal support for activities to improve K- 12 teaching through class size reduction, in-service training, and recruitment. It also more firmly focused federal interest on teacher quality by requiring virtually all teachers to be "highly qualified." Under NCLB, each SEA receiving ESEA Title I-A funding had to have a plan to ensure that, by no later than the end of the 2005-2006 school year, all teachers teaching in core academic subjects[48] within the state be designated a *highly qualified teacher*.

NCLB specified a lengthy definition of the requirements a teacher must fulfill to achieve highly qualified status and subsequent regulations specified the complex procedures that states and LEAs must undertake to demonstrate compliance with the new requirements.[49] As part of its plan, each Title I-funded state had to establish annual measurable objectives for each LEA and school that included, at a minimum, annual increases in the percentage of highly qualified teachers at each LEA and school to ensure that the 2005-2006 deadline was met. States and LEAs were also required to publicly issue annual reports describing progress on the state-set objectives. To assist states and localities in meeting these new requirements, NCLB increased federal teacher program funding and replaced the Eisenhower Professional Development and Class Size Reduction programs with a new formula grant program (discussed further in the next section of this report).

NCLB added to the ESEA the first federal definition of "professional development" to include activities that, among other things, improve teachers' knowledge of the academic subjects and enable teachers to become highly qualified; improve classroom management skills; are sustained, intensive, and classroom-focused instead of one-day, off-site workshops; advance understanding of effective instructional strategies; provide training in the use of technology; are regularly evaluated for their impact on increased teacher effectiveness and improved student academic achievement; provide instruction in methods of teaching children with special needs and English language learners; include instruction in the use of data and assessments; and include instruction in ways to work more effectively with parents.[50]

Compensation, Recruitment, and School Leadership

In recent years, Congress has broken new ground in the area of teacher compensation, expanded federal support for teacher recruitment, and modified the federal role in the preparation of teachers and school leadership. The results of these actions are briefly mentioned here; the programs created are discussed in detail in the next section, which describes all current federal teacher programs.

The 109th Congress established the Teacher Incentive Fund through the FY2006 appropriations legislation (P.L. 109-149) which provided $100 million for competitive grants to support teacher compensation reform. The 110th Congress passed the America COMPETES Act of 2007 (P.L. 110-69) which authorized two new programs that encourage science, technology, engineering, and mathematics (STEM) majors to concurrently obtain teaching certification, support current teachers' pursuit of STEM master's degrees, and bring STEM professionals into teaching. The 110th Congress further enhanced teacher recruitment by amending the HEA through the College Cost Reduction and Access Act of 2007 (P.L. 110-84). The amendments authorized a new TEACH grant program that provides scholarships worth $4,000 a year for prospective teachers who agree to serve in hard-to-staff schools and expanded the existing loan forgiveness opportunities for certain teachers. The HEA was amended again, in the second session of the 110th Congress, through the Higher Education Opportunity Act of 2008 (P.L. 110-315). This legislation amended the Title II, Part A program by targeting grant activities on pre-baccalaureate teacher preparation, teacher residencies, and school leadership development.

Effectiveness

Most recently, Congress has signaled that, as opposed to continuing to emphasize teacher quality, increasingly federal policy may focus on teacher effectiveness. The 111th Congress enacted the American Recovery and Reinvestment Act (ARRA; P.L. 111-5), which was signed by the President on February 17, 2009. The ARRA authorized and appropriated $4 billion for the Race to the Top competitive grant program which is intended to initiate reforms around four areas: (1) adopting standards and assessments that prepare students to succeed in college and the workplace and to compete in the global economy; (2) building data systems that measure student growth and success, and inform teachers and principals about how they can improve instruction; (3) *recruiting, developing, rewarding, and retaining effective teachers and principals, especially where they are needed most*; and (4) turning around the lowest-achieving schools.

In November 2009, the Department of Education published a notice of final priorities for the Race to the Top program. Included in the notice was the first federal definition of an "effective teacher," which

> means a teacher whose students achieve acceptable rates (e.g., at least one grade level in an academic year) of student growth (as defined in this notice). States, LEAs, or schools must include multiple measures, provided that teacher effectiveness is evaluated, in significant part, by student growth (as defined in this notice). Supplemental measures may include, for example, multiple observation-based assessments of teacher performance.51

The next section of this report further discusses the Race to the Top program along with the other major federal teacher programs in detail.

CURRENT FEDERAL TEACHER PROGRAMS

This section provides descriptions of the major federal programs currently authorized to address K-12 teaching. The primary focus of this discussion is on the programs in the ESEA as amended by NCLB. Federal programs authorized in the HEA and elsewhere are also described.

Elementary and Secondary Education Act

Teacher and Principal Training and Recruiting Fund

In amending and reauthorizing the ESEA, NCLB continued Title II as the primary title for teacher programs.[52] As amended, ESEA, Title II-A replaced the Eisenhower Professional Development and Class Size Reduction programs (hereinafter referred to as Eisenhower and CSR, respectively) with a new state formula grant program authorized at $3. 175 billion for FY2002 and such sums as may be necessary for the five succeeding fiscal years.[53] The fund awards formula grants to SEAs which then award formula subgrants to LEAs. The FY2010 appropriation provided $2.948 billion for this purpose.

State Allocation Formula

The allocation formula for Title II-A provides each state with a base guarantee of funding equal to the amount it received for FY2001 under the Eisenhower and CSR programs. Any excess funding is allocated by formula among the states based 35% on school-aged population (5-17) and 65% on school-aged population in poverty. Each state is assured 0.5% of this excess. At the state level, 95% of the state grant is to be distributed as subgrants to LEAs, 2.5% for local partnerships (the Secretary calculates an alternative percentage if 2.5% of the state grant would generate a total for all states in excess of $125 million), and the remainder for state activities.

LEA Subgrants

LEA subgrant funding is distributed first as a base guarantee of the FY2001 Eisenhower and CSR grants to individual districts, with the remainder distributed by formula based 20% on school- aged population and 80% on school-aged population in poverty.

LEAs are authorized to use their funding for one or more of various specified activities. Among the authorized activities are the following:

- assistance to schools in the recruitment and retention of highly qualified teachers (see definition above), principals, and, under certain conditions, pupil services personnel;
- assistance in recruiting and hiring highly qualified teachers through such means as scholarships and signing bonuses;
- use of these teachers to reduce class sizes;
- initiatives to increase retention of highly qualified teachers and principals, particularly in schools with high percentages of low-achieving students, through mentoring, induction services during the initial three years of service, and financial incentives for those effectively serving all students;
- professional development, including professional development that involves technology in teaching and curriculum and professional development delivered through technology;
- improvement of the quality of the teaching force through such activities as tenure reform, merit pay, and teacher testing in their subject areas; and
- professional development for principals and superintendents.

The majority of Title II-A funds are used for class size reduction and professional development. In recent years, professional development has replaced class size reduction as the single largest area of spending. The percentage of funds used for reducing class size decreased from 57% in 2002-2003 to 38% in 2008-2009, and the percentage of funds used for professional development increased from 27% in 2002-2003 to 39% in 2008-2009.[54]

Partnership Subgrants

Funds are awarded competitively to partnerships that must include an IHE and its division preparing teachers and principals; an IHE school of arts and sciences; and a high-need LEA (defined as one with at least 10,000 poor children or a child poverty rate of at least 20% that, in addition, has either a high percentage of out-of-field teachers or a high percentage of teachers with emergency, provisional, or temporary certificates). Other entities, such as charter schools or another LEA, may be part of these partnerships. Partnerships must use their funds for professional development in the core academic subjects for teachers, highly qualified paraprofessionals, and principals.

State Activities

States must use their funding for one or more of several specified activities. Among these activities are the following: teacher and principal certification reform; mentoring and intensive professional development for teachers and principals, including those new to their careers; assistance to LEAs and schools in the recruitment and retention of highly qualified teachers, principals, and, under certain conditions, pupil services personnel; tenure reform; subject matter testing for teachers; projects to promote teacher and principal certification reciprocity across states; training to help teachers integrate technology into the curriculum and instruction; assistance to help teachers become highly qualified by the end of the fourth year of state funding; and a clearinghouse for teacher recruitment and placement.

Accountability

If, after the second year of the plan to ensure that all teachers are highly qualified (see previous section), an LEA has failed to make progress toward the annual objectives in such plan, it must develop an improvement plan. Failure after the third year coupled with failure to make *adequate yearly progress*[55] for three consecutive years requires the SEA to identify the professional development the LEA will use and, generally, precludes use of Title I-A funds for the hiring of paraprofessionals. In addition, the SEA provides funding directly to schools in the LEA to enable their teachers to choose their own professional development activities.

National Activities

The Secretary of Education is authorized to use national activities funding for several specific activities. These funds support an Advanced Credentialing program to encourage teachers to pursue advanced certification by the National Board for Professional Teaching Standards or the National Council on Teacher Quality. In FY20 10, $10.6 million is appropriated for Advanced Credentialing. National activities also support a School Leadership program for the recruitment of principals to high-need LEAs. In FY2010, $29.2 million was appropriated for School Leadership.

Mathematics and Science Partnerships

Title II-B authorizes funding for partnerships to improve math and science instruction. An eligible partnership must include an SEA, the engineering, mathematics, or science department of an IHE, and a high-need LEA. Other entities such as LEAs and charter schools may be included as well. The annual authorization of appropriations is $450 million for FY2002 and such sums as may be necessary for the next five fiscal years. When the annual appropriation is less than $100 million, the program's three-year grants are awarded competitively; otherwise, funds are awarded to SEAs based on school-aged population in poverty with a 0.5% small state minimum. The FY20 10 appropriation was $180 million.

Partnerships must use their grants for one or more of several specific activities. Among them are the following: professional development to improve math and science teachers' subject knowledge; activities to promote strong teaching skills among these teachers and teacher educators; math and science summer workshops or institutes with academic year followup; recruitment of math, science, or engineering majors to teaching through signing and performance incentives, stipends for alternative certification, and scholarships for advanced course work; development or redesign of more rigorous, standards-aligned math and science curricula; distance learning programs for math and science teachers; and opportunities for math and science teachers to have contact with working mathematicians, scientists, and engineers.

The Secretary is to consult and coordinate activities with the Director of the National Science Foundation, particularly regarding the appropriate roles of the two entities in workshops, institutes, and partnerships.

Each partnership must have an evaluation and accountability plan that includes objectives measuring the impact of the funded activities. Among these objectives must be improvement of student achievement on state math and science assessments.

NSF's Mathematics and Science Partnership Program

The NSF has been implementing a Mathematics and Science Partnership program as well, authorized by the National Science Foundation Authorization Act of 2002. The FY20 10 appropriation level for this program was $58.2 million. This is a competitive grant program designed to improve the content knowledge of teachers and the performance of students in the areas of mathematics and science. Grantees are to engage in three kinds of activities: partnerships between IHEs and local school districts, projects focusing on research and evaluation of these efforts and technical assistance, and partnerships supporting teacher institutes.

Innovation for Teacher Quality

Troops-to-Teachers

Title II Part C, Subpart 1, Chapter A authorizes funding and administration of the Troops-toTeachers program, an effort to facilitate the movement of members of the armed forces into K-12 teaching. This legislation authorizes the Secretary of Education to enter into a memorandum of agreement with the Department of Defense for the actual administration of the program, which was first enacted in the FY1993 Defense Authorization Act. The program assists eligible members of the armed forces to become certified as elementary or secondary school teachers or vocational technical teachers. A single authorization of appropriations of $150 million for FY2002 and such sums as may be necessary for the next five fiscal years is provided for the Troops-to-Teachers program and the Transition to Teaching program, of which the Secretary is to reserve not more than $30 million in FY2002 for the Troops-to-Teachers program. The FY2010 appropriation provided $14.4 million for this program.

Transition to Teaching

This is a continuation of a program to recruit mid-career professionals and others to teaching that was first initiated through the Consolidated Appropriations Act of 2001. Title II Part C, Subpart 1, Chapter B authorizes the Secretary to competitively award five-year partnership grants to SEAs, high need LEAs, and higher education institutions for the establishment of state and local "teacher corps" projects. These projects are to recruit highly qualified mid-career professionals, highly qualified paraprofessionals, and recent college graduates to teach in high need schools. Among the activities these programs can support are financial incentives effective for retaining teachers in high need schools in high need LEAs;

pre- and post-placement support such as mentoring; payments for the costs of hiring these teachers or subsidies to participants; and state or regional clearinghouses for recruitment and placement. Participating teachers are to be placed in high need schools within high-need LEAs with a priority on schools in areas with the highest percentages of low-income students. Participants have a three-year service commitment. Projects failing to make substantial progress by the end of their third year toward goals and objectives established in their applications have their grants revoked. The FY2010 appropriation provided $43.7 million for this program.

Teacher Incentive Fund

The Teacher Incentive Fund (TIF) was first authorized and funded through the FY2006 Labor-HHS-Education Appropriations Act (P.L. 109-149) which provided $261 million for activities authorized under Title V, Part D of the ESEA. A portion of these funds ($100 million) was reserved for activities under Subpart 1 which gives the Secretary general authority to award discretionary grants, "to support nationally significant programs to improve the quality of elementary and secondary education."

The act stipulates that these $100 million are to be used for five-year grants competitively awarded to local education agencies (including charter schools) or states individually or in partnership with each other or with a non-profit organization. According to the act, the goal of these projects is to "develop and implement performance-based teacher and principal compensation systems in high-need schools."

The act further requires that TIF project compensation reforms "must consider gains in student academic achievement as well as classroom evaluations conducted multiple times during each school year" among other factors and provide educators with incentives to take on additional responsibilities and leadership roles. The Secretary is given a 5% set-aside to support the Center for Educator Compensation Reform[56] which raises national awareness about alternative and effective strategies for educator compensation reform and provides technical assistance to TIF grantees.

Beginning in 2007, the FY2006 appropriation was used to fund 34 TIF projects; no funds were appropriated for TIF in FY2007. Program funds may be used to pay the costs of developing and implementing performance-based compensation systems for the benefit of teachers and principals in high-need schools. For example, in addition to costs associated with the incentives given to teachers and principals, other project costs could include professional development activities for those teachers in high-need schools, evaluation and analysis tools, project staff salaries at the applicant level, and reasonable travel necessary for project development and implementation.

The Appropriations Acts for FY2008 and FY2009 each provided $97.2 million to continue the original projects. An additional $200 million was appropriated for FY2009 under the ARRA; new grantees supported with these additional funds were announced in September 2010. The FY20 10 appropriation provided $400 million for the TIF program.

Ready to Teach

ESEA, Title V, Part D also authorizes the Ready to Teach program which supports two types of competitive grants to nonprofit telecommunications entities: (1) grants to carry out a national telecommunications-based program to improve teaching in core curriculum areas, and (2) digital educational programming grants that enable eligible entities to develop, produce, and distribute educational and instructional video programming. National telecommunications-based program grants are generally five-year awards. Digital educational programming grants must last three years, be matched by applicants, and must be based on challenging state academic content and student academic achievement standards in reading or mathematics. The FY20 10 appropriation provides $10.7 million for Ready to Teach.

Higher Education Act

The HEA, as amended by the Higher Education Opportunity Act (HEOA, P.L. 110-3 15), addresses K-12 teacher issues through programs supporting the improvement of teacher preparation and recruitment. Title II of the HEA authorizes grants for improving teacher education programs, strengthening teacher recruitment efforts, and providing training for prospective teachers. This title also includes the reporting requirements for states and higher education institutions regarding the quality of teacher education programs. Title IV of the HEA authorizes TEACH Grants to encourage more students to prepare for a career in teaching and student loan forgiveness for individuals teaching in certain high-need subjects. Title VIII of the HEA authorizes support for Teach for America which recruits recent college graduates into teaching.

Teacher Quality Partnership Grants

Title II, Part A of the HEA authorizes Teacher Quality Partnership grants to improve the quality of teachers working in high-need schools and early childhood education programs by improving the preparation of teachers and enhancing professional development activities for teachers; holding teacher preparation programs accountable for preparing effective teachers; and recruiting highly qualified individuals into the teaching force. The FY20 10 appropriation provided $43 million for Teacher Quality Partnerships.

Eligible Partnerships

To be eligible, partnerships must include a high-need LEA; a high-need school or high-need early childhood education program (or a consortium of high-need schools or early childhood education programs served by the partner high-need LEA); a partner IHE; a school, department, or program of education within the partner IHE; and a school or department of arts and sciences within the partner IHE. A high-need LEA must serve either (1) not less than 20%, or (2) not fewer than 10,000 children who are from families below the poverty line.

Partnership Activities

Partnership grant funds are authorized to be used for either a Pre-Baccalaureate Preparation program, a Teacher Residency program, or both. Funds may also be used for a Leadership Development program, but only in addition to one of these other two uses. Activities authorized by the HEOA amendments are described below.

Pre-Baccalaureate Preparation Program. Grants are provided to implement a wide-range of reforms in teacher preparation programs and, as applicable, preparation programs for early childhood educators. These reforms may include, among other things, implementing curriculum changes that improve, evaluate, and assess how well prospective teachers develop teaching skills; using teaching and learning research so that teachers implement research-based instructional practices and use data to improve classroom instruction; developing a high-quality and sustained pre-service clinical education program that includes high-quality mentoring or coaching; creating a high-quality induction program for new teachers; implementing initiatives that increase compensation for qualified early childhood educators who attain two-year and four-year degrees; developing and implementing high-quality professional development for teachers in the partner high-need LEAs; developing effective mechanisms, which may include alternative routes to state certification, to recruit qualified individuals into the teaching profession; and strengthening literacy teaching skills of prospective and new elementary and secondary school teachers.

Teacher Residency Program. Grants are provided to develop and implement teacher residency programs that are based on models of successful teaching residencies and that serve as a mechanism to prepare teachers for success in high-need schools and academic subjects. Grant funds must be used to support programs that provide, among other things, rigorous graduate-level course work to earn a master's degree while undertaking a guided teaching apprenticeship; learning opportunities alongside a trained and experienced mentor teacher; and clear criteria for selecting mentor teachers based on measures of teacher effectiveness. Programs must place graduates in targeted schools as a cohort in order to facilitate professional collaboration and provide a one-year living stipend or salary to members of the cohort, which must be repaid by any recipient who fails to teach full time at least three years in a high-need school or subject area.

Leadership Development Program. Grants are provided to develop and implement effective school leadership programs to prepare individuals for careers as superintendents, principals, early childhood education program directors, or other school leaders. Such programs must promote strong leadership skills and techniques so that school leaders are able to: create a school climate conducive to professional development for teachers; understand the teaching and assessment skills needed to support successful classroom instruction; use data to evaluate teacher instruction and drive teacher and student learning; manage resources and time to improve academic achievement; engage and involve parents and other community stakeholders; and understand how students learn and develop in order to increase academic achievement. Grant funds must also be used to develop a yearlong clinical education program, a mentoring and induction program, and programs to recruit qualified individuals to become school leaders.

Enhancing Teacher Education

The HEOA amendments established five new programs in HEA, Title II, Part B, Enhancing Teacher Education including Subpart 1, Preparing Teachers for Digital Age Learners; Subpart 2, Hawkins Centers of Excellence; Subpart 3, Teach to Reach Grants; Subpart 4, Adjunct Teacher Corps; and Subpart 5, Graduate Fellowships to Prepare Faculty in High-Need Areas. None of these programs have received funding.

TEACH Grants

The College Cost Reduction and Access Act of 2007 (P.L. 110-84) authorized the TEACH Grant program, which provides scholarships worth $4,000 a year for prospective teachers. Eligible recipients must be high-achieving (at least a 3.25 GPA) undergraduate, post-baccalaureate, and graduate students who commit to teaching a high-need subject in a high-need elementary or secondary school for four years. High-need subjects include mathematics, science, foreign languages, bilingual education, special education, and reading. High-need schools are those located in an LEA that is eligible for ESEA, Title I funds.

TEACH Grant recipients agree to serve full-time in a high-need subject at a high-need school for not less than four years within eight years of graduation. For students who fail to fulfill this service requirement, grants are converted to Direct Unsubsidized Stafford Loans with interest accrued from the date the grants were awarded. The FY2010 appropriation for the program was $23 million.

Debt Relief from Student Loans

Qualifying teachers may receive relief from HEA, Title VI Stafford Loan debt.[57] Loan debt can be forgiven for individuals teaching in low-income elementary or secondary schools who are new borrowers on or after October 1, 1998.[58] To be eligible for repayment, borrowers have to teach on a full-time basis for five consecutive years in a Title I school.[59] After completion of that service, up to $5,000 in loan debt can be forgiven. Math, science, and special education teachers in low- income schools are eligible for relief of up to $17,500 in loan debt.

Teach for America

HEA, Title VIII-F, authorizes the Secretary to award a five-year grant to Teach for America, Inc. (TFA), a nonprofit organization that recruits recent college graduates who commit to teach in high-need LEAs. Grant funds may be used for the following activities: (1) recruiting and selecting teachers through TFA's highly selective national process; (2) providing pre-service training to such teachers through a rigorous summer institute that includes hands-on teaching experience and significant exposure to education coursework and theory; (3) finding placements for these teachers in schools and positions designated by high-need local educational agencies as high-need placements serving underserved students; and (4) providing ongoing professional development activities for these teachers during their first two years in the classroom, including regular classroom observations and feedback, and ongoing training and support. The FY20 10 appropriation provided $18 million for Teach for America.

Other Federal Programs

Teachers for a Competitive Tomorrow

The America COMPETES Act of 2007 (P.L. 11 0-69)[60] authorized two new programs to improve K-12 teaching: (1) a Baccalaureate Degree program that encourages STEM majors to concurrently obtain teaching certification and (2) a Master's Degree program to upgrade the skills of current teachers through two to three years of part-time study or to support one-year programs to bring STEM professionals into teaching. The program requires that grantees put particular emphasis on encouraging members of groups that are underrepresented in the teaching of STEM subjects or critical foreign languages to participate in the program. In addition, the program gives priority to grantees whose primary focus is on placing participants in high-need LEAs. The FY2010 appropriation provided $1.1 million for each of these programs.

Tax Provisions

Teachers may take an above-the-line deduction from their federal taxable income of up to $250 a year for classroom expenses (including those for books, supplies, computer equipment, other equipment, and supplementary materials used in the classroom) incurred by teachers and others in schools.[61]

Race to the Top

The ARRA authorized the Race to the Top (RTTT) program and appropriated $4 billion which the Secretary may use to award discretionary RTTT grants to states.[62] Section 14006(c) of the ARRA requires at least 50% of RTTT funding to states to be sub-granted to participating LEAs according to their relative shares of funding under the ESEA, Title I-A. States have considerable flexibility in awarding or allocating the remaining 50% of their RTTT awards, which are available for state-level activities, disbursements to LEAs, and other purposes as the state may propose in its application.

The purpose of the RTTT program is to encourage the development and implementation of educational reforms in four areas: (1) adopting standards and assessments that prepare students to succeed in college and the workplace and to compete in the global economy; (2) building data systems that measure student growth and success, and inform teachers and principals about how they can improve instruction; (3) recruiting, developing, rewarding, and retaining effective teachers and principals, especially where they are needed most; and (4) turning around the lowest-achieving schools. The second and third of these reform areas have particular importance for federal teacher policy.

State Eligibility and Data Systems

To be eligible to compete for RTTT funds, a state must have its application for funds under the State Fiscal Stabilization Fund[63] approved by the Secretary and, at the time the state submits its RTTT application, "there must not be any legal, statutory, or regulatory barriers at the state level to linking data on student achievement (as defined in this notice) or student growth (as defined in this notice) to teachers and principals for the purpose of teacher and principal evaluation."[64] Moreover, priority in the grant competition is given to applications in which the state plans to expand statewide longitudinal data systems to include or integrate data on subgroups of students with human resources data on teachers, principals, and other staff.

Applications must explain the extent to which the state's data system would (1) provide teachers, principals, and administrators with the information and resources they need to inform and improve their instructional practices, decision-making, and overall effectiveness; (2) support LEAs and schools in providing effective professional development to teachers, principals, and administrators; and (3) make data available and accessible to researchers so that they have detailed information with which to evaluate the effectiveness of instructional materials, strategies, and approaches for educating different types of students.

LEA Evaluation of Teacher Effectiveness

To be eligible for participation, LEAs must sign a memorandum of understanding with the state that demonstrates they are, "strongly committed to the state's plans and to effective implementation of reform in the four education areas," including reforms of their teacher evaluation systems.[65] In reforming these systems, participating LEAs must consider several factors when evaluating teachers' effectiveness. According to ED's guidance, "The Department believes that teacher and principal evaluations and related decisions should be based on multiple measures of teacher performance. The Department also believes that student growth should be one of those measures and should be weighted as a significant factor."[66]

ED's RTTT regulations define an "effective teacher" as "a teacher whose students achieve acceptable rates (e.g., at least one grade level in an academic year) of student growth (as defined in this notice)."[67] That is, to be considered effective, teachers must raise their students' learning to a level at or above what is expected within a typical school year. The guidance additionally points out that the focus of evaluating an effective teacher should be student *growth*, not one-time measures of student achievement or proficiency.

These reforms must also produce evaluation results that have actionable consequences. First, they must differentiate teacher and leader effectiveness using multiple rating categories. Second, LEAs must use these evaluations to inform decisions regarding (1) coaching, induction support, and/or professional development; (2) compensating, promoting, and retaining teachers and principals; (3) granting tenure and/or full certification; and (4) removing ineffective tenured and untenured teachers and principals after they have had ample opportunities to improve. Third, states must ensure the equitable distribution of effective teachers based on definitions that are comparable across classrooms in each LEA and across classrooms statewide.

Forty-six states and the District of Columbia applied for RTTT funds. In March 2010, ED announced two winners of the first phase of awards; Delaware received $100 million and Tennessee received $500 million. Winners of the second phase of awards were announced in August 2010. Nine states and the District of Columbia were awarded grants ranging from $75 million to $400 million, depleting the balance of the $4 billion. In its budget request for FY2011, the Administration requested $1.35 billion additional funds for a third phase of awards.

ESEA Reauthorization

The authorization for ESEA programs expired at the end of FY2008, and the 112th Congress is expected to consider whether to amend and extend the ESEA.[68] This section discusses teacher policy issues that may arise as Congress proceeds with reauthorization. The Administration's proposal for ESEA reauthorization address some of these issues.

Administration's Blueprint

In March 2010, ED released *A Blueprint for Reform: The Reauthorization of the Elementary and Secondary Education Act.*[69] The second of five major priorities set out in the *Blueprint*, Great Teachers and Leaders in Every School, addresses changes to the various federal teacher and leadership programs discussed earlier in this report.[70] In general, the Administration's proposal would consolidate and refocus current federal programs on the conditions that allow teachers and leaders, "to get meaningful information about their practice, and support them in using this information to ensure that all students are getting effective teaching."[71] The *Blueprint* places emphasis on improving the evaluation of teacher and leader effectiveness, rewarding and advancing effective teachers and leaders, and strengthening the recruitment and preparation of teachers and leaders.

Effective Teachers and Leaders

The Administration proposes to continue formula grants to states under the ESEA, Title II-A. The program would be refocused on improving the effectiveness of school staff and renamed Effective Teachers and Leaders State Grants. In response to the NCLB "highly-qualified teacher" requirement, LEAs use of Title II-A funds increasingly focused on in-service teacher professional development.[72] The proposed program would refocus Title II-A grants toward reforming teacher and principal evaluation systems through requirements modeled on the RTTT.[73] Specifically, the proposed program would require states and LEAs to put in place three policies and systems:

1. Statewide definitions of "effective teacher," "effective principal," highly effective teacher," and "highly effective principal" developed in collaboration with stakeholders that are "based in significant part on student growth" and also include other measures, such as classroom observations;
2. State-level data systems that link information on teacher and principal preparation programs to the job placement, student growth, and retention outcomes of their graduates; and
3. District-level evaluation systems that (1) meaningfully differentiate teacher and principal effectiveness in at least three performance levels, (2) are consistent with state definitions of effectiveness, (3) provide meaningful feedback that informs professional development, and (4) are developed in collaboration with stakeholders.[74]

Teacher and Leader Innovation Fund

Under the *Blueprint*, ED proposes to merge two existing competitive grant programs that reward teacher performance and career advancement—the Teacher Incentive Fund and Advanced Credentialing—into a new competitive grant program called the Teacher and Leader Innovation Fund. According to the *Blueprint*, the new program would build on the strengths of the Teacher Incentive Fund and support compensation reforms and complementary reforms of teacher and principal development and evaluation, teacher placement, and other practices. It would support states and districts willing to "implement ambitious reforms to better identify, recruit, prepare, develop, retain, reward, and advance effective teachers, principals, and school leadership teams."[75] These reforms would be required to differentiate among teachers and principals on the basis of their students' growth and other measures and must use this information to differentiate credentialing, professional development, retention, advancement, and rewards for effectiveness.

Teacher and Leader Pathways

ED proposes to merge several existing competitive grant programs into a new competitive grant program called Teacher and Leader Pathways. Five current competitive grant programs would be combined under this new program into two activities: Teacher Pathways and Transformational Leaders. Four current programs[76] would be consolidated into a Teacher Pathways program to strengthen traditional and alternative pathways into teaching by providing competitive grants to programs that would (1) prepare teachers to teach to college- and career-ready standards; (2) meet the needs of high-need areas, including rural areas, or high-need fields; and (3) recruit and prepare high-performing college graduates or non-traditional teacher candidates, such as mid- career professionals and military veterans. The fifth current program, School Leadership, would become a Transformational Leaders program.

Reauthorization Issues

This section discusses teacher policy issues addressed in the *Blueprint* as well as additional issues that may arise during ESEA reauthorization. These issues include

- teacher and principal effectiveness,
- compensation and high-stakes decision-making,
- equitable distribution of teachers,
- preparation and certification, and
- professional development.

Teacher and Principal Effectiveness

Federal policy has, until very recently, been silent on what constitutes effective teaching. The definition of an effective teacher and the evaluation of teachers' performance have largely remained the responsibility of school leadership within broad parameters outlined at the district level; indeed, few states have intervened in this process. Still, Congress has shown increasing interest in growing federal involvement in this area; most recently through passage of RTTT and several hearings on the topic. Among other questions that may arise during ESEA reauthorization, Congress may consider

- whether definitions of teacher effectiveness and principal effectiveness should be written into federal law;
- whether HOUSSE[77] procedures currently laid out in NCLB to identify highly-qualified teachers can be adapted to reform teacher evaluation;
- whether federal accountability requirements for student achievement can be amended to facilitate their use in teacher evaluation;

- whether the federal investment in teacher and principal training should be targeted at improving evaluation systems;
- whether the best policy levers for reforming teacher evaluation systems to emphasize effectiveness occur at the state, district, or school level; and
- whether value-added methods for determining the effectiveness of individual teachers, principals, schools, or districts is currently feasible across grades and subject areas and should be required by federal policy.

Compensation and High-Stakes Decision-Making

Along with increasing the federal role in the evaluation of teacher and principal effectiveness, Congress has shown interest in influencing the use of these evaluations. The TIF requires that grantees reform compensation systems to reward teacher performance with bonuses and other financial incentives. RTTT requires that grantees go further and use evaluations to inform high- stakes decisions such as the granting of tenure, awarding full certification, and removing ineffective teachers. With the knowledge that these decisions are often made at the local level of our educational system, Congress may consider

- whether the federal government will have a sustained role in teacher and principal compensation and whether this role will focus on seeding efforts to develop the capacity to link compensation to performance;
- whether performance-based teacher compensation efforts have triggered reforms in other areas such as evaluation procedures, leadership development, and data systems;
- whether successful reforms in a limited set of school districts can be replicated by scaling up the federal investment; and
- whether federal policy should address other barriers (i.e., beyond failure to identify poor teacher performance) that limit the role of teacher evaluations in high-stakes decision-making.

Equitable Distribution of Teachers

NCLB requires that *highly-qualified teachers* be equitably distributed among classrooms and schools.[78] Although some claim that high-poverty schools are less likely to have highly qualified teachers,[79] given that nearly all teachers are considered highly qualified,[80] it is not clear whether this requirement has proven useful. Congress included similar provisions concerning the equitable distribution of teacher effectiveness in RTTT. However, instead of binary categories—highly qualified or not highly qualified—the new program requires states to define and identify "effective" and "highly effective" teachers. If distribution issues arise during ESEA reauthorization, Congress may consider

- whether federal policy should require states, districts, and/or schools to distinguish multiple levels of teacher quality and/or effectiveness in order to better examine questions of equity;
- whether requirements for distribution of teacher quality and/or effectiveness should be integrated with requirements for "comparability of services" under Title I-A;[81]

- whether current seniority rules for teacher-to-school assignment, often written into collective bargaining agreements, that contribute to the uneven distribution of teachers, should be addressed by the federal government; and
- whether other policy levers, such as pay incentives, are effective at improving equity and should be expanded.

Preparation and Certification

The federal government currently plays a somewhat limited role with regard to support for pre- service teacher preparation. Fewer than one-in-twenty teacher preparation programs receive funding through HEA, Title II-A.[82] All such programs at institutions receiving assistance through the HEA must adhere to the accountability provisions in Title II-A, including reporting requirements regarding pass rates on teacher certification exams. When Congress reauthorized the HEA through the HEOA, Title II-A was authorized through FY20 11 (rather than the FY20 14 authorization provided most of the rest of the HEA). This early expiration provides Congress with an opportunity to simultaneously reauthorize two of the major federal teacher programs (ESEA, Title II-A and HEA, Title II-A). In taking this opportunity, Congress may consider

- whether a portion of the comparatively large federal investment supporting in-service teacher training (under ESEA, Title II-A) should be reallocated to pre- service preparation;
- whether current support for traditional teacher preparation programs under HEA, Title II-A needs to be reworked in light of the growth of alternative routes to certification;
- whether accountability for teacher preparation programs under HEA, Title II-A should be designed to promote the most effective training practices[83] rather than identify so-called "failing" programs; and
- whether certification reform efforts supported by the initial round of HEA, Title II-A State Grants should be renewed in light of recent Congressional interest in incorporating teacher effectiveness into the awarding of full certification to teachers.

Professional Development

ESEA, Title II-A funds are increasingly being used by school districts to support additional in- service professional development.[84] However, this training is often delivered in a sporadic and uncoordinated fashion and teachers often find it of little use in the classroom.[85] As federal mandates expand the collection of student achievement data, teachers have little access to the training needed to use this data effectively.[86] Should improving teacher training become an issue during ESEA reauthorization, Congress may consider

- whether to amend the current, lengthy definition of "professional development"[87] and/or create mechanisms to enforce the practices described in the definition;
- whether to hold schools and/or professional development providers accountable for improving teachers' effectiveness; and
- whether strengthening incentives to improve student achievement is a better way to improve teacher training than to define what that training should entail.

End Notes

[1] For more information on this requirement, see CRS Report RL33333, *A Highly Qualified Teacher in Every Classroom: Implementation of the No Child Left Behind Act and Reauthorization Issues for the 111th Congress*, by Jeffrey J. Kuenzi.

[2] For example, the House Education and Labor Committee held a hearing on September 30, 2009, "to examine the progress states and school districts have made toward ensuring that every child is taught by an effective teacher." http://edlabor.house.gov/hearings/ 2009/09/teacher-equity

[3] For more information on this topic, see CRS Report R41051, *Value-Added Modeling for Teacher Effectiveness*, by Erin D. Lomax and Jeffrey J. Kuenzi.

[4] For more information on teacher compensation, see CRS Report R40576, *Compensation Reform and Incentive Pay for Teachers*, by Jeffrey J. Kuenzi.

[5] Thomas D. Snyder, Sally A. Dillow, and Charlene M. Hoffman, *Digest of Education Statistics 2008 (NCES 2009-020)*, U.S. Department of Education, National Center for Education Statistics, Washington, DC, March 2009, http://nces.ed.gov/programs/digest/. Hereinafter cited as *Digest of Education Statistics*, 2008.

[6] Unless otherwise noted, these data are from Jared Coopersmith and Kerry Gruber, *Characteristics of Public, Private, and Bureau of Indian Education Elementary and Secondary School Teachers in the United States: Results From the 2007-08 Schools and Staffing Survey (NCES 2009-324)*, U.S. Department of Education, National Center for Education Statistics, Washington, DC, June 2009, http://nces.ed.gov/pubsearch/ pubsinfo.asp?pubid=2009324. Hereinafter cited as *Characteristics of School Teachers.*

[7] *Characteristics of School Teachers*, Table 3.

[8] *Characteristics of School Teachers*, Table 2.

[9] *Characteristics of School Teachers*, Table 4.

[10] Thomas G. Carroll and Elizabeth Foster, *Who Will Teach? Experience Matters*, National Commission on Teaching and America's Future, Washington, DC, January 2010, http://www.nctaf.org/NCTAFWho WillTeach.pdf.pdf.

[11] William J. Hussar and Tabitha M. Bailey, *Projections of Education Statistics to 2018*, U.S. Department of Education, National Center for Education Statistics, Washington, DC, September 2009, http://nces.ed.gov/ pubsearch/pubsinfo.asp?pubid=2009062.

[12] According to a national survey of teachers and principals conducted by the National Center on Teaching and America's Future. For a discussion of the survey results, see Tom Carroll and Elizabeth Foster, *Learning Teams: Creating What's Next*, National Commission on Teaching and America's Future, Washington, DC, April 2009, http://www.nctaf.org /documents/NCTAFLearningTeams408REG2.pdf.

[13] CRS analysis of the U.S. Department of Education, National Center for Education Statistics, School and Staffing Survey (SASS), "Public Teacher Data File," 2003-04, http://nces.ed.gov/surveys/sass/.

[14] Sharon E. Anderson and C. Dennis Carroll, *Teacher Career Choices*, U.S. Department of Education, Timing of Teacher Careers Among 1992–93 Bachelor's Degree Recipients, Washington, DC, March 2008, p. NCES 2008-153, http://nces.ed.gov/pubs2008/ 2008153.pdf.

[15] *Digest of Education Statistics*, 2008.

[16] Robin R. Henke et al., *America's Teachers: Profile of a Profession*, 1993-94, U.S. Department of Education, NCES 97-460, Washington, DC, July 1997, http://ies.ed.gov/pubsearch/ pubsinfo.asp?pubid=97460.

[17] Richard M. Ingersoll, "The Teacher Shortage: Myth or Reality?," *Educational Horizons*, Spring 2003, p. 147, http://www.pilambda.org/horizons/v81-3/Ingersoll.pdf.

[18] Michael Panty et al., *Condition of Education 2009*, U.S. Department of Education, Washington, DC, May 8, 2009, Table 31-1, http://nces.ed.gov/pubsearch/pubsinfo. asp?pubid=2009081.

[19] In general, the terms licensure and certification are used interchangeably in this report to describe the state-administered process of granting a teacher the authority to teach. State-by-state information on certification and licensure is compiled by the National Association of State Directors of Teacher Education and Certification and made available in a knowledgebase at http://www.nasdtec.org/.

[20] These are terms given to such temporary licenses by the states of California and Minnesota, respectively; similar terms exist in most other states.

[21] Information on these programs is available at http://www.teachforamerica.org/ and http:// www.ibm.com/ibm/ ibmgives/news/transition_to_teaching.shtml.

[22] Further information is available at the National Center for Alternative Certification, http://www.teach-now.org/.

[23] Ellen Behrstock and Jane G. Coggshall, Teacher Hiring, Placement, and Assignment Practices, National Comprehensive Center for Teacher Quality, Washington, DC, December 2009, http://www.tqsource.org/ publications/ KeyIssue_HiringPlacementAssignment.pdf.

[24] Edward Liu and Susan Moore Johnson, "New Teachers' Experiences of Hiring: Late, Rushed, and Information-Poor," Educational Administration Quarterly, vol. 42, no. 3 (2006), pp. 324-3 60.

[25] Lora Cohen-Vogel and La'Tara Osborne-Lampkin, “Allocating Quality: Collective Bargaining Agreements and Administrative Discretion over Teacher Assignment,” *Educational Administration Quarterly*, vol. 43, no. 4 (October 2007), pp. 433-461.

[26] Cynthia D. Prince, *Changing Policies to Close the Achievement Gap: A Guide for School System Leaders* (Blue Ridge Summit, PA: Rowman & Littlefield Education, 2004), p. 14.

[27] Marguerite Roza and Paul Hill, “How Within-District Spending Inequities Help Some Schools to Fail,” *in Brookings Papers on Education Policy*, ed. Diane Ravitch (Washington, DC: Brookings Institution Press, 2004).

[28] Richard M. Ingersoll, *Who Controls teachers' Work? Power and Accountability in America's Schools* (Cambridge, MA: Harvard University Press, 2006), p. 121.

[29] Cynthia D. Prince, *Changing Policies to Close the Achievement Gap: A Guide for School System Leaders* (Blue Ridge Summit, PA: Rowman & Littlefield Education, 2004).

[30] A review of teacher evaluation policies can be found in, Carrie Mathers, Michelle Oliva, and Sabrina W. M. Laine, *Improving Instruction Through Effective Teacher Evaluation*, National Comprehensive Center for Teacher Quality, Washington, DC, February 2008, http://www.tqsource.org/publications/February2008 Brief.pdf. In addition, the Center maintains a database of teacher contracts in the nation's 50 largest districts, which includes some information on teacher evaluation at http://www2.tqsource.org/resources

[31] Chris Brandt et al., *Examining district guidance to schools on teacher evaluation policies in the Midwest Region*, U.S. Department of Education, Washington, DC, November 2007, http://ies.ed.gov/ncee/edlabs/ regions/midwest/pdf/ REL_2007030_sum.pdf.

[32] Morgaen L. Donaldson and Heather G. Peske, *Supporting Effective Teaching Through Teacher Evaluation, Center for American Progress*, Washington, DC, March 10, 2010, p. 10, http://www.americanprogress.org/ issues/2010/03/ teacher_evaluation.html.

[33] Daniel Weisberg et al., *The Widget Effect: Our National Failure to Acknowledge and Act on Differences in Teacher Effectiveness*, The New Teacher Project, New York, NY, June 1, 2009, http://www.widgeteffect.org.

[34] Kate Walsh, *2009 State Teacher Policy Yearbook, National Council on Teacher Quality*, Washington, DC, January 28, 2010, http://www.nctq.org/stpy09/.

[35] Thomas Toch and Robert Rothman, *Rush to Judgement: Teacher Evaluation in Public Education, Education Sector*, Washington, DC, January 2008, http://www.education sector.org/usr_doc/RushToJudgment_ES_ Jan08.pdf.

[36] For more information on these models, see CRS Report R41051, *Value-Added Modeling for Teacher Effectiveness*, by Erin D. Lomax and Jeffrey J. Kuenzi.

[37] Union contracts may incorporate aspects of state tenure laws. For state-by-state information on teacher tenure and contract laws, see Michael Colasanti, *Teacher Tenure/Continuing Contract Laws: Updated for 2007*, Education Commission of the States, Denver, CO, August 2007, http://www.ecs.org/html/Document.asp? chouseid=7564.

[38] CRS analysis of the U.S. Department of Education, National Center for Education Statistics, School and Staffing Survey (SASS), “Public Teacher Data File,” 2003 -04, http://nces.ed.gov/surveys/sass/.

[39] Mitch Price, *Teacher Union Contracts and High School Reform*, Center on Reinventing Public Education, Bothell, WA, January 2009, p. 27, http://www.crpe.org/cs/crpe/download/ csr_files/pub_crpe_unioncont_ jan09.pdf.

[40] Frederick M. Hess and Coby Loup, *The Leadership Limbo: Teacher Labor Agreements in America's Fifty Largest School Districts*, Thomas B. Fordham Institute, Washington, DC, February 2008, p. 29, http://www.aei.org/paper/ 27672.

[41] *Digest of Education Statistics*, 2008.

[42] Sylvia A. Allegretto, Sean P. Corcoran, and Lawrence Mishel, How Does Teacher Pay Compare?, Economic Policy Institute, August 2004.

[43] Jay P. Greene and Marcus A. Winters, *How Much Are Public School Teachers Paid?,* Manhattan Institute for Policy Research, Civic Report, No. 50, January 2007.

[44] For more on teacher compensation reforms, see CRS Report R40576, *Compensation Reform and Incentive Pay for Teachers*, by Jeffrey J. Kuenzi.

[45] Although federal aid to improve K-12 teaching has historically come from multiple federal agencies, ED has always been the primary source.

[46] In FY2010, the total amount appropriated for all teacher programs under ED was $3.4 billion. The FY1998 amount of $498 million is equivalent to $646 million in constant FY2010 dollars; adjusted using the GDP (chained) price index published by the Office of Management and Budget, *Historical Tables, Budget of the United States Government, Fiscal Year 2011*, Washington, DC, February 2010, Table 10.1, http://www.whitehouse.gov /omb/budget/fy2011/assets/ hist.pdf.

[47] At that time, the HEA provided teachers an additional recruitment incentive by offering borrowers of certain student loans debt forgiveness in return for teaching at high poverty schools.

[48] According to ESEA Section 9101(11), "The term 'core academic subjects' means English, reading or language arts, mathematics, science, foreign languages, civics and government, economics, arts, history, and geography."

[49] For more information on this issue, see CRS Report RL33333, *A Highly Qualified Teacher in Every Classroom: Implementation of the No Child Left Behind Act and Reauthorization Issues for the 111th Congress*, by Jeffrey J. Kuenzi.

[50] ESEA, Section 9101(34).

[51] U.S. Department of Education, "Race to the Top Fund; Final Rule," *74 Federal Register* 59804, November 18, 2009, http://edocket.access

[52] The No Child Left Behind Act included the Paul D. Coverdell Teacher Protection Act of 2001, which provides liability protection to school employees (including teachers, administrators, and school board members) acting to control, discipline, expel, or suspend a student or to maintain order in the classroom or school.

[53] This authority was automatically extended through FY2008 under the General Education Provisions Act (20 USC 1226a). Although the ESEA has not been reauthorized, unless otherwise noted, funds continue to be appropriated for the ESEA programs described in this report.

[54] U.S. Department of Education, *Findings from the 2008-2009 Survey on the Use of Funds Under Title II, Part A*, Washington, DC, July 2009, http://www2.ed.gov/programs/ teacherqual/data2009.doc.

[55] Adequate yearly progress refers to progress made toward proficiency benchmarks under the reauthorized ESEA. For more information on this topic, see CRS Report RL33749, *The No Child Left Behind Act: An Overview of Reauthorization Issues for the 111th Congress*, by Rebecca R. Skinner.

[56] For more information about the Center for Educator Compensation Reform, see http://cecr.ed.gov/.

[57] For more information on student loans and options for forgiveness and repayment benefits, see CRS Report R40 122, *Federal Student Loans Made Under the Federal Family Education Loan Program and the William D. Ford Federal Direct Loan Program: Terms and Conditions for Borrowers*, by David P. Smole.

[58] That is, an individual with an outstanding loan balance on a student loan before October 1, 1998, is ineligible for this program, unless the loan balance is paid in full before again borrowing under the program.

[59] At least one of these school years must be after the 1997-1998 school year. Borrowers whose five-year period of service began on or after October 30, 2004, must be highly qualified teachers, as defined in the Elementary and Secondary Education Act (ESEA), § 9101.

[60] For more information on the America COMPETES Act, see CRS Report R40519, *America COMPETES Act and the FY2010 Budget*, by John F. Sargent Jr.

[61] CRS Report RS2 1682, *The Tax Deduction for Classroom Expenses of Elementary and Secondary School Teachers*, by Linda Levine.

[62] An additional $350 million was appropriated for a separate Race to the Top Assessment Program, http://www2.ed.gov/programs/racetothetop-assessment

[63] RTTT is part of the $53.6 billion ARRA appropriation of which $48.6 billion is to be awarded by formula. More information on this program can be found in CRS Report R40151, *Funding for Education in the American Recovery and Reinvestment Act of 2009 (P.L. 111-5)*, by Rebecca R. Skinner, David P. Smole, and Ann Lordeman, and at http://www2.ed.gov/policy

[64] U.S. Department of Education, "Race to the Top Fund; Final Rule," *74 Federal Register* 59692, November 18, 2009, http://edocket.access

[65] U.S. Department of Education, *Race to the Top Program: Executive Summary*, Washington, DC, November 2009, p. 6, http://www2.ed.gov/programs/racetothetop/executive-summary.pdf.

[66] U.S. Department of Education, *Race to the Top Program: Guidance and Frequently Asked Questions*, May 2010, p. 19, http://www2.ed.gov/programs/racetothetop/faq.pdf.

[67] U.S. Department of Education, "Race to the Top Fund; Final Rule," *74 Federal Register* 59804, November 18, 2009, http://edocket.access

[68] This authority was automatically extended through FY2008 under the General Education Provisions Act (20 USC 1226a). Although the ESEA has not been reauthorized, funds continue to be appropriated.

[69] Hereinafter referred to as the *Blueprint*, U.S. Department of Education, *A Blueprint for Reform: The Reauthorization of the Elementary and Secondary Education Act*, Washington, DC, March 2010, http://www2.ed.gov/policy blueprint/.

[70] The discussion of these proposals draws on additional details presented in the Administration's proposed budget for FY2011, U.S. Department of Education, *Justifications of Appropriation Estimates to the Congress: Fiscal Year 2011*, Washington, DC, 2010, http://www2.ed.gov/about/overview/budget/budget11/justifications/ index.html, hereinafter referred to as the Justifications.

[71] *Blueprint*, p. 13.

[72] For more information on this requirement, see CRS Report RL33333, *A Highly Qualified Teacher in Every Classroom: Implementation of the No Child Left Behind Act and Reauthorization Issues for the 111th Congress*, by Jeffrey J. Kuenzi.

[73] *Justifications*, p. F-27.

[74] *Blueprint,* pp. 14-15. The *Blueprint* notes that during the transition to using these new definitions, ED will maintain provisions of current law relating to "highly-qualified teachers" with additional flexibility.

[75] *Blueprint,* p. 16.

[76] Transition to Teaching, Teacher Quality Partnerships, Teach for America, and Teachers for a Competitive Tomorrow. The proposal would transfer the Troops to Teachers program to the Department of Defense in FY2011, U.S. Department of Education, *Fiscal Year 2011 Justifications of Appropriation Estimates to the Congress*, v. 1, p. F-136.

[77] According to NCLB, a teacher who is not new to the teaching profession may demonstrate subject matter knowledge through a state-defined *High Objective Uniform State Standard* of Evaluation (HOUSSE) process. In defining its HOUSSE, the state must set standards for both grade appropriate academic subject knowledge and teaching skills that are aligned with challenging state academic and student achievement standards.

[78] ESEA, Section 111 1(b)(8)(C).

[79] Stephen Sawchuk, "The Latest on States' 'Highly Qualified' Teacher Counts," *Education Week*, August 13, 2009.

[80] According to the most recent figures, from the 2007-2008 school year, 95% of all core academic classes are taught by highly qualified teachers; the figure is 99% in more than a dozen states. U.S. Department of Education, *A Summary of Highly Qualified Teacher Data,* Washington, DC, May 2009, http://www2.ed.gov/ programs/teacherqual/ data2009.doc.

[81] ESEA, Section 1 120A(c) requires LEAs to ensure, among other things, "equivalence among schools in teachers" in order to receive Title I-A funds.

[82] In FY2009, ED supported 48 teacher preparation programs through Teacher Quality Partnership grants. According to American Association of Colleges for Teacher Education, there are over 800 teacher preparation programs at colleges and universities and nearly 200 alternative certification programs nationwide. Additional federal support is provided to alternative routes to certification though the appropriation for Teach for America.

[83] National Research Council, *Preparing Teachers: Building Evidence for Sound Policy*, Washington, DC, April 9, 2010, http://www.nap.edu/nap-cgi/report.cgi?record_id =12882&type=pdfxsum.

[84] U.S. Department of Education, *Findings from the 2008-2009 Survey on the Use of Funds Under Title II, Part A*, Washington, DC, July 2009, http://www2.ed.gov/programs/ teacherqual/data2009.doc.

[85] Linda Darling-Hammond et al., *Professional Learning in the Learning Profession: A Status Report on Teacher Development in the United States and Abroad*, National Staff Development Council, Dallas, TX, February 2009, http://www.nsdc.org/news/ NSDCstudy2009.pdf.

[86] Alliance for Excellent Education, *Achieving a Wealth of Riches: Delivering on the Promise of Data to Transform Teaching and Learning*, Policy Brief, Washington, DC, August 2009, http://www.all4ed.org/files/ AchievingWealthOfRiches.pdf.

[87] ESEA, Section 9101(34).

In: Elementary and Secondary Education Act
Editors: D. M. Brown and A. Davies

ISBN: 978-1-61942-694-8

Chapter 3

COMPENSATION REFORM AND THE FEDERAL TEACHER INCENTIVE FUND

Jeffrey J. Kuenzi

SUMMARY

Congress has historically recognized the importance of teacher quality in improving the academic performance of elementary and secondary school students; however, federal policy has only recently begun to address the impact of teacher compensation systems on both quality and performance. Growing concern about the dominant feature of these systems—the single salary schedule—has led to a variety of compensation reform efforts around the country. These efforts include pay-for-performance incentives that attempt to align teacher compensation more closely with student achievement, as well as other reforms that link increased pay to improved teacher competency or to service in hard-to-staff positions.

Congress provided significant support to several existing compensation reform efforts by enacting the Teacher Incentive Fund (TIF) through the Labor-HHS-Education Appropriations Act of 2006 (P.L. 109-149). The concise passage that provides program authority for TIF states that funds are intended to "develop and implement performance-based teacher and principal compensation systems in high-need schools." Little additional guidance has been provided with respect to how these reforms are to be implemented.

Subsequent congressional action to extend the TIF has left the authorizing language largely unchanged. Prior to the TIF, federal education policy had not significantly addressed the nature of teacher compensation. Nevertheless, significant amounts of funding from several federal programs support the salaries of specific kinds of teachers, including teachers and paraprofessionals serving educationally disadvantaged students, newly hired teachers, and special education teachers.

As Congress moves to reauthorize the Elementary and Secondary Education Act (ESEA), proposals to leverage federal education spending to reform teacher compensation systems may receive serious consideration. Beyond recent increases in TIF appropriations through the American Recovery and Reinvestment Act (P.L. 111-5) and the Omnibus Appropriations Act of 2009 (P.L. 111-8), Congress may also consider altering and expanding the federal role in this area. Some proposals that would make changes to the federal effort in this area received attention in recent congressional sessions. These include a *discussion draft* for ESEA reauthorization circulated by the leadership of the House Education and Labor Committee as well as legislation to create *Innovation Districts* as part of the Obama Administration's education agenda.

This report is intended to discuss a variety of issues that relate to compensation reform and the proposals Congress may consider during ESEA reauthorization. The report provides background on the teacher pay system, discusses the basic elements of compensation reform, and describes several reform efforts that are currently underway around the country. The report concludes with a discussion of recent legislative action and issues for ESEA reauthorization.

OVERVIEW

Congress has historically recognized the importance of teacher quality in improving the academic performance of elementary and secondary school students. The latest amendments to the Higher Education Act (HEA) align with past efforts to improve quality through support and accountability for teacher preparation programs. The Elementary and Secondary Education Act (ESEA) has long sought to improve quality by supporting better professional development, effective recruitment and retention, and smaller class sizes. In perhaps its most direct effort to improve teacher quality, the 107th Congress established new federal highly qualified teacher requirements through the No Child Left Behind Act of 2001 (NCLB, P.L. 107-110). In recent years, researchers and policy-makers have begun to consider and implement ways to use compensation reform to improve teacher quality; however, federal policy up to this point has not been heavily focused on the issue of teacher pay.

There is growing concern that the single salary schedule currently in place in nearly all of the nation's schools may be a barrier to improving quality. Many believe that teachers' pay should be used to leverage changes in behavior, knowledge, and skills, and make teaching more financially attractive to successful teachers and to highly able individuals outside of teaching. The recent policy focus on student academic achievement has led some reformers to advocate for various systems of pay-for-performance based on achievement gains, including the use of value-added methods. Others argue that pay differentiation should reward a broader set of factors. These reforms include incentives based on such things as teacher evaluations, advanced credentials, career ladders, and service in hard-to-staff schools or high-need subject areas.

Apart from the recently enacted Teacher Incentive Fund (TIF), federal education policy has not significantly addressed the nature of teacher compensation. Nevertheless, significant amounts of funding from several federal programs support the salaries of certain kinds of teachers, including teachers and paraprofessionals serving educationally disadvantaged students under the compensatory education program (ESEA, Title I-A), newly hired teachers under the continuation of activities provided by the Class Size Reduction program (antecedent to ESEA, Title II-A) and special education teachers (under the Individuals with Disabilities Education Act).

As Congress moves to reauthorize the ESEA, proposals to leverage federal education spending to reform teacher compensation systems may receive serious consideration. Congress could scale up the current federal role in compensation reform through continued expansion of the TIF program; which is basically providing funding for promising programs that already exist (mainly) at the local level. However, Congress may also consider alternative approaches that would alter or expand the federal role. An example of such a proposal would be to strengthen current language supporting pay reform under ESEA Title II (Sections 2113 and 2123).

This report is intended to discuss a variety of issues that relate to compensation reform and the proposals Congress may consider during ESEA reauthorization. The report first provides background on the teacher pay system, including the history behind the development of the dominant feature of this system—the single salary schedule. Second, the report discusses the basic elements of compensation reform, namely performance-based pay, competency-based pay, and service-based pay. The third section of the report describes several reform efforts that are currently underway around the country at the national, state, and local levels. Finally, the report concludes with a discussion of recent legislative action and issues for ESEA reauthorization.

BACKGROUND ON TEACHER COMPENSATION

The origins of the current system of teacher compensation can be traced to the turn of the 20th century and the labor movement's drive to improve pay equity in public education and the civil service at large. Prior to that time, "room and board" and "grade-based" compensation models allowed large discrepancies to develop, particularly along racial and gender lines.[1] By the 1920s, new systems of uniform pay steps were taking hold to ensure teachers with the same years of experience and education level would receive the same salary.[2] These systems came to be known as the single salary schedule and have been nearly universal in public schools since the mid-20th century; adopted in 97% of all schools by 1950 and operational in 96% of schools in 2000.[3]

Teacher salary schedules are primarily determined at the level of the individual school district.[4] They are often the subject of negotiation between local school boards and teacher unions where applicable. This salary schedule bases a teacher's pay primarily on two factors—the number of years of teaching experience the individual has and the number of educational credits and degrees the individual has earned. Increases in both teaching experience and credits/degrees lead to increases in salary, up to absolute limits imposed by the applicable pay schedule.

Critics view the single salary schedule as largely rewarding longevity and the accumulation of college credits, not classroom effectiveness. Some researchers have found that the schedule's main factors—experience and level of education—have relatively little beneficial impact on classroom effectiveness as measured by the achievement of a teacher's students. Hanushek and Rivkin have concluded: "The results [of a review of the available research] are startlingly consistent in finding no strong evidence that teacher-student ratios, teacher education, or teacher experience have an expected positive effect on student achievement."[5] Other research challenges these conclusions. For example, based on their analysis of the literature, Rob Greenwald et al. concluded: "[R]esource variables that attempt to describe the quality of teachers (teacher ability, teacher education, and teacher experience) show very strong relations with student achievement."[6]

Regardless of the strength of the relationship between teacher quality and student achievement, the single salary schedule (and perhaps low overall pay, see box below) is argued by some to fail to draw the highest caliber of potential teachers into the field; to fail to reward teachers who are exceptionally productive; or to fail to allocate the supply of teachers to fields where they are most needed (like math and science). Criticism of the single salary schedule has undergirded efforts to implement performance-based pay plans in elementary and secondary education.

ARE TEACHER SALARIES LOW?

The answer to this question is hotly debated among education researchers. Complicating this debate are thorny methodological issues concerning how to calculate the number of days per year or hours per week teachers actually work as well as how to factor non-monetary benefits like sick leave, health care, and pensions into total compensation. Research comparing teachers' salaries to those earned by individuals with similar skill sets or similar jobs produce a range of estimates. On the low end of this range is research by the Economic Policy Institute[7] which shows that teachers earned 12% less per week in 2002 compared to accountants, reporters, registered nurses, computer programmers, clergy, personnel officers, and vocational counselors and inspectors. On the other end, according to a Manhattan Institute study of 2005 teacher salaries,[8] public school teachers at that time were paid 11% more than the average professional worker in a similar list of occupations.

ELEMENTS OF COMPENSATION REFORM

Teacher compensation reform efforts have a long history and have fallen into and out of favor in public schools repeatedly throughout the 20th century.[9] Throughout this history there has been a consistent tension in the balance between rewarding *inputs* versus *outputs*. Put simply, should teachers be given additional pay for improving the skills and abilities they bring into the classroom or should they get additional pay for improving the skills and abilities their students carry away from school? Reflecting this debate, a recent review of the history of compensation reforms described the two classic approaches as (1) knowledge-based pay and (2) merit-based pay.[10]

Many writing in this area conflate these two reforms (among other reforms) under terms like "performance-based pay" and "pay-for-performance." To avoid confusion, in this report, the term *performance-based pay* is used to refer strictly to output-based compensation reforms that reward teachers for improving student performance. Input-based incentives (such as rewards for improving a teacher's knowledge) are referred to as *competency-based pay*. In addition to these two types of reform, there exists a third category that will be called *service-based pay*. These reforms include financial rewards for those teaching in hard-to-staff schools and hard-to-staff subject areas, but can also include rewards for those who move up the career ladder to serve in more advanced roles (e.g., team leadership) and take on additional responsibilities (e.g., mentoring).

Performance-Based Pay

In the labor market generally, performance-based pay policies attempt to correlate employee pay directly with employee output and take the form of either individual incentive plans or group incentive plans. Performance-based pay is consistent with widely held beliefs that employees should be rewarded based on effort and with theories of human motivation which contend that effective motivation is predicated on a close relationship between performance and rewards.[11]

Most employers rely principally on time-based pay (paying employees on an hourly or salaried basis) but incorporate some form of performance-based pay on an adjunct basis. Implementation of performance-based pay requires supervisory time and, consequently, entails costs for employee monitoring among other managerial problems.[12] However, it is presumed that because of the additional incentives to individual performance, less supervision will be required than under strictly time-based pay. These performance incentives may reward productive workers with larger annual wage increases (or one-time bonuses) on an individual basis.

As an alternative to supporting individual performance, group incentive plans reward organization-wide effort. Because group incentive plans ideally foster cooperation and teamwork rather than competition among coworkers, they overcome one of the potential limitations of individual incentive plans. On the other hand, group incentive plans are sometimes criticized for not sufficiently recognizing individual effort. In practice, many employers rely on both group and individual incentives to try and enhance individual performance and teamwork. Gain-sharing plans, which tie part of pay to some measure of group effort, often include some components of individual performance plans, thereby potentially enhancing group and individual effort. Gain- sharing rewards are tied to improvements in organizational performance attributable to factors controllable by employees. Thus, gain-sharing plans affect performance by influencing employee motivation and organizational culture.

Merit Pay for Teachers

The first wave of performance-based pay reforms for teachers mainly took the form of so-called *merit pay*. Merit pay is a, “system that hinges on student outcomes attributed to a particular teacher or group of teachers rather than on ‘inputs’ such as skills or knowledge.”[13] Following the release of *A Nation at Risk*[14] in 1983, a significant number of public school districts began considering merit pay as a supplement to the single salary schedule.[15] These merit pay systems provided bonuses to individual teachers, groups of teachers, or schools based on any number of factors including student performance, classroom observations, and teacher portfolios.

A 2002 report by the Progressive Policy Institute found that the most common form of merit pay were school-based performance awards.[16] These bonus awards were based on the aggregate performance of schools that may include a wide range of possible measures. Student-related measures may include achievement levels, attendance rates, dropout rates (for secondary schools), participation rates in advanced placement courses (for secondary schools), and college going rates (for secondary schools). Measures of school performance need not be student-based. For example, they may include the extent of parental and community involvement in school activities, or whether the schools have developed and implemented new curricula. The awards are made to individual schools for use at the school level. Some, but not all, of the initiatives being implemented that include school-based performance awards require the distribution of these awards to individual teachers as additional compensation.

Early pay reform efforts demonstrate that measuring teacher performance is quite difficult. Many highly valued activities by teachers are qualitative, and as a consequence, hard to measure:

> One key problem in predicting teacher quality is that managers using the criteria demand quantitative measurements, while the factors that actually relate to classroom performance are typically qualitative and vague. Even if the factors important in producing a good teacher were known, specifying true quality and implementation standards would still be exceedingly difficult. [17]

Historically, merit pay reforms foundered frequently on the evaluation portion of the plans which often involved subjective assessments of teacher performance by principals, teachers, or others. In many instances, teachers considered this process to be ill-defined, overly subjective, or basically biased. Measuring performance remains one of the biggest obstacles to these reforms. Heneman et al. point out that teachers do not necessarily object to merit pay itself, "but the way in which plans were designed, implemented, and administered."[18]

Measuring Performance and Value-Added Modeling

In recent years, much has changed in the area of measuring teacher performance. With the growth of student assessments and related data systems, student test scores are increasingly used as a measure of teacher effectiveness. To many advocates, test scores are viewed as a more quantitative and less subjective way of gauging teacher performance than traditional evaluation procedures. Debate over the use of student test scores for this purpose focuses on the attribution of changes in student test scores to the effectiveness of an individual teacher, given the multitude of other factors, including family background and the quality of previous teachers, that are known to influence achievement. In addition, issues arise concerning the validity and reliability of the testing instruments, and whether such assessment instruments measure the full range of student outcomes that policymakers and others desire. Goldhaber summarizes the debate this way, "while such research has taught us valuable lessons about the appropriate ways to measure teacher effectiveness, it is an overstatement to suggest that debates about how precisely to measure teacher contributions to student learning are anywhere close to settled."[19]

One avenue of research that has attempted to address the debate over the use of student assessments for teacher evaluation has come to be known as *value-added modeling* (VAM). Most notably tied to the work of William Sanders at the University of North Carolina and later at the SAS Institute, Inc.,[20] VAM attempts to estimate the improvement in student achievement that can be attributed to teachers' interventions net of the effect of all other factors. In its pure form, these procedures use linked student-teacher unit records to identify teacher effects; however, at the present time such data systems exist in only a handful of states.[21] A recent comprehensive review of VAM research undertaken by the RAND corporation declared the lack of these data systems to be "among the greatest challenges facing VAM" and concluded that "the research base is currently insufficient to support the use of VAM for high-stakes decisions."[22]

Competency-Based Pay

In contrast to performance-based pay incentives that attempt to reward teacher output, other pay reform programs reward teachers for improving inputs thought to lead to better student performance. In the private sector, such reforms are often referred to as "competency pay" in which employees receive pay increases or bonuses for obtaining skills needed by the employer.[23] Odden and Kelley have identified several ways in which competency-based pay reforms have been implemented in public schools including financial incentives for obtaining additional licensure or certification, such as National Board Certification, and teacher performance as measured by a standards-based teacher evaluation system.[24]

Advanced Certification

Obtaining additional formal training leading to an advance degree is built into the current salary schedule; however, teachers are increasingly being offered financial incentives to obtain additional certification. Teachers may receive extra pay for obtaining certification in a second or third subject area or for earning advanced certification. Probably the best known and most widespread example of the latter is additional compensation awarded to teachers who become certified by the National Board for Professional Teaching Standards (NBPTS). Such certifications are growing in popularity among a significant number of states and school districts, with many of them adopting incentives designed to reward teachers for becoming NBPT S-certified, and in some cases these rewards are quite large.[25]

Teacher Evaluation

In standards-based teacher evaluation systems, teachers' performance is evaluated against a set of standards that define a competency model of effective teaching.[26] Such systems replace the traditional teacher evaluation system and seek to provide a more thorough description and accurate assessment of teacher performance. A popular competency model of teacher performance intended to apply to all grade levels and subjects is the so-called "Framework for Teaching," developed by Charlotte Danielson. The framework attempts to describe the full range of teacher performance, from beginner to expert. It defines four performance domains: planning and preparation, the classroom environment (classroom management), instruction, and professional responsibilities. For each domain there is a set of specific performance components, each of which has one or more elements (a total of 66). Each element has four performance levels/standards, defined by specific behavioral rubrics.

Service-Based Pay

This section discusses two teacher compensation reforms that involve increased pay for teachers who fill *hard-to-staff* positions or take on advanced responsibilities. Compared to the reforms described above, these reforms have a relatively short history. The notion of hard-to-staff teaching positions was recognized recently as a turnover and distributional problem rather than a result of a labor shortage.[27] Thus, recruitment policies have been tailored to encourage teachers to move into schools and subjects which are experiencing the greatest demand. Meanwhile, retention policies often seek to keep veteran teachers by providing them with incentives to advance their educational roles.

Hard-to-Staff Positions

Teaching jobs can be deemed "hard-to-staff" for several reasons. For one, the position may be in a school that presents undesirable working conditions. Second, the subject area or academic background required for the position may be in a field that commands higher pay in non-teaching professions. Finally, the population of students served by the position may require special skills or may be otherwise difficult to teach.

Hard-to-staff schools might be most directly identified by human resource data such as unfilled vacancies at the start of the school year and the rate of teacher turnover; however, often proxy measures are used such as poverty rates, school lunch subsidies, crime statistics, and Medicaid enrollment. Incentive pay is provided for teachers willing to work in these hard-to-staff schools even though research suggests that money alone is insufficient to attract and retain them in such schools.[28]

Pay for high-need subject areas can be thought of as an attempt to meet the "market demand" for a particular set of skills (e.g., additional pay for teachers with math degrees who could earn more in the private sector). While this can be considered a type of knowledge-based pay system, it fits more in the service-pay category because, unlike pay systems for knowledge and skills (which are generally designed to be consistent from year-to-year), pay systems for high-need subjects areas may shift as the needs of a given school change from year-to-year. The same can be said for those teaching high-need student populations such as students with disabilities and migratory students.

Advanced Responsibilities

Professional development has traditionally been provided to teachers through in-service workshops, conferences and training sessions. Over 90% of teachers participate in some professional development activities in this manner.[29] In many cases, an outside consultant or curriculum expert is brought in on a staff-development day to give teachers a one-time training seminar on a general pedagogic or subject-area topic. Criticism of this model has led to more ongoing and intense professional development activities. One of the new delivery methods for ongoing professional development has been for veteran teachers to take on mentoring roles as "master" teachers.[30] Teachers that assume such expanded responsibilities may be offered additional pay and release time to assist in the development of new teachers. Initiatives like these that provide incentives for teachers to take on advanced roles are often referred to as *Career Ladder* programs.

CURRENT TEACHER INCENTIVE PAY EFFORTS

The teacher compensation reforms discussed above have not been implemented on a widespread basis. Two surveys conducted by the National Education Association (NEA) found that fewer than one in ten teachers receive some form of "performance-based or incentive pay (e.g., merit pay, stipends for teaching in critical shortage areas, incentives for National Board Certification, etc.)." More specifically, the NEA found that 5% of teachers surveyed during the 1995-1996 school year and 8% of those surveyed during the 2000-2001 school year were receiving this type of pay.[31] Data from a more recent survey conducted by the Department of Education suggest that compensation reforms may be spreading. The 2003-2004 Schools and Staffing Survey (SASS) found that 14% of teachers reported receiving a "merit pay bonus [or a] state supplement" to their regular salary.[32]

The Federal Role

As with educational expenditures in general, the federal government plays a somewhat limited role with respect to teacher compensation. Federal education appropriations have historically accounted for less than 10% of all education spending. In the 2005-2006 school year, a total of $529 billion was spent on public elementary and secondary education; $39 billion (7.4%) of these funds came through ED.[33] That same year, $274 billion of the total was spent on instruction and nearly all ($246 billion) of that amount was used for staff salaries and benefits.[34] A recent ED study found that roughly half of the major sources of federal K-12 education funds are used by schools and districts for instructional staff (e.g., 59% of Title I funds, 63% of Title II funds, and 55% of Title III funds).[35] Even with these large shares of the federal effort going to instructional staff, it is still a very small proportion of all spending on teacher salaries and benefits. With respect to Title I, the ED report concluded that, "In an average-size Title I school of 500 students, Title I resources added a total of 3.5 full-time equivalent (FTE) staff, including 1.9 teachers, 1.2 teacher aides, and 0.4 non-instructional staff."[36]

Until recently, the federal role has also been limited in terms of the *way* in which teachers are compensated. Prior to the creation of the Teacher Incentive Fund (TIF), this role was limited to the inclusion of pay reforms among a list of allowable uses of funds under the two main federal teacher programs. The HEA, Title II-A, Teacher Quality Enhancement Grants program (enacted through the 1998 HEA amendments) authorized participating states to develop "performance- based compensation systems."[37] Although the 2008 amendments to the HEA eliminated the Title II grants to states, the retained Title II partnership grant program contains support for activities that may include "bonus, differential, incentive, or performance pay" for mentor teachers.[38] The ESEA, Title II-A, Improving Teacher Quality State Grants program (enacted through the NCLB amendments of 2001) allows grantees to use these funds for, among many other activities, "merit pay programs" to promote teacher retention.[39] According to a recent study, only 4% of ESEA, Title II-A funds were used for "scholarships, signing bonuses, or other financial incentives, such as differential pay" or "merit pay programs."[40]

The establishment of the TIF represents a notable change in the federal stance on teacher compensation. Rather than simply allowing states and districts to use federal funds for incentive pay (as is the case under the ESEA and HEA, Title II programs), the TIF actively seeks out and supports promising pay reform efforts. Though limited in scope, this program establishes a targeted federal role in supporting compensation reforms. Funding has always been one of the major barriers to the development of pay reform. The merit pay reforms of the 1970s and 1 980s came in the form of bonuses (instead of salary increases) that did not outlive periodic budget shortfalls.[41] Unlike that previous wave of reforms, current efforts depend heavily on outside financing such as foundation support to supplement funds from state and local budgets.[42]

The Teacher Incentive Fund

The TIF represents the paramount federal effort to reform teacher compensation. This program was first funded through the FY2006 Labor-HHS-Education Appropriations Act (P.L. 109-149) which provided $261 million for activities authorized under Title V, Part D of the ESEA. A portion of these funds ($99 million) was reserved for activities under Subpart 1 which gives the Secretary general authority to award discretionary grants "to support nationally significant programs to improve the quality of elementary and secondary education."

The act stipulates that these $99 million are to be used for five-year grants competitively awarded to local education agencies (including charter schools) or states individually or in partnership with each other or with a non-profit organization. According to the act, the goal of these projects is to "develop and implement performance-based teacher and principal compensation systems in high-need schools."

The act further requires that TIF project compensation reforms "must consider gains in student academic achievement as well as classroom evaluations conducted multiple times during each school year" among other factors and provide educators with incentives to take on additional responsibilities and leadership roles. The Secretary is given a 5% set-aside to support the Center for Educator Compensation Reform[43] which raises national awareness about alternative and effective strategies for educator compensation reform and provides technical assistance to TIF grantees.

Beginning in 2007, the FY2006 appropriation was used to fund 34 TIF projects; no funds were appropriated for TIF in FY2007. Program funds may be used to pay the costs of developing and implementing performance-based compensation systems for the benefit of teachers and principals in high-need schools. For example, in addition to costs associated with the incentives given to teachers and principals, other project costs could include professional development activities for those teachers in high-need schools, evaluation and analysis tools, project staff salaries at the applicant level, and reasonable travel necessary for project development and implementation.

The FY2008 Consolidated Appropriations Act (P.L. 110-161) contained the same authorizing language that was in the FY2006 Appropriations Act and provided $97.3 million to continue funding for all 34 projects.[44] The Omnibus Appropriations Act of 2009 (P.L. 111-8) appropriated $97.3 million to support the 34 continuation awards. These FY2009 funds were supplemented with an additional $200 million under the American Recovery and Reinvestment Act (P.L. 111-5). These additional funds were used to award 60 new TIF grants. The Consolidated Appropriations Act of 2010 (P.L. 111-117) provided $400 million to support 94 continuation awards and 65 new TIF grants.[45]

National Programs

CRS was able to identify four fairly sizable non-federal national-level efforts to reform teacher compensation currently in existence. In keeping with the TIF approach of funding promising pay reforms, each of these four efforts receives financial support from the TIF as well as from private sources. The most prominent of these is the Teacher Advancement Program (TAP).

Teacher Advancement Program

The Teacher Advancement Program (TAP) grew out of the Milken Family Foundation's earlier support for the Milken Educator Awards. TAP was launched in 1999 as a comprehensive strategy to find and reward excellent teachers. In 2005, TAP began operating under the National Institute for Excellence in Teaching (NIET), an independent 501(c)(3) public charity. Under the NIET, TAP currently receives support from over a dozen major foundations as well as through a federal TIF grant.[46] The TAP model of reform has four components: (1) multiple career paths; (2) ongoing applied professional growth; (3) instructionally focused accountability; and (4) performance-related compensation.

Multiple Career Paths. TAP's multiple career paths allow high quality teachers to pursue a variety of positions, advance professionally, and earn higher salaries without leaving the classroom. If teachers demonstrate consistent success, they have the opportunity to become career, master, or mentor teachers and earn salary increases of up to $15,000.

Ongoing Applied Professional Growth. The program allocates time during the instructional day for teachers to meet and collaborate on instructional and curricular issues. These meetings are either group- or individual-focused and often scheduled with a TAP-identified mentor or master teacher.

Instructionally-focused Accountability. Instructionally-focused accountability refers to TAP's mechanism for evaluating teachers. In an effort to assess teacher performance appropriately, TAP employs a grading rubric to measure systematically a teacher's content knowledge, instructional methods, and student learning gains. These evaluations are ultimately used to determine a teacher's career ladder advancement within the school.

Performance-related Compensation. TAP 's performance-related compensation scheme rewards teachers across three dimensions: (1) student performance; (2) increased roles and responsibilities; and (3) classroom teaching performance. High-performing teachers can earn salary increases of up to $4,000 annually.

TAP currently operates in more than 125 schools in 9 states and 50 districts. Another 10 states presently are pursuing program implementation in routinely low-performing schools. In the aggregate, there are approximately 3,500 teachers and 56,000 students in TAP schools across the country.

Other National Programs

Three other national programs exist, but on a much more limited scale compared to TAP. The *Institute for Compensation Reform and Student Learning*, operated by the Community Training and Assistance Center (CTAC), assists in the implementation of performance pay initiatives in about 16 locations including a TIF-funded project in the Charlotte-Mecklenburg, North Carolina school district. The *Partnership for Innovation in Compensation for Charter Schools*, coordinated by the Center for Educational Innovation (CEI), received a TIF grant to implement performance pay in 10 charter schools in New York City and also provides support to other charter schools around the country. The *Effective Practice Incentive Community*, established by New Leaders for New Schools (NLNS), received a TIF grant to implement performance pay in 66 charter schools affiliated with the National Charter School Consortium. NLNS is also partnered with three other TIF grantees in the Memphis, Denver, and District of Columbia school systems.

State Programs

CRS was able to identify seventeen states that currently have teacher compensation reform efforts underway. This section discusses initiatives in three states – Minnesota, Arizona, and Texas – these are among the more prominent efforts underway. An Appendix at the end of this report provides a table which identifies the main components of all of the aforementioned state-level programs.

Minnesota Quality Compensation Program

In 2005, the Minnesota legislature approved the Quality Compensation (Q-Comp) program.[47] Q- Comp incorporates both career ladder and traditional professional development for teachers, while compensating teachers according to state approved measures of student achievement. The program was funded at $13 million in FY2006, $76 million in FY2007, and $64 million in FY2008. Under Q-Comp guidelines, 60% of any compensation increase must be based on district professional standards and on classroom-level student achievement gains.

School districts wishing to participate in the program must submit a Q-Comp proposal to the state department of education. Districts with approved plans are awarded up to $260 per student to support implementation and sustenance of their compensation plan. The number of participating districts has grown from 22 in 2005-06 to 43 in 2008-09; the state's 15 TAP schools (all located in the Minneapolis school district) receive Q-Comp funds.

Arizona Career Ladder Program and Classroom Site Fund

Since 1993, 28 of Arizona's 200 school districts have participated in the state's Career Ladder Program (which began as a pilot program in 1985).[48] As of 2006, the same 28 districts continued to participate. At that time, these districts enrolled 31% of the state's 865,000 students and employed 40% of the state's 43,000 teachers. Roughly seven in ten of all eligible teachers participate in the program. Arizona Revised Statute 15-918 requires that participating districts must provide for: (1) increasingly higher levels of pupil academic progress as measured by objective criteria; (2) increasingly higher levels of teaching skills; (3)

increasingly higher levels of teacher responsibility; (4) professional growth; and (5) equal teacher pay for equal teacher performance.

In 2000, Proposition 301 was passed by 53% of Arizona voters. This initiative established the Classroom Site Fund which provides funding, from a dedicated sales tax, for districts to participate in some form of pay-for-performance plan for teachers. Career Ladder districts, as well as districts with other forms of diversified compensation programs in place, already meet this requirement. In FY2007, sales tax collections plus other sources of revenue for this fund totaled more than $400 million. Districts are required to direct 20% of the funds received toward increasing teachers' base pay and another 40% toward performance pay.

Texas Educator Excellence Award Programs

In 2006, the Texas Legislature enacted the three Educator Excellence Award programs, creating one of the largest state-level performance-related pay program in the nation.[49] For FY2008, these programs were appropriated $340 million including (1) $10 million for the Governor's Educator Excellence Grant, (2) $100 million for the Texas Educator Excellence Grants, and (3) $230 million for a district-level grant yet to be named.

Governor's Educator Excellence Grants (GEEG). Under this program, funds are distributed through formula grants to schools that are in the top third of Texas schools in terms of percentage of economically disadvantaged students. To be eligible, schools must also meet certain performance criteria on the state's pupil assessment, the Texas Assessment of Knowledge and Skills. Approximately 100 schools qualified in 2008 and individual campus-award amounts varied according to student enrollment, ranging from $60,000 to $220,000. GEEG schools are required to use 75% of these funds for direct incentives to full-time teachers based both on improvement in student achievement and on teacher effectiveness in collaborating with colleagues. The other 25% may be spent on (1) direct incentives to other school employees (including principals) who contribute to improved student achievement, (2) professional development, (3) teacher mentoring and induction programs, (4) stipends for participation in after-school programs, (5) signing bonuses for teachers in hard-to-staff subjects, and/or (6) programs to recruit and retain effective teachers.

Texas Educator Excellence Grants (TEEG). The eligibility criteria, purposes, and activities supported under this program are nearly identical to those of the GEEG program; however, schools must be in the top half of Texas schools in terms of percentage of economically disadvantaged students. GEEG grantees are not eligible for TEEG grants. TEEG grantees must reapply annually, while GEEG grants are awarded for a period of three years. For the 2006–07 school year (the most recent data available), 1,163 campuses were eligible for grants and award amounts ranged from $40,000 to $295,000.

District-Level Grants. All districts in the state are eligible for funding under this program and they may apply for funds for all campuses or for selected campuses. Districts are required to use at least 60% of funds to directly reward classroom teachers based on improvements in student achievement. The remaining funds may be used: (1) as stipends for mentors or teacher coaches, teachers certified in hard-to-staff subjects, or teachers who hold post-baccalaureate degrees; (2) as awards to principals based on improvements in student achievement; or (3) to implement components of the TAP.

State Program Inventory

Table A-1 (in the Appendix to this report) displays information for all state-level teacher compensation reform programs CRS was able to identify as of December of 2008. These programs were identified through three main sources: (1) the National Center on Performance Incentives (NCPI) based at Vanderbilt University, (2) the U.S. Department of Education, Office of Academic Improvement and Teacher Quality Programs, and (3) the Education Commission for the States, Teacher Quality and Leadership Institute. Detailed information on these programs was collected through a variety of secondary sources, including (1) an extensive review of the academic literature and educational press, (2) a thorough search of the internet for project websites, (3) a review of documentation made available by state education departments, policy centers, associations and commissions, and (4) numerous discussions with experts and practitioners in the field. The table lists the project name for each program in the left-hand column, while the remaining columns provide program information including the method of program funding, the criteria used to award performance incentives, and the extent of district or school eligibility and/or participation.

At the present time, CRS has identified 20 teacher compensation reform programs in 17 states. Every program uses student performance as a criteria for rewarding teachers with incentive pay. At least 7 of the 20 programs also base incentive pay on some form of teacher evaluation. As many as eight programs provide additional pay for teachers who move up the career ladder. At least nine offer extra pay to those who teach in high-need schools and/or hard-to-staff subjects. Programs vary in terms of school and district eligibility—some offer incentives to just a few schools or districts, others make all LEAs eligible, still others *require* all LEAs to participate. Programs also vary in the amount and type of incentive awarded—some offer a school-wide increase of a few hundred dollars per student, others give individual teachers as little as $1,000 or as much as $11,000.

At least 10 of the state programs deliver funds for incentive awards through a formula. These programs provide supplemental formula funding (often on a per pupil basis) to schools or districts that apply to be included in the program. Such funding strategies exemplify an alternative to the TIF approach of awarding competitive grants to a select set of promising reform efforts.

Local Programs

CRS has identified over 80 teacher compensation reform efforts that exist at the local level in 25 states and the District of Columbia. This section discusses initiatives in three locations—Denver, CO; Guilford County, NC; and Hamilton County, TN—these are among the more prominent local efforts and are profiled to provide a sense of how local efforts are structured. An Appendix at the end of this report provides a table (Table A-2) which identifies the main components of all identified local-level programs.

Denver Professional Compensation Systems for Teachers

In 1999, the Denver Classroom Teachers Association and the Denver Public Schools reached agreement on an alternative teacher pay plan that linked pay to student achievement and professional evaluations.[50] Following refinement of the pilot model by teachers, principals, administrators, and community members, the Professional Compensation Systems for Teachers (ProComp) was adopted in 2004 by the Board of Education and members of the Denver Classroom Teachers Association.

Passage of a 2005 ballot initiative provided $25 million in dedicated tax funds for the program. In 2007, the Denver public school district was awarded a Federal TIF grant. Together, these funds will be used to expand ProComp to nearly 90% of the district's 150 K-12 public schools. The district has also created the ProComp Teacher Compensation Trust; with a balance of $44 million in 2007, the fund is projected to last for many years.

ProComp has four components that enable teachers to increase their salary by as much as 18%, including (1) knowledge and skills; (2) professional evaluation; (3) market incentives; and (4) student growth. Teachers may get up to a 9% increase for completing an advanced degree or certification, 2% for professional development, and 3% for a satisfactory evaluation. Student achievement growth, which includes both teacher and school-wide growth awards, can generate up to a 6% increase. Filling a hard-to-staff position or teaching in a hard-to-staff school can each return a 3% salary increase.

Mission Possible—Guilford County, NC

In 2006, Guilford County Schools launched the Mission Possible program—a comprehensive teacher incentive plan that combines multiple components to keep and attract highly effective teachers and administrators.[51] Twenty high-need schools were initially selected to participate in the program; an additional eight schools were added in 2007 following receipt of a TIF grant. The addition of a $2 million grant from the University of North Carolina system and Action Greensboro to support a math incentive pilot program, called Cumulative Effect, brought the total number of participating schools up to 30 for the 2007-2008 school year.

In addition to a variety of teaching supports (including ongoing training and collaboration and reduced class sizes), Mission Possible teachers and administrators receive recruitment incentives and performance incentives. Mission Possible financial incentives are based on grade levels and subjects that are part of state and national accountability requirements. Teacher performance bonuses are based on student achievement in math and English and range from $2,500 to $4,000. Bonuses are paid the following school year in late November after the NC Department of Public Instruction releases student data. Guilford County Schools conducts a student-teacher linkage verification, and SAS, Inc. generates value-added data for each teacher.

Benwood Initiative—Hamilton County, TN

In 2001, the Benwood Foundation agreed to spend $5 million over five years and the Chattanooga-based Public Education Foundation added another $2.5 million to establish a performance incentive program in the nine lowest performing schools in the Hamilton County School District.[52] In 2006, the two groups added another $7 million and $1 million, respectively, for another five-year phase to expand, what came to be known as the Benwood Initiative, to 16 additional schools.

In addition to several activities to support effective teaching, the program provides salary bonuses of up to $2,000 per teacher based on school-wide improvement in student achievement on the Tennessee Value-Added Assessment System.[53] Principals may receive up to a $10,000 bonus for school-wide student improvement. Teachers may also receive a $5,000 bonus after three years of growth in student achievement. The program also offers recruitment and retention incentives including a forgivable loan that can be used by staff to purchase a home near their schools.

Local Program Inventory

Table A-2 (in the Appendix to this report) displays all 82 identified local-level teacher compensation reform programs known to exist as of December of 2008. These programs were identified through the same sources as the state-level programs discussed above. Every program used student performance as a criteria for rewarding teachers with additional compensation and most programs also included a teacher evaluation component. In addition to these incentives, many programs incorporate service-based incentives.

Tying teacher compensation to student performance is the one element every performance pay initiative has in common. Although achievement is measured in a wide variety of ways and factored into teachers' pay differently across programs, generally speaking, it is gauged through school-wide improvement in student performance on academic assessments and accounts for at least half of the overall incentive award. Some programs apply *value-added modeling* (VAM) techniques that link student achievement to teacher performance and provide individual teacher awards based on these data; however, VAM-based incentives are more commonly awarded on a school-wide basis. Roughly three-quarters (59) of the programs complement school-wide awards with individual teacher awards based on traditional teacher evaluation systems. Roughly three-quarters (58) of the programs also incorporate career ladder incentives for teachers and about one- quarter (21) of the programs provide pay incentives to those who agree to serve in high-need schools or teach hard-to-staff subjects.

Of the 82 pay reform initiatives, most (72 programs) are influenced by either TIF funding or TAP assistance (or both). TIF funds support 30 of these programs; the smallest of the five-year TIF grants provides $1.6 million for two schools that comprise the Mare Island Technology Academy's "New 3Rs" program in Vallejo, California, while the largest provides $29.2 million for 11 schools participating in "Project EXCELL" in Tucson, Arizona's Amphitheater Unified School District #10. More typical of TIF grantees, the Mission Possible program (discussed above) received an $8 million award. According to Amy Holcombe of Guilford County Schools, this grant doubled the $4 million the district recieved from foundation and local funds.[54] Information on whether this proportion of federal to non-federal funds is typical of TIF grantees is not available; however, grantees are required to meet 75% of their costs through non-federal funds by the final (5th) year of the grant.

Forty-seven of the 82 local programs included in Table A-2 are affiliated with the TAP program. According to Kristan Van Hook, TAP 's Senior Vice President, the funds used to support incentive awards under these programs come from non-TAP sources.[55] Van Hook further indicated that districts working with TAP often use their federal Title II funds to support their performance pay activities. Results from ED's most recent survey on the use of Title II funds suggests that nationally this is a rare occurrence. The Department's report states that among the districts surveyed only, "Four percent of Title II, Part A funds were spent on mechanisms and strategies to help schools recruit and retain highly qualified teachers, principals and specialists in core academic areas, such as scholarships, loan forgiveness, signing bonuses or *differential pay* for teachers" [emphasis added].[56] Still, it is quite possible that the small fraction of the nation's 14,000 school districts which are working with TAP may use their Title II funds very differently than the typical district. At the same time, anecdotal evidence collected in this research suggests that, apart from TIF support, a great deal of the funds used to award performance incentives may come from private sources—such as grants and donations received from foundations.

RECONSIDERING THE FEDERAL ROLE

As Congress considers education legislation, including bills to reauthorize the ESEA, proposals to leverage federal education spending to reform teacher compensation systems may receive serious attention. The debate over expansion of the federal involvement in this area will likely raise questions about what role the federal government should play in reforming teacher compensation given that most funding for teacher compensation is provided at the local and state levels. Recent legislative action has mostly involved proposals that simply would expand the TIF approach of funding a limited number of promising reform efforts already underway, mainly at the local level. Although bills to expand TIF funding were not passed in the 109th Congress and the 110th Congress kept program funding level, the 111th Congress tripled TIF appropriations for FY2009. Meanwhile, the program authority continues to provide only minimal guidance as to how these funds should be used.

In recent sessions, Congress has considered alternative approaches that would have begun to alter or expand federal support for teacher incentives and compensation reform. During the last two Congresses, debate over this issue occurred both within efforts to amend the TIF and also around broader legislative activities. This section will discuss these recent congressional actions including two bills that were introduced to reauthorize the HEA and would also have amended the TIF program authority; two bills that would have established a new program, for so-called *Innovation Districts,* in which performance incentives for teachers were to play a major role; and several hearings in which a broader debate over the federal role in teacher compensation reform occurred. Following a review of recent congressional action is a discussion of some of the issues that may be raised as the process for reauthorizing the ESEA continues to unfold.

Recent Congressional Action

Amending and Extending TIF

During the 109th Congress, three bills were introduced to amend or increase funding for the TIF. Two of the bills simply would have increased funding, while the third bill (H.R. 609) would have moved TIF authority from Title V-D of the ESEA to Title II-D of the HEA. The latter bill also further specified eligible entities and program activities, and would have required new nonfederal matching funds as well as a program evaluation. During the 110th Congress, this HEA reauthorization bill was reintroduced as H.R. 3746 and retained the TIF provisions; however, action on the bill stopped with committee referral. The HEA was eventually reauthorized by the Higher Education Opportunity Act (HEOA, P.L. 110-3 15); neither the HEOA nor the House and Senate-passed bills (H.R. 4137 and S. 1642) contained the TIF provisions of the earlier reauthorization proposals.

Three other TIF-related bills were introduced during the 110th Congress. The Teacher Incentive Fund Act (H.R. 1761) would have clarified and expanded the program's provisions, similar to the H.R. 3746, and would have codified TIF authority in ESEA, Title II, Part C; the same provisions were included in a bill introduced in the Senate (S. 1775). Action on both of these bills stopped with committee referral. Finally, the 110th Congress reauthorized TIF through the FY2008 Consolidated Appropriations Act (P.L. 110-161) using the same authorizing language that was initially passed in the FY2006 appropriations act.

The FY2006 authorizing language was again used to appropriate funds for TIF under the American Recovery and Reinvestment Act (P.L. 111-5), the Omnibus Appropriations Act of 2009 (P.L. 111-8), and the Consolidated Appropriations Act of 2010, (P.L. 111-117).

Incentive Pay Legislation

Apart from the TIF bills just discussed, few bills related to teacher performance pay have been introduced in Congress. One notable exception was the Innovation Districts for School Improvement Act (introduced in the 109th Congress as S. 2441 and reintroduced in the 110th as S. 114) that would have required participating districts to establish metrics to evaluate teacher effectiveness and, "develop a differentiated pay scale to provide incentives for effective teaching, teaching specific subject areas, and teaching in specific schools, including hard-to-staff schools." The bills' provisions regarding these incentives were more specific than either the existing TIF language or the bills to amend the TIF, particularly with regard to district cooperation with teachers, union representatives, and the community. Another bill, the Teacher Excellence for All Children (TEACH) Act (introduced in the 109th Congress as H.R. 2835 and S. 1218 and reintroduced in the 110th as H.R. 2204 and S. 1339) would have required participating districts to award "premium pay" to those teaching "shortage" subjects in high-need schools and deemed exemplary "based on strong learning gains for students." Neither the Innovation Districts bill nor TEACH Act legislation moved beyond committee referral; although some non-performance pay provisions in the TEACH Act were enacted through the HEA reauthorization bill (P.L. 110-31 5).[57]

ESEA Reauthorization Hearings

Early in the 110th Congress, both the House and Senate held hearings on the quality of K-12 teaching in which issues related to teacher incentives and performance pay figured prominently. Intended as early steps in the ESEA reauthorization process, testimony at these hearings often raised issues regarding compensation reform and several members asked specific questions about performance pay and other incentives. On March 6, 2007, the Health, Education, Labor, and Pensions Committee held a hearing entitled, "NCLB Reauthorization: Strategies for Attracting, Supporting and Retaining High Quality Educators" (S. Hrg. 110-154). On May 11, 2007, the Education and Labor Committee held a hearing entitled, "ESEA Reauthorization: Boosting Quality in the Teaching Profession" (Serial No. 110-34).

The overarching sentiment among the education experts tapped for these panels was in favor of providing incentives to promote teacher quality. Several spoke in support of the pay incentive components of TIF and TAP; some comments were in response to committee members questions about the issue and several mentioned the need to use a variety of evaluation methods in addition to measures of student performance. One witness on the Senate panel submitted additional material following the hearing in which she argued against the use of value-added modeling for measuring the performance of individual teachers.[58]

In September 2007, the majority and minority leadership of the Education and Labor Committee released a discussion draft of proposed legislation to reauthorize the ESEA. Title II of the draft proposed the establishment of a discretionary grant program (similar to the TEACH Act proposal) which would have awarded "premium pay" to "exemplary teachers" serving in high-need schools. The draft required that LEAs, in collaboration with local teacher organizations, develop a system to identify "exemplary teachers" that must be

(1) based on strong learning gains for students;
(2) based on classroom observation and feedback at least four times annually;
(3) conducted by multiple sources, including master teachers and principals; and
(4) evaluated against research-validated rubrics that use planning, instructional, and learning environment standards to measure teaching performance.[59]

The Committee held an all-day, six-panel hearing on September 10, 2007, for comments on the discussion draft. The "Teaching and School Leadership" panel included representatives from the Nation's two largest teacher unions – the National Education Association (NEA) and the American Federation of Teachers (AFT). Both representatives spoke out strongly against the premium pay provisions. In his prepared statement, Reg Weaver, President of the NEA, stated his organization's position plainly, "The NEA opposes federal requirements for a pay system that mandates teacher pay based on student performance or student test scores."[60] The AFT opposition was less blunt; Vice-President, Antonia Cortese, expressed concern about the proposal's "top- down" approach which "jeopardizes buy-in" from teachers.

Other members of the panel spoke favorably of the proposal's potential to remedy inequities in the distribution of quality teachers. Specifically, both Kati Haycock, President of the Education Trust, and Kristan Van Hook, of the National Institute for Excellence in Teaching, praised the use of premium pay to encourage teachers to work in hard-to-staff schools and career ladders to reward professional advancement. Ms. Van Hook discussed her support for performance pay at great length; emphasizing the importance of implementing such incentives as part of a "comprehensive approach, such as that that is taken in the bill before you today."[61]

Issues for ESEA Reauthorization

Staying the Course with TIF

Should the 112th Congress consider compensation reform and teacher incentive pay proposals, it will inevitably be thinking about whether to stay the course with TIF. As it stands, the program is very broadly defined and has been implemented at the local level in varying ways. Should the federal role in this area continue to be a supporter of local pay reform experimentation and provider of seed money to encourage financial commitments from local, state, and other sources for these reforms? In light of recent appropriations and accompanying non-federal matching requirement, it appears this view may hold sway in future deliberations. If TIF remains an experimental approach to finding out what works, Congress may consider how long and in how many settings to continue to support this type of effort.

Expanding the Federal Role Beyond TIF

Alternatively, Congress may consider whether the federal role should be expanded beyond TIF. Should this role be greater than funding a limited set of reform efforts designed to meet a few broadly defined objectives? If the federal role is to expand, Congress may need to consider (or set up a process to consider) what elements of teacher compensation reform can or should be written into federal law. Recently considered legislation and testimony before the authorizing committees (mentioned in the previous section) provide some potential avenues for development and also point to potential areas of difficulty. Competency-based and service-based incentives appear to have much support, but some may feel they don't do enough to reward performance. On the other hand, performance-based incentives may be too controversial and may be difficult to enact on a large scale and in a manner that would achieve intended goals.

State or Local Reform?

Another element of the debate over pay reforms may occur around what level of the educational system these reforms are best applied. That is, either under TIF or through a different program, Congress may consider whether it wants federal involvement in this area to focus on state reforms or local reforms. Programs reviewed in the previous section of this report show reforms occurring at both levels in numerous locations throughout the country. Should future federal policy development encourage states to be more involved in compensation reform or instead provide direct support to local efforts? Scaling up federal support for TIF may be easier to implement at the local level, while an expanded federal role that includes more specified program activities may be better suited to the state level.

Leveraging ESEA Title II-A

The debate over local versus state reform may also involve proposals to amend the ESEA Title II- A state formula grant program. Currently, most of these funds go through state education agencies to local school districts and are mainly used for class size reduction and professional development; however, "merit pay" is also included in the program's authorized activities. Congress could consider placing greater priority on addressing compensation reform through ESEA Title II-A by strengthening current language (Sections 2113 and 2123).

Measuring Teacher Performance

Performance measurement may be the most hotly contested issue in the compensation reform debate. Current federal law governing TIF requires that teacher performance be based on student achievement and teacher evaluation, but does not provide any detail as to how this should occur. Traditional teacher evaluation has been common for decades, while, performance evaluation tied to student achievement is a more recent development. Significant improvements have been made in the effort to connect student achievement to teacher performance, particularly in certain subjects like math. Still, the research in this area provides reason for Congress to give serious thought to issues such as the use of value-added methods for high-stakes decision-making for individual teachers. One reason these methods are hard to apply to individual teachers is that, to produce reliable results, the statistical modeling employed requires large amounts of data. For example, an elementary school teacher with an average class size of 15 students assessed twice a year would produce too few data points on which to reliably estimate teacher effects apart from non-teacher effects.[62]

Individual versus School-wide Incentives

The problems associated with measuring individual teacher performance explain much of why school-wide incentives are the dominant mode for delivering performance rewards. Simply put, measuring a school's performance is easier than measuring an individual teacher's performance. Critics of school-wide awards point out that they fail to incentivize individual effort and defeat the purpose of compensation reform. The counter-argument holds that school-wide awards encourage cooperation and collegiality which are critical to the success of broad-based, systemic reform. Congress may wish to consider the extent to which school and individual performance goals can or should be collectively targeted by pay incentive programs.

Developing Data Systems

Data systems for both student achievement and teacher performance have greatly improved in recent years; however, these systems have by no means reached universal or consistent application. In addition to the many technical obstacles that remain when it comes to compiling the data many feel are needed to measure and reward teacher performance, there are also political barriers to linking teacher and student records; some states have moved to prohibit this practice. Congress should be award of the data limitations and obstacles and may want to consider basing performance incentives on data elements and linkages that can be expected to be consistently available.

Appendix. Inventory of State- and Local-Level Incentive Pay Reforms, as of May 2009

CRS has constructed inventories of state and local programs, which are presented below. It is important to emphasize that these inventories are not comprehensive.

Ideally, compiling complete inventories of all pay incentive programs would involve a proactive, investigative approach such as surveying all school districts or conducting a nationwide sample of school personnel.[63] Given the limitations on our resources, however, CRS has collected information through somewhat less systematic methods based on secondary sources. These methods include (1) an extensive review of the academic literature and educational press, (2) a thorough search of the Internet for project websites, (3) a review of documentation made available by state education departments, policy centers, associations, and commissions, and (4) numerous discussions with experts and practitioners in the field. These inventories are provided to offer a sense of the landscape of programs in operation in states and localities. CRS believes this is useful in conveying basic information about the structure of programs and the range of characteristics programs feature.

The inventories are not all-inclusive, and CRS can not be certain about the extent to which they reflect the actual universe of programs. On the following pages, Table A-1 contains the inventory of state-level incentive pay reforms and Table A-2 contains the inventory of local-level reforms.

Table A-1. State-Level Teacher Incentive Pay Reforms

State	Project Name	Funding Method and/or Supplement	Student Performance	Teacher Evaluation	Advanced Responsibility	High-Need/ Hard-to-Staff	Eligible or Participating Schools/ LEAs	Incentive Range or Maximum Amount	Source
			Incentive Criteria						
AK	Alaska School Performance Incentive Program		Y				All LEAs	$2,500-5,500	NCPI, ECS
AZ	Arizona Career Ladder	Formula	Y	Y	Y		28 LEAs		NCPI, ECS
AZ	Classroom Site Fund	Sales Tax	Y	Y			All LEAs		NCPI, ECS
AR	Comprehensive Testing and Accountability Program	Formula	Y						NCPI, ECS
FL	Merit Awards Program (replaced STAR in 2007)	Formula	Y						NCPI, ECS
GA	Georgia Salary Structure Components	Discretionary	Y		Y	Y		5%	NCPI, ECS
ID	Idaho State Teacher Advancement and Recognition System		Y		Y	Y		$1,200-3,600	NIET
MN	Quality Compensation Program	Formula	Y	Y	Y		22 LEAs	$260/ Student	NCPI, ECS
MS	Mississippi Performance Based Pay Plan		Y			Y	All LEAs		ECS
NC	ABCs of Public Education	Formula	Y			Y		$1,500	NCPI, ECS
OH	Ohio Teacher Incentive Fund	TIF	Y	Y	Y		4 LEAs	$2,000-6,000	ED, NCPI
OK	Academic Achievement Awards	Discretionary	Y				43 Schools		NIET
OR	Creative Leadership and Student Success	Formula	Y	Y	Y		3 LEAs	$200-400 /Student	NCPI
SC	South Carolina Teacher Incentive Fund	TIF	Y	Y	Y	Y	23 Schools	$2,000-10,000	ED, NCPI
SD	Technology and Innovations in Education	TIF	Y				11 Schools		ED, NCPI

State	Project Name	Funding Method and/or Supplement	Student Performance	Teacher Evaluation	Advanced Responsibility	High-Need/ Hard-to-Staff	Eligible or Participating Schools/ LEAs	Incentive Range or Maximum Amount	Source
			Incentive Criteria						
TX	Governor's Educator Excellence Grant	Formula	Y			Y	99 Schools		NCPI, ECS
TX	Texas Educator Excellence Grant	Formula	Y			Y	1,200 Sch.		NCPI, ECS
TX	District Awards for Teacher Excellence	Formula	Y	Y	Y	Y	All LEAs		NCPI, ECS
UT	Utah Performance Plan	Formula	Y				All LEAs	$1,000	NCPI
VA	Incentives for Hard-to-Staff Schools		Y			Y		$3,000	ECS
State Total			20	7	8	9			

Source: CRS synthesis of available information based on a review of the literature on pay for performance programs including academic publications, educational press, government documentation, and other sources of information made available by policy centers, associations, and commissions.

Key: NCPI = National Center on Performance Incentives, Policy Information Resource, http://www. performanceincentives.org/ statebystate_resources/ index.asp;

NIET = National Institute for Excellence in Teaching, Teacher Advancement Program website, http://www. talentedteachers.org/; ED = Department of Education, Teacher Incentive Fund grantee profiles, http://cecr.ed.gov/initiatives/grantees/profiles.cfm;

ECS = Education Commission for the States, Teacher Compensation Database, http://www.ecs.org/ html/educationissues/ teachingquality/NCLB-HQTP/ t_comp.asp.

Note: Information current as of December 2008. An empty cell indicates data were not available in the materials reviewed for this inventory.

Table A-2. Local-Level Teacher Incentive Pay Reforms

State	Project Name and Location	TIF/TAP Support	Student Performance	Teacher Evaluation	Advanced Responsibility	High-Need/ Hard-to-Staff	Eligible or Participating Schools /LEAs	Incentive Range or Maximum Amount	Source
			Incentive Criteria						
AL	Transformed Schools Program, Mobile County		Y	Y			5 Sch.	$4,000-12,000	NCIP, ECS
AK	Alaska Teacher and Principal Incentive Project - Chugach School District, Anchorage	TIF	Y				4 LEAs		ED, NCPI
AR	Lincoln Consolidated School District	TAP	Y	Y	Y			$2,000-6,000	NIET
AR	Little Rock School District	TAP	Y	Y	Y			$2,000-6,000	NIET
AZ	Project EXCELL - Amphitheater Unified School District, Tucson	TIF	Y	Y	Y	Y	11 Sch.		ED, NCPI
AZ	University Public Schools, Mesa	TAP	Y	Y	Y			$2,000-6,000	NIET
CA	Quest for Success - Lynwood Unified School District	TIF	Y		Y	Y	17 Sch.		ED, NCPI
CA	The New 3Rs: Rigor, Results, and Rewards - Mare Island Tech. Academy, Vallejo	TIF	Y				2 Sch.		ED, NCPI
CA	Vaughn Next Century Learning Center, Los Angeles		Y		Y		1 Chrtr.	$2,000-14,700	NCPI, ECS
CO	Performance-Based Compensation Program - Eagle County School District RE 50J	TIF+TAP	Y	Y	Y	Y	13 Sch.	$2,000-6,000	ED, NCPI
CO	Recognizing Engagement in the Advancement of Learning -Harrison School District 2, Colorado Springs	TIF	Y	Y	Y	Y	21 Sch.		ED, NCPI
CO	Professional Compensation w/ NLNS, Denver	TIF	Y	Y	Y	Y			ED, NCPI, ECS
CO	Douglas County		Y	Y	Y			$4,800-7,300	

State	Project Name and Location	TIF/TAP Support	Student Performance	Teacher Evaluation	Advanced Responsibility	High-Need/ Hard-to-Staff	Eligible or Participating Schools /LEAs	Incentive Range or Maximum Amount	Source
			Incentive Criteria						
CO	Fort Lupton Teacher Incentive Fund -Weld County School District	TIF	Y			Y	4 Sch.		ED, NCPI
CO	Academy School District 20, Colorado Springs	TAP	Y	Y	Y			$2,000-6,000	NIET
DC	Washington, DC Charter Schools	TAP	Y	Y	Y			$2,000-6,000	NIET
DC	Washington, DC Public Schools w/ NLNS	TIF	Y						ED, NCPI
FL	Rewards and Incentives for School Educators - Miami-Dade Co. PS	TIF	Y	Y	Y	Y	36 Sch.		ED, NCPI
FL	Recognizing Excellence in Achievement and Professionalism, Orlando	TIF	Y					$4,000-5,000	ED, NCPI
FL	Gadsden County School District	TAP	Y	Y	Y			$2,000-6,000	NIET
IL	Recognizing Excellence in Academic Leadership - Chicago Public Schools	TIF+TAP	Y	Y	Y	Y	40 Sch.	$2,000-6,000	ED, NCPI
IN	Archdiocese of Indianapolis	TAP	Y	Y	Y			$2,000-6,000	NIET
LA	Algiers Charter Schools Assoc. w/ NIET, New Orleans	TIF+TAP	Y	Y	Y		7 Chrtr.	$2,000-6,000	ED, NIET
LA	Ascension Public Schools, Donaldsonville	TAP	Y	Y	Y			$2,000-6,000	NIET
LA	Caddo Public Schools, Shreveport	TAP	Y	Y	Y			$2,000-6,000	NIET
LA	Desoto Parish Schools, Mansfield	TAP	Y	Y	Y			$2,000-6,000	NIET
LA	East Baton Rouge Parish School System	TAP	Y	Y	Y			$2,000-6,000	NIET
LA	Jefferson Parish Public Schools, Marrerro	TAP	Y	Y	Y			$2,000-6,000	NIET
LA	Natchitoches Parish School Board	TAP	Y	Y	Y			$2,000-6,000	NIET

Table A-2. (Continued)

State	Project Name and Location	TIF/TAP Support	Student Performance	Teacher Evaluation	Advanced Responsibility	High-Need/ Hard-to-Staff	Eligible or Participating Schools /LEAs	Incentive Range or Maximum Amount	Source
			Incentive Criteria						
LA	Rapides Parish School Board, Greensboro	TAP	Y	Y	Y			$2,000-6,000	NIET
LA	Recovery School District, New Orleans	TAP	Y	Y	Y			$2,000-6,000	NIET
LA	St. Barnard Parish Public Schools	TAP	Y	Y	Y			$2,000-6,000	NIET
MD	Financial Incentive Rewards for Supervisors and Teachers, Upper Marlboro	TIF	Y			Y			ED, NCPI
MA	Teacher Excellence Incentive Project, Roslindale	TIF	Y			Y	1 Chrtr.		ED, NCPI
MN	Minneapolis Public Schools	TAP	Y	Y	Y			$2,000-6,000	NIET
MN	Minneapolis Charter School	TAP	Y	Y	Y			$2,000-6,000	NIET
NV	Las Vegas Charter School	TAP	Y	Y	Y			$2,000-6,000	NIET
NM	Performance-Based Compensation Program, Rio Rancho	TIF	Y			Y	4 LEAs		ED, NCPI
NY	NYC Partnership for Innovation in								
	Compensation for Charter Schools w/ CEI, New York	TIF	Y	Y		Y	10 Chrtr.		ED, NCPI
NY	Admin. Pay Incentive - Elmira City		Y				1 LEA		NCPI
NC	Leadership for Educators' Advanced Performance - Charlotte-Mecklenburg Schools w/ CATC	TIF	Y	Y		Y	16 Sch.	$1,400	ED, NCPI, ECS
NC	Charlotte-Mecklenburg County Schools		Y	Y	Y	Y			ECS
NC	Teacher Compensation Plan - Winston-Salem/ Forsyth County Schools		Y						NCPI

State	Project Name and Location	TIF/TAP Support	Student Performance	Teacher Evaluation	Advanced Responsibility	High-Need/ Hard-to-Staff	Eligible or Participating Schools /LEAs	Incentive Range or Maximum Amount	Source
			Incentive Criteria						
NC	Cumberland County Schools, Fayetteville	TIF	Y			Y			ED, NCPI
NC	Wake County Schools	TAP	Y	Y	Y			$2,000-6,000	
NC	Mission Possible - Guilford County Schools, Greensboro	TIF	Y					$4,000-5,000	ED, NCPI, ECS
OH	Cincinnati Public Schools	TAP	Y	Y	Y			$2,000-6,000	NIET
OH	Columbus Public Schools	TAP	Y	Y	Y			$2,000-6,000	NIET
OK	System to Motivate and Reward Teachers, Beggs	TIF	Y	Y			8 LEAs		ED, NCPI
PA	Principal Incentive Program, Pittsburgh	TIF	Y				64 Sch.		ED, NCPI
PA	School District of Philadelphia (public charters)	TIF+TAP	Y	Y	Y		6-12 Chrtr.	$2,000-6,000	ED, NCPI, NIET
SC	Anderson School District Four, Pendleton	TAP	Y	Y	Y			$2,000-6,000	NIET
SC	Beaufort County School District	TAP	Y	Y	Y			$2,000-6,000	NIET
SC	Dillon School District Two	TAP	Y	Y	Y			$2,000-6,000	NIET
SC	Darlington County School District	TAP	Y	Y	Y			$2,000-6,000	NIET
SC	Florence School Districts 1 & 3 and Laurens School District 56, Lake City	TIF+TAP	Y	Y	Y	Y	6 Sch.	$2,000-6,000	ED, NCPI, NIET
SC	Georgetown County School District	TAP	Y	Y	Y			$2,000-6,000	NIET
SC	Hampton School District 2	TAP	Y	Y	Y			$2,000-6,000	NIET
SC	Marlboro County School District	TAP	Y	Y	Y			$2,000-6,000	NIET
SC	Pickens County School District	TAP	Y	Y	Y			$2,000-6,000	NIET

Table A-2. (Continued)

State	Project Name and Location	TIF/TAP Support	Student Performance	Teacher Evaluation	Advanced Responsibility	High-Need/ Hard-to-Staff	Eligible or Participating Schools /LEAs	Incentive Range or Maximum Amount	Source
			Incentive Criteria						
SC	Richland School District 2		Y					$7,500-15,000	.
SC	Spartanburg School District 7	TAP	Y	Y	Y			$2,000-6,000	NIET
SC	Sumter School District 17	TAP	Y	Y	Y			$2,000-6,000	NIET
TN	Benwood Initiative - Hamilton County Schools, Chattanooga		Y				9 Sch.	$7,000-10,000	ECS
TN	Memphis City Schools w/ NLNS	TIF	Y				17 Sch.		ED, NCPI
TN	Knox County School District	TAP	Y	Y	Y			$2,000-6,000	NIET
TX	Principal and Teacher Incentive Pay Program, Dallas	TIF	Y		Y	Y			ED, NCPI
TX	Aldine Independent School District, Houston		Y			Y		$500-18,000	NCPI, ECS
TX	Austin Independent School District		Y	Y	Y				NCPI, ECS
TX	Strategies for Motivating and Rewarding Teachers, Houston	TIF	Y				27 Sch.	$7,000	ED, NCPI
TX	Teachers and Principals Awarded for Student Achievement, San Antonio	TIF	Y		Y	Y	6 Sch.		ED, NCPI
TX	University of Texas, Austin	TIF	Y			Y	27 Sch.		ED, NCPI
TX	Hays Consolidated Independent School District, Kyle	TAP	Y	Y	Y			$2,000-6,000	NIET
TX	Judson Independent School District, Live Oak	TAP	Y	Y	Y			$2,000-6,000	NIET
TX	Lancaster Independent School District	TAP	Y	Y	Y			$2,000-6,000	NIET

State	Project Name and Location	TIF/TAP Support	Student Performance	Teacher Evaluation	Advanced Responsibility	High-Need/ Hard-to-Staff	Eligible or Participating Schools /LEAs	Incentive Range or Maximum Amount	Source
			Incentive Criteria						
TX	Lytle Independent School District	TAP	Y	Y	Y			$2,000-6,000	NIET
TX	Manor Independent School District	TAP	Y	Y	Y			$2,000-6,000	NIET
TX	Richardson Independent School District	TAP	Y	Y	Y			$2,000-6,000	NIET
WY	Laramie County School District #2	TAP	Y	Y	Y			$2,000-6,000	NIET
WY	Sheridan County School District #2	TAP	Y	Y	Y			$2,000-6,000	NIET
Local Total			82	59	58	21			

Source: CRS synthesis of available information based on a review of the literature on pay for performance programs including academic publications, educational press, government documentation, and other sources of information made available by policy centers, associations, and commissions.

Key: NCPI = National Center on Performance Incentives, Policy Information Resource, http://www.performanceincentives.org/ statebystate_resources/index.asp;

NIET = National Institute for Excellence in Teaching, Teacher Advancement Program website, http://www.talentedteachers.org/;

ED = Department of Education, Teacher Incentive Fund grantee profiles, http://cecr.ed.gov/initiatives/grantees/profiles.cfm;

ECS = Education Commission for the States, Teacher Compensation Database, http://www.ecs.org/html/ educationissues/ teachingquality/NCLB-HQTP/t_comp.asp.

Note: Information current as of December 2008. An empty cell indicates data were not available in the materials reviewed for this inventory.

End Notes

[1] Protsik, J. (1995). History of teacher pay and incentive reform. Washington: Educational Resources Information Center. Guthrie, J.W., Springer, M.G., Rolle, A.R., Houck, E.A. (2007). Modern Education Finance and Policy. Mahwah, New Jersey: Allyn & Bacon.

[2] Moehlman, A.B. (1927). Public School Finance. New York: New York: Rand McNally & Company. During this period, salary schedules for all civil service workers were developed to combat the "spoils" system. More information on these developments can be found in Phil Gonring, Paul Teske, and Grad Jupp, *Pay-for-Performance Teacher Compensation: An Inside View of Denver's ProComp Plan*, (Cambridge: Harvard Education Press, 2007), p. 8.

[3] Sharpes, D.K. (1987). Incentive pay and the promotion of teaching proficiencies. The Clearinghouse, 60, 407-410. Podgursky, M. (2007). Teams versus Bureaucracies: Personnel Policy, Wage-Setting, and Teacher Quality in Traditional Public, Charter, and Private Schools. In M. Berends, M.G. Springer, and H. Walberg (Eds.), Charter School Outcomes. Mahwah, NJ: Lawrence Erlbaum Associates.

[4] Twenty-one states have a statewide salary schedule that generally sets minimum salary levels. Usually, local districts can exceed these minimum levels when fashioning salary schedules for their teachers. (Education Commission of the States. Statewide Teacher Salary Schedules. ECS Information Clearinghouse. July 2005.) http://www.ecs.org/ clearinghouse/62/43/6243.htm

[5] Handbook of the Economics of Education, Volume 2, 2006, Pages 1051-1078 Chapter 18 Teacher Quality, Eric A. Hanushek and Steven G. Rivkin.

[6] Rob Greenwald et al. "The Effect of School Resources on Student Achievement," *Review of Educational Research*, (Fall 1996) p. 384.

[7] Sylvia A. Allegretto, Sean P. Corcoran, and Lawrence Mishel, *How Does Teacher Pay Compare?*, Economic Policy Institute, August 2004.

[8] Jay P. Greene and Marcus A. Winters, *How Much Are Public School Teachers Paid?*, Manhattan Institute for Policy Research, Civic Report, No. 50, January 2007.

[9] Murnane, Richard J., and David K. Cohen. Merit Pay and the Evaluation Problem: Understanding Why Most Merit Pay Plans Fail and a Few Survive. Institute for Research on Educational Finance and Governance. Stanford University. November 1985.

[10] Podgursky, Michael J. and Matthew G. Springer, *Teacher Performance Pay: A Review*, Working Paper 2006-0 1, Nashville, TN: National Center on Performance Incentives, November, 2006.

[11] Portions of this section were originally published in CRS Report RL3 0217, *Performance-Based Pay for Teachers*, by James B. Stedman and Gail McCallion (out of print; available from the author).

[12] Michael Beer, Mark D Cannon, James N Baron, Patrick R Dailey et al., "Promise and Peril in Implementing Pay-forperformance," *Human Resource Management*, Spring 2004, vol. 43-1.

[13] Ibid.

[14] David Pierpont Gardner et al., *A Nation at Risk: The Imperative For Educational Reform*, National Commission on Excellence in Education, Washington, DC, April 1983, http://www.ed.gov/pubs/NatAtRisk/index.html.

[15] Podgursky, Michael J. and Matthew G. Springer, *Teacher Performance Pay: A Review*, Working Paper 2006-0 1, Nashville, TN: National Center on Performance Incentives, November, 2006.

[16] Hassal, B., *Better Pay for Better Teaching: Making Teacher Pay pay off in the age of accountability*, PPI Policy Report, Washington, DC, 2002.

[17] Hanushek, Eric. Making Schools Work. Washington. The Brookings Institution, 1994. p. 79.

[18] Herbert Heneman III, Anthony Milanowski and Steven Kimball.(RB-46, 2007). Teacher Performance Pay: Synthesis of Plans, Research and Guidelines for Practice. Philadelphia, PA: University of Pennsylvania, Graduate School of Education, Consortium for Policy Research in Education.

[19] Dan Goldhaber, *Teacher Pay Reforms: The Political Implications of Recent Research*, Center for American Progress, December 2006, p. 19.

[20] http://www.sas.com/govedu/edu/bio_sanders.html

[21] National Center on Teaching Quality, *2008 State Teacher Policy Yearbook*, February 2008.

[22] Dan McCaffrey et al., *Evaluating Value-Added Models for Teacher Accountability*, RAND Corporation: Santa Monica, CA, 2003.

[23] Heneman, Robert L.; Ledford, Gerald E., Jr., "Competency Pay for Professionals and Managers in Business: A Review and Implications for Teachers," *Journal of Personnel Evaluation in Education*, v12 n2 p103-21, Jun 1998.

[24] Odden, Allan, and Carolyn Kelley. *Paying Teachers for What They Know and Do: New and Smarter Compensation Strategies to Improve Schools*. 2002.

[25] Dan Goldhaber, *Teacher Pay Reforms: The Political Implications of Recent Research*, Center for American Progress, December 2006.

[26] Herbert G. Heneman III et al., "Standards-Based Teacher Evaluation as a Foundation for Knowledge- and Skill-Based Pay," Philadelhphia: Consortium for Policy Research in Education, RB-45, 2006.

[27] Richard M. Ingersoll, "Teacher Turnover and Teacher Shortages: An Organizational Analysis," American Educational Research Journal, Vol. 38, No. 3 (Autumn, 2001), pp. 499-534.

[25] Dan Goldhaber, *Teacher Pay Reforms: The Political Implications of Recent Research*, Center for American Progress, December 2006.

[26] Herbert G. Heneman III et al., "Standards-Based Teacher Evaluation as a Foundation for Knowledge- and Skill-Based Pay," Philadelhphia: Consortium for Policy Research in Education, RB-45, 2006.

[27] Richard M. Ingersoll, "Teacher Turnover and Teacher Shortages: An Organizational Analysis," American Educational Research Journal, Vol. 38, No. 3 (Autumn, 2001), pp. 499-534.

[28] Berry, Barnett, *Performance Pay for Teachers*, Center for Teaching Quality, March 2007.

[29] Ruth Chung Wei, Linda Darling-Hammond, Alethea Andree, Nikole Richardson, and Stelios Orphanos, *Professional learning in the learning profession: A status report on teacher development in the United States and abroad*, (Dallas, TX: National Staff Development Council, 2009), p. 31.

[30] Some states, such as Massachusetts and Illinois, require NBPTS certification to obtain master teacher status.

[31] National Education Association. *Status of the American Public School Teacher 2000-2001*, Washington, DC, 2003 and *Status of the American Public School Teacher 1996-1997*, Washington, DC, 1997. The survey has not been administered since 2001.

[32] U.S. Department of Education, *Characteristics of Schools, Districts, Teachers, Principles, and School Libraries in the United States, 2003-2004 Schools and Staffing Survey*, NCES 2006-313.

[33] Thomas D. Snyder, Sally A. Dillow, and Charlene M. Hoffman, *Digest of Education Statistics 2008*, U.S. Department of Education, NCES 2009-020, Washington, DC, March 2009, p. 258 & p. 540, http://nces.ed.gov/ pubsearch/pubsinfo.asp?pubid=2009020.

[34] Ibid, p. 260.

[35] Stephanie Stullich et al., *State and Local Implementation of the No Child Left Behind Act, Volume VI—Targeting and Uses of Federal Education Funds*, U.S. Department of Education, Office of Planning, Evaluation and Policy Development, Policy and Program Studies Service, Washington, DC, January 2009, p. 94, http://www.ed.gov/rschstat/ eval/disadv/nclb-targeting/index.html.

[36] Ibid, p. 89.

[37] For a discussion of this program, see CRS Report RL3 1882, *Teacher Quality Enhancement Grants (Title II, Part A of the Higher Education Act): Overview and Reauthorization Issues*, by Jeffrey J. Kuenzi.

[38] For more information on the 2008 amendments to the HEA, see CRS Report RL34654, *The Higher Education Opportunity Act: Reauthorization of the Higher Education Act*, by David P. Smole et al.

[39] For more information on this program, see CRS Report RL30834, *K-12 Teacher Quality: Issues and Legislative Action*, by Jeffrey J. Kuenzi (out of print; available from the author).

[40] U.S. Department of Education, *Findings From the 2007-08 Survey on the Use of Funds Under Title II, Part A*, June 2008.

[41] Richard J. Murnane and David K. Cohen. "Merit Pay and the Evaluation Problem: Understanding Why Most Merit Pay Plans Fail and a Few Survive," Institute for Research on Educational Finance and Governance, Stanford University, November 1985.

[42] Andrew J. Rotherham, *Achieving Teacher and Principal Excellence: A Guidebook for Donors*, Philanthropy Roundtable, 2008. http://www.philanthropyroundtable.org/ files/ TeacherExcellence.pdf

[43] http://cecr.ed.gov/

[44] U.S. Department of Education, *Fiscal Year 2009, Justifications for Appropriation Estimates to the Congress*, vol. 1.

[45] U.S. Department of Education, *Fiscal Year 2011, Justifications for Appropriation Estimates to the Congress*, vol. 1.

[46] Information about TAP and its funders can be found at http://www.talentedteachers.org

[47] Minnesota Office of the Legislative Auditor, "Q Comp: Quality Compensation for Teachers," February 2009.

[48] Information available at http://www.ade.state

[49] Matthew G. Springer et al., *Texas Educator Excellence Grants (TEEG) Program: Year Two Evaluation Report*, National Center on Performance Incentives, Policy Evaluation Report, December 1, 2008.

[50] Phil Gonring, Paul Teske, and Grad Jupp, *Pay-for-Performance Teacher Compensation: An Inside View of Denver's ProComp Plan* (Cambridge: Harvard Education Press, 2007).

[51] Information available at http://gcsnc.com/depts/mission

[52] Elena Silva, "The Benwood Plan: A Lesson in Comprehensive Teacher Reform," Education Sector Reports, April 2008. See also http://www.pefchattanooga.org/tabid/64/Default.aspx.

[53] http://www.shearonforschools.com/TVAAS.html.

[54] Presentation at the Alliance for Excellent Education, Washington, DC, December 10, 2008.

[55] Based on a phone conversation with Ms. Van Hook, January 2009.

[56] U.S. Department of Education, "Findings From the 2007-08 Survey on the Use of Funds Under Title II, Part A," June 2008.

[57] The HEA reauthorization bill (P.L. 110-315) also contained "performance pay" for mentor teachers; however, these incentives are to be "based on the mentor's extra skills and responsibilities," rather than teaching performance.

[58] Additional material submitted by Linda Darling-Hammond, U.S. Congress, Senate Committee on Health, Education, Labor, and Pensions, *NCLB Reauthorization: Strategies for Attracting, Supporting and Retaining High Quality Educators*, 1 10th Cong., 1st sess., March 6, 2007, S.Hrg. 110-154 (Washington: GPO, 2008), p. 93.

[59] Miller/McKeon Discussion Draft of ESEA Reauthorization, pp. 7-8; available from the author.

[60] U.S. Congress, House Committee on Education and Labor, *Reauthorization of the Elementary and Secondary Education Act of 1965*, hearing on the Miller/McKeon Discussion Draft of ESEA Reauthorization, 110th Cong., 1st sess., September 10, 2007, Serial No. 110-61 (Washington: GPO, 2008), p. 238.

[61] Ibid., pp. 259-260.

[62] Based on a phone conversation with Dr. Dale Balou of the National Center on Performance Incentives, March 2008.

[63] The only nationally representative survey of school personnel, the Schools and Staffing Survey conducted by the National Center for Education Statistics, provides little information beyond estimates of how many teachers receive incentive awards.

In: Elementary and Secondary Education Act
Editors: D. M. Brown and A. Davies
ISBN: 978-1-61942-694-8

Chapter 4

THE ELEMENTARY AND SECONDARY EDUCATION ACT, AS AMENDED BY THE NO CHILD LEFT BEHIND ACT: A PRIMER

Rebecca R. Skinner

SUMMARY

The primary source of federal aid to K-12 education is the Elementary and Secondary Education Act (ESEA), particularly its Title I, Part A program of Education for the Disadvantaged. The ESEA was initially enacted in 1965 (P.L. 89-10), and was most recently amended and reauthorized by the No Child Left Behind Act of 2001 (NCLB, P.L. 107-110), which authorized virtually all ESEA programs through FY2008. It is widely expected that the 112th Congress will consider whether to amend and extend the ESEA.

The NCLB initiated a major expansion of federal influence upon several aspects of public K-12 education, primarily with the aim of increasing the accountability of public school systems and individual public schools for improving achievement outcomes of all students, especially the disadvantaged. States must implement in all public schools and school districts a variety of standards-based assessments in reading, math and science; make complex annual adequate yearly progress (AYP) determinations for each public school and district; and require virtually all public school teachers and aides to meet a variety of qualification requirements. State AYP policies must incorporate an ultimate goal of all public school students reaching a proficient or higher level of achievement by the end of the 2013-14 school year. Further, participating states must enforce a series of increasingly substantial consequences for most of their schools and almost all school districts that fail to meet the AYP standards for two consecutive years or more. All of these requirements are associated with state participation in the ESEA Title I-A program.

Other major ESEA programs provide grants to support the education of migrant students; recruitment of and professional development for teachers; language instruction for limited English proficient students; drug abuse prevention programs; after-school instruction and care; expansion of charter schools and other forms of public school choice; education services for Native American, Native Hawaiian, and Alaska Native students; Impact Aid to compensate local educational agencies for taxes foregone due to certain federal activities; and a wide variety of innovative educational approaches or instruction to meet particular student needs.

INTRODUCTION

The primary source of federal aid to K-12 education is the Elementary and Secondary Education Act (ESEA), particularly its Title I, Part A program of Education for the Disadvantaged. The ESEA was initially enacted in 1965 (P.L. 89-10), and was most recently amended and reauthorized by the No Child Left Behind Act of 2001 (NCLB, P.L. 107-110), which authorized virtually all ESEA programs through FY2008. It is widely expected that the 112th Congress will consider whether to amend and extend the ESEA.

The NCLB initiated a major expansion of federal influence on several aspects of public K-12 education, primarily with the aim of increasing the accountability of public school systems and individual public schools for improving achievement outcomes of all students, especially the disadvantaged. Accountability requirements included in Title I-A of the ESEA require states to implement content and performance standards and assessments aligned with these standards for reading/language arts and mathematics for multiple grades. The results of these assessments are used to make complex annual adequate yearly progress (AYP) determinations for each public school and local educational agency (LEA). A series of increasingly substantial consequences must be applied to schools and LEAs that fail to meet the AYP standards for two consecutive years or more. Accountability requirements also extend to virtually all public school teachers and aides with respect to their qualifications.

Beyond Title I-A, other major ESEA programs provide grants to support the education of migrant students; recruitment of and professional development for teachers; language instruction for limited English proficient (LEP) students; drug abuse prevention programs; after-school instruction and care; expansion of charter schools and other forms of public school choice; education services for Native American, Native Hawaiian, and Alaska Native students; Impact Aid to compensate local educational agencies for taxes forgone due to certain federal activities; and a wide variety of innovative educational approaches or instruction to meet particular student needs.

Annual appropriations for ESEA programs are provided through the Departments of Labor, Health and Human Services, and Education, and Related Agencies Appropriations Act. Table A-1 provides FY2009 and FY20 10 appropriations for programs authorized by the ESEA. Final FY20 11 appropriations have not yet been enacted by Congress. Appropriations are currently being provided through March 4, 2011, at the FY20 10 level through the Continuing Appropriations and Surface Transportation Extensions Act, 2011 (P.L. 111-322).[1]

This report provides a brief overview of major provisions of the ESEA. It is organized by title and part of the act. Other CRS reports provide much more detailed discussions and analyses of major ESEA provisions.[2] Appendix B provides a list of selected acronyms used in the report.

TITLE I: IMPROVING THE ACADEMIC ACHIEVEMENT OF THE DISADVANTAGED

The introductory text for ESEA Title I includes the authorization of appropriations for FY2002- FY2007 for each Part of the Title, including school improvement grants (SIGs), and authority for states to reserve 1% of grants under parts A, C, and D, or $400,000 (whichever is greater), for state administration.

School Improvement Grants

Title I-A authorizes the appropriation of such sums as may be necessary for grants to states under Section 1003(g) for School Improvement Grants. States are eligible to apply for these grants, which are allocated in proportion to each state's share of funds received under ESEA Title I, Parts A, C (Migrant Education Program), and D (Neglected and Delinquent Children and Youth). States must use at least 95% of the funds received to make subgrants to LEAs. Subgrants made to LEAs must be between $50,000 and $500,000 for each school identified for improvement, corrective action, or restructuring that will be served through the grant, and must be renewable for up to two additional years if schools meet the goals of their school improvement plans. Subgrants must be used by LEAs to support school improvement. LEAs with the lowest-achieving schools and the greatest commitment to ensuring that such funds are used to provide "adequate resources" to enable the lowest-achieving schools to meet the goals under school and LEA improvement plans must be given priority in the awarding of subgrants.

Through the Consolidated Appropriations Act, 2010 (P.L. 111-117), the School Improvement Grants program was amended to provide a maximum grant of $2 million to each school served using funds appropriated under the American Recovery and Reinvestment Act (ARRA; P.L. 111- 5) or FY2010 appropriations. In addition, provisions in P.L. 111-117 altered school eligibility criteria to receive School Improvement Grants to include any school eligible to receive assistance under Title I-A that has not made AYP for at least two years or is in the state's lowest quintile of performance based on proficiency rates or, for secondary schools, has a graduation rate below 60%.[3]

Part A: Improving Basic Programs Operated by Local Educational Agencies

Title I, Part A, of the ESEA authorizes federal aid to local educational agencies (LEAs) for the education of disadvantaged children. Title I-A grants provide supplementary educational and related services to low-achieving and other students attending pre-kindergarten through grade 12 schools with relatively high concentrations of students from low-income families. It has also become a "vehicle" to which a number of requirements affecting broad aspects of public K- 12 education for all students have been attached as a condition for receiving Title I-A grants.

Title I-A funds are allocated by the U.S. Department of Education (ED) to state educational agencies (SEAs), which then suballocate grants to LEAs. It is one of the few federal K- 12 formula grant programs for which substate grants are, in most cases, calculated by ED. Portions of each annual appropriation for Title I-A are allocated under four different formulas—Basic, Concentration, Targeted, and Education Finance Incentive Grants—although funds allocated under all of these formulas are combined and used for the same purposes by recipient LEAs. Although the allocation formulas have several distinctive elements, the primary factors used in all four formulas are estimated numbers of children aged 5-17 in poor families plus a state expenditure factor based on average expenditures per pupil for public K-12 education. Other factors included in one or more formulas include weighting schemes designed to increase aid to LEAs with the highest concentrations of poverty, and a factor to increase grants to states with high levels of expenditure equity among their LEAs. Each formula also has a LEA hold harmless provision (no LEA may receive less than 85-95% of its previous year grant, depending on the LEA's poverty rate) and a state minimum grant provision (up to either 0.25% or 0.3 5% of state grants, depending on the formula).

Within LEAs, Title I-A funds are used to provide supplementary educational services to students at public schools with the highest percentages or numbers of children from low-income families, as well as eligible students who live in the areas served by these public schools, but who attend private schools.[4] While there are several program rules related to school selection, the participating schools must generally have a percentage or number of children from low-income families that is greater than the LEA's average. LEAs can generally choose to focus Title I-A services on selected grade levels (e.g., only in elementary schools), but they must usually provide services in all schools, without regard to their grade level, where the percentage of students from low-income families exceeds 75%. Once schools are selected, Title I-A funds are allocated among them on the basis of their number of students from low-income families.

There are two basic types of Title I-A programs. *Schoolwide programs* are authorized if the percentage of low-income students served by a school is 40% or higher. In schoolwide programs, Title I-A funds may be used to improve the performance of all students in a school. For example, funds might be used to provide professional development services to all of a school's teachers, upgrade instructional technology, or implement new curricula. The other major type of Title I-A school service model is the *targeted assistance* program (TAP). This was the original type of Title I-A program, under which Title I-A-funded services are generally limited to the lowest achieving students in the school. For example, students may be "pulled out" of their regular classroom for several hours of more intensive instruction by a specialist teacher each week, or they may receive such instruction in an after-school program, or funds may be used to hire a teacher's aide who provides additional assistance to low achieving students in their regular classroom.

A number of major accountability requirements apply to public schools in a state that participates in the Title I-A program. Participating states[5] must administer annual, standards-based assessments in reading/language arts and mathematics to students in each of grades 3-8, plus at least once in grades 10-12. Beginning with the 2007-2008 school year, such assessments must also be administered to students in each of three grade levels (3-5, 6-9, and 10-12) in science. Student performance standards for all required assessments must include at least three performance levels: advanced, proficient, and basic. The state assessments must meet a variety of criteria regarding accommodations for students with disabilities and LEP students, and linkages between state content standards, student performance standards, and assessments. Participating states must also administer annual assessments of English language proficiency to all of their LEP students, and participate in National Assessment of Educational Progress (NAEP) tests of 4th and 8th grade students in reading and math every two years.

States participating in Title I-A must use results of the required reading and math assessments to make annual adequate yearly progress determinations. AYP standards must be applied to all public schools, LEAs, and to states overall. However, under the ESEA, consequences for failing to meet AYP standards need only be applied to schools and LEAs participating in Title I-A, and consequences for states as a whole are limited to potential identification and provision of technical assistance. AYP is defined primarily on the basis of the percentage of students scoring at a proficient or higher level of achievement. AYP standards must also include at least one additional academic indicator; in the case of high schools, this must be the graduation rate.

AYP calculations must be disaggregated—that is, determined separately for several demographic groups, as well as for an "all students" group. The specified groups include economically disadvantaged students, LEP students, students with disabilities, and students in major racial and ethnic groups. However, student groups need not be considered if their number is so small that results would not be statistically significant or the identity of students might be divulged (minimum group size). In order to make AYP, at least 95% of students overall and 95% of each demographic group must participate in assessments. Schools or LEAs meet AYP standards only if they meet the required threshold levels of performance on assessments, other academic indicators, and test participation with respect to all of the designated student groups that meet the minimum group size criterion selected by the state. The primary structure for AYP determination under the ESEA applies the same required threshold level of achievement to all students and schools statewide (a "status" model). The ESEA also includes a "safe harbor" provision, under which AYP may be met by a student group if it experiences a 10% reduction, compared to the previous year, in the number of students below proficiency. In recent years, there has been increasing interest in using "growth" models to determine AYP, by which the achievement of individual students is tracked from year to year. Interested states may apply to receive a waiver from the Secretary of Education (hereafter referred to as the Secretary) to implement a growth model.

The ESEA requires states to identify LEAs and schools that fail to meet AYP standards for two consecutive years for improvement. Students attending these schools must be provided with options to attend other public schools that make AYP. If a Title I-A school fails to meet AYP standards for a third year, students from low-income families must be offered the opportunity to receive instruction from a supplemental educational services (SES) provider of their choice. One or more additional "corrective actions," such as implementing a new curriculum, must be taken with respect to Title I-A schools that fail to meet AYP for a fourth year. Those that fail to meet AYP standards for a sixth year must develop a "restructuring" plan, involving such actions as reopening as a charter school. If a school fails to make AYP for a subsequent year, the school must implement its restructuring plan. Procedures analogous to those for schools apply to LEAs that receive Title I-A grants and fail to meet AYP requirements.

Finally, states participating in Title I-A are required to provide that all public school teachers in core subjects are "highly qualified." In order to be deemed a highly qualified teacher (HQT), all such public school teachers must hold at least a bachelor's degree, have obtained full state certification or passed the state teacher licensing examination, and must hold a license to teach. In addition, teachers who are new to the profession must demonstrate subject area knowledge, including (if teaching at a secondary level) passing a state academic test or completing an academic major, graduate degree, or advanced certification in each subject taught. A public school teacher who is *not* new to the profession may also be deemed to be "highly qualified" by demonstrating competence in all subjects taught "based on a high objective uniform State standard of evaluation" (HOUSSE). Further, paraprofessionals (aides) providing instruction in Title I-A programs must have either: (a) completed at least two years of higher education; or (b) earned an associate's (or higher) degree; or (c) met a "rigorous standard of quality."

Part B: Student Reading Skills Improvement Grants

Subpart 1 of Title I-B authorizes the Reading First program. Under Reading First, grants are allocated among participating states in proportion to their estimated number of children aged 5-17 in poor families, with each state receiving at least 0.25% of the total funds available for state grants. SEAs then make competitive subgrants to LEAs, with priority given to LEAs in which the estimated number of children aged 5-17 in poor families is at least 6,500 or the poverty rate for 5- 17 year-olds is at least 15%. LEAs are to use these funds to improve reading programs for students in grades K-3 in schools that either have percentages of students from low-income families that are among the highest in the LEA or have been identified for improvement under Title I-A. The supported reading instruction must be grounded in scientifically based reading research. Subpart 1 also authorizes targeted assistance performance awards to states that have demonstrated improvements in student reading performance. This program is not currently funded.

The Early Reading First program is authorized under *Subpart 2* of Title I-B. Early Reading First provides competitive grants to LEAs and/or programs serving preschool children for activities, grounded in scientifically based reading research, that are intended to help preschool children acquire knowledge and skills necessary for learning to read. This program is not currently funded.

Subpart 3 of Title I-B authorizes the William F. Goodling Even Start Family Literacy Programs. Under Even Start, funds are allocated to states in proportion to grants under Title I-A, with a minimum state grant amount of the greater of $250,000 or 0.5% of total funding for state grants. Within states, funds are competitively awarded to partnerships of LEAs and other entities to provide a combination of services to parents and children, from birth to age 7, including early childhood education, adult basic education, and parenting skills training to parents lacking a high school diploma.

Subpart 4 of Title I-B authorizes grants to LEAs to improve the services provided by school libraries. If annual appropriations are less than $100 million (as has been the case each year thus far), competitive grants to LEAs are made directly by ED; if appropriations were $100 million or above, grants would be made by formula to SEAs, in proportion to Title I-A grants, and SEAs would make competitive grants to LEAs.

Part C: Education of Migratory Children

Title I-C authorizes grants to SEAs for the education of migratory children and youth. Funds are allocated by formula on the basis of each state's number of migratory children and youth aged 3- 21 and the Title I-A state expenditure factor. ED may also make grants for the coordination of services and transfer of educational records for migratory students.

Part D: Prevention and Intervention Programs for Children and Youth Who Are Neglected, Delinquent, or At-Risk

Title I-D authorizes a pair of programs intended to improve education for students who are neglected, delinquent, or at risk of dropping out of school. *Subpart 1* authorizes grants for the education of children and youth in *state* institutions for the neglected or delinquent, including community day programs and adult correctional institutions. Funds are allocated to states on the basis of the number of such children and youth plus the Title I-A state expenditure factor. A portion of each state's grant is to be used to provide transition services to children and youth transferring to regular public schools. *Subpart 2* provides aid for programs operated by LEAs in collaboration with *locally operated* correctional facilities, and in coordination with the Title I-A program.

Part E: National Assessment of Title I

Title I-E requires ED to conduct a national assessment of Title I programs, including a national longitudinal study of schools participating in Title I-A and an evaluation of assessments used to meet the accountability requirements of Title I-A. Part E also authorizes grants for the demonstration of innovative practices in serving students assisted under Title I programs, and grants to the Close-Up Foundation for civic education programs.

Part F: Comprehensive School Reform

Title I-F authorizes grants via SEAs to LEAs to implement comprehensive reform strategies in schools participating in Title I-A. This program is not currently funded.

Part G: Advanced Placement Programs

Title I-G authorizes grants to SEAs to pay advanced placement test fees on behalf of low-income individuals, as well as grants to SEAs, LEAs, or nonprofit educational entities with relevant expertise, to support activities intended to expand access to advanced placement programs for low-income individuals.

Part H: School Dropout Prevention

At annual appropriations levels of $75 million or less (as has been the case each year thus far), Title I-H authorizes competitive grants to SEAs or LEAs for dropout prevention and reentry programs in high schools with dropout rates above the state average plus middle schools whose graduates attend these high schools. At annual appropriations levels above $75 million but less than $250 million, competitive grants would be made to SEAs for dropout prevention and reentry services to be provided via competitive subgrants to LEAs. If annual appropriations were $250 million or above, grants would be made by formula (in proportion to Title I-A grants) to SEAs, with competitive subgrants to LEAs. At all funding levels, the Secretary of Education is authorized to carry out a variety of activities as part of a "coordinated national strategy" for dropout prevention and reentry.

Part I: General Provisions

Title I-I provides for the development of federal regulations for Title I programs, state administration of these programs, and a selected number of LEA Title I-A audits. Part I also prohibits federal control of the "specific instructional content, academic achievement standards and assessments, curriculum or program of instruction" of states, LEAs, or schools (Sec. 1905), and states that nothing in Title I is to be "construed to mandate equalized spending per pupil for a State, local educational agency, or school" (Sec. 1906).

TITLE II: PREPARING, TRAINING, AND RECRUITING HIGH-QUALITY TEACHERS AND PRINCIPALS

Part A: Teacher and Principal Training and Recruiting Fund

Subpart 1 authorizes a program of state grants that may be used for a variety of purposes related to recruitment, retention, and professional development of K- 12 teachers and principals. In the allocation of funds, each state first receives an amount equal to its FY200 1 grant under two antecedent programs (the Eisenhower Professional Development and the Class Size Reduction programs), and remaining funds, if any, are allocated as follows: 35% on the basis of total population aged 5-17, and 65% on the basis of population aged 5-17 in poor families, with a state minimum grant amount of 0.5% of funds available for state grants. SEAs may reserve a share of funds for administration and statewide services, such as teacher or principal support programs or certification reform, and must suballocate at least 95% of grants to LEAs under *Subpart 2*. In making grants to LEAs under Subpart 2, each LEA first receives an amount equal to its FY2001 grant under the two antecedent programs noted above, and remaining funds, if any, are allocated as follows: 20% on the basis of total population aged 5-17, and 80% on the basis of population aged 5-17 in poor families. LEAs may use these grants for purposes that include recruiting and retaining highly qualified teachers, and professional development activities for teachers and principals, consistent with a locally developed needs assessment.

Subpart 3 authorizes grants to partnerships for sustained, high quality professional development services for teachers, principals, and paraprofessionals. Eligible partnerships must include an institution of higher education (IHE) with a teacher or principal education department, a school of arts and sciences within an IHE, a high-need LEA[6] (defined as an LEA with either a school-age child poverty rate of 20% or with 10,000 school-age children in poor families, and a high percentage of teachers who are not fully certified or who are not teaching in fields or grade levels for which they were trained), and possibly additional organizations. Additional provisions of Part A authorize national activities, such as support for principal recruitment, advanced certification, and early childhood educator professional development programs, plus a National Panel on Teacher Mobility.

Part B: Mathematics and Science Partnerships

Part B authorizes grants to eligible partnerships—that include an SEA (if annual appropriations are $100 million or above), an engineering, mathematics, or science department of an IHE, and a high-need LEA (as defined in Part A)—for activities that include professional development, summer workshops or institutes, and recruitment of mathematics and science teachers, as well as development of rigorous curricula in these fields. Title II-B funds are allocated to states by formula if appropriations are equal to or greater than $100 million, as has been the case in recent years.

Part C: Innovation for Teacher Quality

Subpart 1 authorizes a pair of programs designed to encourage former members of the armed services to become teachers (Troops to Teachers), and to support alternative certification programs for mid-career professionals and others to become teachers through nonstandard routes, especially in high-need LEAs (as defined in Part A) or schools (Transition to Teachers). *Subpart 2* authorizes grants to a nonprofit organization, the National Writing Project, which, through a series of contracts with IHEs and other nonprofit entities, provides professional development training to teachers of writing. *Subpart 3* authorizes a pair of grants to nonprofit organizations, the Center for Civic Education and the National Council on Economic Education, as well as other organizations experienced in the development of civic and economic educational materials for use in the schools of other nations. These grants are used to support civic education in U.S. schools, plus civic and economic educational exchange programs between the United States and Central or Eastern European nations, Ireland, or any developing country. *Subpart 4* authorizes the Teaching of Traditional American History program, under which competitive grants are made for instructional improvement to partnerships that include an IHE, a nonprofit history or humanities organization, and a library or museum. *Subpart 5* sets limits on the liability of teachers for actions taken to maintain classroom discipline; it applies to states that receive funds under any ESEA program.

Part D: Enhancing Education through Technology

Subpart 1 of Part D authorizes grants to SEAs and LEAs to increase access to educational technology, support the integration of technology into instruction, enhance technological literacy, and support technology-related professional development of teachers. Funds are allocated to states in proportion to Title I-A grants, with a state minimum grant amount of 0.5% of total funding for state grants. At least 95% of state grants must be allocated to LEAs (and consortia of LEAs and other entities)—50% by formula, in proportion to Title I-A grants, and 50% competitively. *Subpart 2* authorizes support for national activities related to educational technology, including development of a national long range technology plan. *Subpart 3* authorizes the Ready-to-Learn Television program, under which support is provided to one or more public telecommunications entities to support the production and distribution of educational programs for preschool and elementary school students and their parents to support school readiness and student academic achievement. *Subpart 4* requires LEAs or schools receiving aid under Part D to establish and implement Internet safety policies designed to prevent minors from accessing material that is obscene, includes child pornography, or is harmful to minors, and prevent adults from accessing material that is obscene or includes child pornography.

Title III: Language Instruction for Limited English Proficient and Immigrant Students

Title III of the ESEA authorizes funds to support the education of LEP and immigrant students. For fiscal years in which appropriations equal or exceed $650 million, Title III, Part A, the English Language Acquisition, Language Enhancement, and Academic Achievement Act, is in effect. If appropriations are less than $650 million, Title III, Part B, Improving Language Instruction Educational Programs, is in effect. Since FY2002, appropriations have exceeded $650 million, meaning only Title III, Part A has been in effect. Therefore, only Part A is discussed below.

Part A: English Language Acquisition, Language Enhancement, and Academic Achievement Act

Title III-A was designed to help ensure that LEP students, including immigrant students, attain English proficiency, develop high levels of academic attainment in English, and meet the same state academic content and student academic achievement standards that all students are expected to meet. Formula grant allocations are made to states based on the proportion of LEP students and immigrant students in each state relative to all states. These amounts are weighted by 80% and 20%, respectively, resulting in a formula allocation based primarily on the number of LEP students in each state. States make subgrants to eligible entities (often LEAs) based on the relative number of LEP students in schools served by the eligible entity.

States are also required to reserve up to 15% of the state allocation to make grants to eligible entities that have experienced a significant increase in the number of immigrant students enrolled in schools in the geographic area served by the eligible entity.

Eligible entities receiving subgrants are required to use funds for two activities. Funds must be used to increase the English language proficiency of LEP students by providing high-quality instructional programs that are grounded in scientifically based research that demonstrates the program is effective in increasing English language proficiency and student academic achievement in core academic subjects. Funds must also be used to provide high-quality professional development to school staff or community-based personnel that work with LEP students. Eligible entities receiving grants from the funds reserved specifically for immigrant students are required to use these funds to support activities that "provide enhanced instructional opportunities" for immigrant students.

Each SEA is required to develop and hold eligible entities responsible for meeting annual measurable achievement objectives (AMAOs) for LEP students. AMAOs must include objectives for the following measures:

- Annual increases in the number or percentage of students making progress in attaining English proficiency;
- Annual increases in the number or percentage of students attaining English proficiency by the end of each school year; and
- AYP targets for LEP students on annual assessments (under Title I-A).

While Title III-A focuses on the education of LEP students, Title I-A also contains provisions that specifically apply to this student population. For example, Title I-A requires that LEAs annually assess the English proficiency of all students with limited English proficiency (Section 1111(b)(7)). These assessments must measure students' speaking, listening, reading, and writing skills in English.

National Programs (Sections 3131 and 3303)

In the reservations of funds made under Title III-A, funds are provided to support two specific national programs: (1) the National Professional Development Project; and (2) the National Clearinghouse. Under the National Professional Development Project, grants are awarded on a competitive basis for a period of up to five years to IHEs working in consortia with SEAs or LEAs to provide for professional development activities that will improve classroom instruction for LEP students and to help personnel working with these students to meet professional standards (e.g., licensure, certification). The National Clearinghouse is responsible for collecting, analyzing, synthesizing, and disseminating information about language instruction educational programs for LEP students and related programs.

TITLE IV: 21ST CENTURY SCHOOLS

Title IV of the ESEA authorizes the Safe and Drug-Free Schools and Communities program (Part A) and the 21st Century Community Learning Centers (Part B). It also includes requirements related to the provision of services for children in smoke-free environments (Part C).

Part A: Safe and Drug-Free Schools and Communities

Title IV-A is the federal government's major initiative to prevent drug abuse and violence in and around schools. One-half of state grant funds is allocated on the basis of total population aged 5- 17, and one-half is allocated in proportion to Title I-A concentration grants, with a minimum grant amount of the greater of 0.5% of total funding for state grants or each state's grant for FY2001. SEAs subsequently make formula grants to LEAs based on each LEA's share of total Title I-A funding (60%) and share of enrollment in public and private nonprofit elementary and secondary schools (40%). Title IV-A also provides funds to state governors to create programs to deter youth from using drugs and committing violent acts in schools. Funds are not currently provided for state grants. National programs supporting a variety of national leadership projects designed to prevent drug abuse and violence in elementary and secondary schools (e.g., the Safe Schools/Healthy Students initiative) are also funded under Title IV-A.

Part B: 21st Century Community Learning Centers

Title IV-B supports activities provided during nonschool hours that offer learning opportunities for school-aged children. Formula grants are made to states based on the proportion of Title I-A funds received by each state relative to the total amount of funding provided through Title I-A. States subsequently award grants to local entities (e.g., LEAs, community-based organizations) on a competitive basis for a period of three to five years. SEAs are required, to the extent possible, to distribute funds equitably among the various geographic areas within the state, including urban and rural communities. Eligible entities are to serve primarily students who attend schools eligible for schoolwide programs under Title I-A and the families of these students. Eligible entities may use funds for before- and after-school activities that advance student academic achievement. The program's focus, however, is currently on providing after-school activities for children and youth, and literacy-related activities for their families.

Part C: Environmental Tobacco Smoke

Title IV-C prohibits smoking in facilities providing elementary or secondary education or library services to children, if the services are funded directly or indirectly by the federal government, or the facility is constructed, operated, or maintained using federal funds.

TITLE V: PROMOTING INFORMED PARENTAL CHOICE AND INNOVATIVE PROGRAMS

Part A: Innovative Programs

Part A authorizes the Innovative Programs block grant program, under which aid is provided to SEAs and LEAs that can be used for an especially wide range of educational services and activities. Part A grants are allocated to states on the basis of total population aged 5-17, with a state minimum grant amount of 0.5% of total funding for state grants. At least 85% of Title V-A funds must be allocated by SEAs to LEAs on the basis of state-developed formulas that take into consideration each LEA's enrollment of students in public and private schools, with adjustments to provide increased grants per pupil to LEAs with the greatest numbers or percentages of "high cost" students, including those from economically disadvantaged families and those living in sparsely populated areas or areas of concentrated poverty.

Of the Part A funds that may be retained by states, no more than 15% may be used for administrative costs; remaining funds reserved by states are to be used for one or more of seven specified types of programs and services, including the broad categories of statewide education reform, school improvement programs and technical assistance activities. LEAs may use their Part A funds for any of 27 different types of "innovative assistance programs." While several of these are relatively specific (e.g., programs to provide same gender schools and classrooms), others are more general (e.g., promising education reform projects). This program is not currently funded.

Part B: Public Charter Schools

Subpart 1 authorizes grants to SEAs or, if a state's SEA chooses not to participate, charter school developers, to support the development and initial implementation of public charter schools. Priority in awarding grants is to be given to states with charter school policies meeting such criteria as holding charter schools accountable for meeting clear and measurable objectives, or establishing one or more public chartering agencies that are not LEAs. Up to 5% of program funds may be reserved by ED for technical assistance to, as well as studies of, charter schools. Subpart 1 also includes general provisions for allocations to charter schools under ESEA and other federal formula grant programs. *Subpart 2* authorizes ED to make grants to three or more entities to demonstrate innovative ways to help charter schools acquire appropriate facilities. *Subpart 3* authorizes competitive grants to SEAs, LEAs, or partnerships of these entities with nonprofit organizations for programs to expand public school options for K-12 students.

Part C: Magnet Schools Assistance

Part C provides grants to plan and operate magnet schools—public schools of choice designed to encourage voluntary enrollment by students of different racial backgrounds.

Part D: Fund for the Improvement of Education

Part D authorizes a series of competitive grant programs intended to support a variety of innovative K-12 educational activities. *Subpart 1* includes both a broad authority for innovative activities selected at the discretion of the Secretary of Education, and a series of required studies (on unhealthy public school buildings, exposure of children to violent entertainment, and sexual abuse in schools).[7] A number of specific activities are authorized in *Subparts 2-21*. The availability of funds for any of these subparts, and the level of actual discretion for the Secretary, within a single appropriations authorization for all of Part D, is determined through annual appropriations legislation.

The specific programs authorized in *Subparts 2-21* of Part D include Elementary and Secondary School Counseling Programs; Partnerships in Character Education; Smaller Learning Communities; Gifted and Talented Students; Star Schools Program; Ready to Teach; Foreign Language Assistance Program; Physical Education; Community Technology Centers; Educational, Cultural, Apprenticeship, and Exchange Programs for Alaska Natives, Native Hawaiians, and Their Historical Whaling and Trading Partners in Massachusetts; Excellence in Economic Education; Grants to Improve the Mental Health of Children; Arts in Education; Parental Assistance and Local Family Information Centers; Combating Domestic Violence; Healthy, High-Performance Schools; Grants for Capital Expenses of Providing Equitable Services for Private School Students; Additional Assistance for Certain Local Educational Agencies Impacted by Federal Property Acquisition; and the Women's Educational Equity Act.

TITLE VI: FLEXIBILITY AND ACCOUNTABILITY

Part A: Improving Academic Achievement

Subpart 1 of Part A authorizes grants to states for the development and enhancement of assessments meeting the requirements of Title I-A. In the allocation of funds, each state first receives $3 million per year, and remaining funds, if any, are allocated in proportion to population aged 5-17. If appropriations exceed a "trigger" amount (currently $400 million), funds in excess of the trigger amount are awarded competitively to states for assessment-related activities.

Subpart 2 of Part A allows most *LEAs* to transfer up to 50% of their formula grants among selected ESEA programs, and to transfer funds from these programs *into*, but *no funds out of*, Title I-A. *States* may transfer up to 50% of the funds under the selected ESEA programs over which they have authority, except for administrative funds, among a number of ESEA programs. States may also transfer these funds into, but not out of, Title I-A.

Subpart 3 of Part A authorizes a pair of regulatory flexibility programs, State-Flex and Local- Flex. Under State-Flex, up to seven states may consolidate all of their state administration and state activity funds under a number of ESEA programs and use these funds for any purpose authorized under any ESEA program. Under a companion Local-Flex authority, a limited number of LEAs may consolidate all of their funds under a number of ESEA programs, and use these funds for any purpose authorized under any ESEA program.

Under both the state and local flexibility demonstration programs, a limited number of specified types of requirements— including those regarding civil rights, fiscal accountability (particularly the requirement that funds be used only to supplement, and not supplant, nonfederal funds), and equitable participation by private school students and teachers—may *not* be waived.

Subpart 4 of Part A requires the Secretary of Education to review whether participating states overall (i.e., not individual LEAs or schools) meet the adequate yearly progress requirements of Title I-A and the annual measurable achievement objectives of Title III-A. The Secretary is to provide technical assistance to states that fail to meet either of these requirements for two consecutive years, and to submit reports to Congress listing such states.

Part B: Rural Education Initiative

Part B includes Rural Education Achievement Program (REAP) initiatives that are designed to assist rural LEAs that may lack the resources to compete effectively for competitive grants and that may receive grants that are too small to be effective in meeting their specified purposes. *Subpart 1* of Part B authorizes the Small, Rural School Achievement Program (SRSA), that provides flexibility in the use of funds under several ESEA programs to rural LEAs with fewer than 600 students (or meeting certain other criteria). Eligible LEAs may also receive additional grants, although these are offset by amounts received under certain ESEA programs. *Subpart 2* authorizes the Rural and Low-Income School Program (RLIS), under which grants are made to rural LEAs that do not receive grants under the SRSA program and that have a school-age child poverty rate of 20% or more. The RLIS grants may be used for a variety of ESEA-related purposes.

Part C: General Provisions

Part C contains one of several prohibitions against federal control of educational curriculum, standards, and assessments (others may be found in Title I-I and Title IX-E of the ESEA, as well as other statutes). Title VI-C also contains a number of provisions regarding the National Assessment of Educational Progress that were primarily designed to support the NAEP participation requirements under Title I-A.

TITLE VII: INDIAN, NATIVE HAWAIIAN, AND ALASKA NATIVE EDUCATION

Part A: Indian Education

Subpart 1 of Part A authorizes grants to LEAs and to schools operated or funded by the Bureau of Indian Affairs (BIA).[8] Eligible LEAs must meet Indian student enrollment thresholds of at least 10 students or 25% of total enrollment (the thresholds do not apply if the LEA is located in Alaska, California, or Oklahoma, or on or near an Indian reservation).

Formula grants are allocated on the basis of the number of Indian students and the greater of the average expenditure per pupil for the state or 80% of the national average. The formula grants may be consolidated with grants under other federal education programs serving Indian students (under a demonstration project authority); and may be used for comprehensive programs of educational services for Indian students, such as culturally related activities and curriculum content, substance abuse prevention, and family literacy programs. *Subpart 2* of Part A authorizes competitive grants to SEAs, LEAs, Indian tribes and organizations, BIA operated or supported schools, Indian institutions (such as IHEs), or consortia of these entities for such activities as early childhood education and teacher professional development. *Subpart 3* authorizes a variety of national activities intended to improve education for Indian students, such as research, postsecondary education fellowships, programs for gifted and talented Indian students, adult education programs, and education planning and administration grants to Indian tribes. *Subpart 4* establishes the National Advisory Council on Indian Education, and authorizes a preference for Indian applicants under Part A grant programs.

Part B: Native Hawaiian Education

Part B authorizes a consolidated program of competitive grants to Native Hawaiian educational or community-based organizations, or other public or private nonprofit organizations with experience in operating Native Hawaiian programs, or consortia of these entities to provide a wide variety of services intended to improve education for Native Hawaiians. In the awarding of grants, priority is to be given to activities that are intended to: improve reading skills for Native Hawaiian students in grades K-3; meet the needs of at-risk children and youth; increase participation by Native Hawaiians in fields or disciplines in which they are underemployed; or increase the use of the Hawaiian language in instruction. Specifically authorized activities include early childhood education and care, postsecondary education scholarships, and services for Native Hawaiian students with disabilities. Title VII-B also establishes a Native Hawaiian Education Council, and supports the establishment of individual island councils.

Part C: Alaska Native Education

Part C authorizes competitive grants for a variety of activities and services intended to improve education for Alaska Natives. Eligible grantees include Alaska Native organizations, entities with experience operating Alaska Native programs or instruction in Alaska Native languages, or other organizations, including SEAs and LEAs, in consortia with Alaska Native organizations. Priority is to be given to applicants that include Alaska Native regional nonprofit organizations. Authorized uses of grants include the development of curriculum materials that address the special needs of Alaska Native students, family literacy services, support for Alaska Native students in teacher preparation programs, home instruction programs, and cultural education and exchange programs.

TITLE VIII: IMPACT AID

Title VIII of the ESEA, Impact Aid, compensates LEAs for "substantial and continuing financial burden" resulting from federal activities. These activities include federal ownership of certain lands, as well as the enrollments in LEAs of children of parents who work and/or live on federal land (e.g., children of parents in the military and children living on Indian lands). The federal government provides compensation because these activities deprive LEAs of the ability to collect property or other taxes from these individuals (e.g., members of the Armed Forces living on military bases) even though the LEAs are obligated to provide free public education to their children. Thus, Impact Aid is intended to compensate LEAs for the resulting loss of tax revenue.

Title VIII authorizes several types of Impact Aid payments. These include payments under Section 8002, Section 8003, Section 8007, and Section 8008.[9] Each of these types of payments is discussed briefly below.

Section 8002. Section 8002 compensates LEAs for the federal ownership of certain property. To qualify for compensation, the federal government must have acquired the property, in general, after 1938, and the assessed value of the land at the time it was acquired must have represented at least 10% of the assessed value of all real property within an LEA's area of service.

Section 8003. Section 8003 compensates LEAs for enrolling "federally connected" children. These are children who reside with a parent who is a member of the Armed Forces living on or off federal property; reside with a parent who is an accredited foreign military officer living on or off federal property; reside on Indian lands; reside in low-rent public housing; or reside with a parent who is a civilian working and/or living on federal land.

Two payments are made under Section 8003. Section 8003(b) authorizes "basic support payments" for federally connected children. Basic support payments are allocated directly to LEAs by ED based on a formula that uses weights assigned to different categories of federally connected children and cost factors to determine maximum payment amounts. Section 8003(d) authorizes additional payments to LEAs based on the number of certain children with disabilities who are eligible to receive services under the Individuals with Disabilities Education Act (IDEA). Payments are limited to certain IDEA-eligible children, most notably those whose parents are members of the Armed Forces (residing on or off military bases), and those residing on Indian lands. Section 8003 payments account for more than 90% of total Impact Aid appropriations.

Section 8007. Section 8007 provides funds for construction and facilities upgrading to certain LEAs with high percentages of children living on Indian lands or children of military parents. These funds are used to make formula and competitive grants.

Section 8008. Section 8008 provides funds for emergency repairs and comprehensive capital improvements to 24 schools that ED currently owns but LEAs use to serve federally connected children.[10] Two of the schools are located on closed military bases and operated by

ED, and the remaining facilities are operated by LEAs. Statutory language requires ED to transfer ownership of these facilities to LEAs or other entities.

TITLE IX: GENERAL PROVISIONS

Part A: Definitions

Part A provides definitions of a variety of terms used frequently throughout the ESEA, such as "local educational agency," "state educational agency," "highly qualified teacher," "limited English proficient," "professional development," "scientifically based research," and "state."

Part B: Flexibility in the Use of Administrative and Other Funds

Part B authorizes SEAs and LEAs to consolidate and jointly use funds available for administration under multiple ESEA programs. In order to qualify for this flexibility, SEAs must demonstrate that a majority of their resources are provided from nonfederal sources.

Part C: Coordination of Programs; Consolidated State and Local Plans and Applications

Part C authorizes SEAs and LEAs to prepare single, consolidated plans and reports for all "covered" ESEA programs (in general, these are the formula grant programs administered via SEAs).

Part D: Waivers

Under this provision, the Secretary of Education is authorized to waive most requirements associated with any program authorized by the ESEA, if specifically requested by SEAs, LEAs, Indian tribes or schools (via their LEAs).

Part E: Uniform Provisions

Subpart 1 of Part E contains provisions for the participation of private school students and staff in those ESEA programs where such participation is authorized.[11] Under the relevant ESEA programs, services provided to private school students or staff are to be equitable in relation to the number of such students or staff eligible for each program; are to be secular, neutral and nonideological, with no funds to be used for religious worship or instruction; and are to be developed through consultation between public and private school officials.

Provision is made for bypassing SEAs and LEAs that cannot or have not provided equitable services to private school students or staff, and serving private school students and staff in these areas through neutral, third-party organizations. Provision is also made for the submission of complaints regarding implementation of these requirements. Subpart 1 also prohibits federal control of private or home schools, or the application of any ESEA requirement to any private school that does not receive funds or services under any ESEA program.

Subpart 2 of Part E contains a general definition of "maintenance of effort," as applied in several ESEA programs; requires ED to publish guidance on prayer in public schools, and requires LEAs receiving ESEA funds to certify to their SEAs that they do not limit the exercise of "constitutionally protected prayer" in public schools; requires recipient SEAs, LEAs, and public schools that have a "designated open forum" to provide equal access to the Boy Scouts; prohibits the use of ESEA funds to "promote or encourage sexual activity;" prohibits federal control of educational curriculum, content or achievement standards, building standards, or allocation of resources; prohibits federally sponsored testing of students or teachers; and requires LEAs receiving funds under any ED program to provide to the armed services access to directory information on secondary school students, unless students or their parents request that such information not be released (this provision does not apply to certain religiously affiliated private schools). Finally, under an "Unsafe School Choice Option," students in states receiving ESEA funds who attend a "persistently dangerous" public school, or who are victims of violent crime at school, are to be offered the opportunity to transfer to a safe public school.

Part F: Evaluations

Part F authorizes ED to reserve 0.5% of the funds appropriated for ESEA programs, other than Titles I and III, for program evaluations, if funds for this purpose are not separately authorized.

APPENDIX A. APPROPRIATIONS FOR PROGRAMS AUTHORIZED BY THE ESEA

Table A1. Programs Authorized by the Elementary and Secondary Education Act (ESEA) and FY2009 and FY2010 Appropriations (dollars in thousands)

Count	Program/Activity	ESEA Citation	FY2009 Regular Appropriations	FY2009 ARRA Appropriations	FY2010 Appropriations
1	School Improvement Grants	Title I, Section 1003(g)	$545,633	$3,000,000	$545,633
2	Grants to Local Educational Agencies (LEAs)	Title I-A	$14,492,401	$10,000,000	$14,492,401
3	Reading First	Title I-B-1	$0	$0	$0
4	Early Reading First	Title I-B-2	$112,549	$0	$0
5	Even Start	Title I-B-3	$66,454	$0	$66,454
6	Improving Literacy through School Libraries	Title I-B-4	$19,145	$0	$19,145
7	Migrant Education Program	Title I-C	$394,771	$0	$394,771
8	Neglected and Delinquent	Title I-D	$50,427	$0	$50,427
9	National Assessment of Title I	Title I-E	$9,167	$0	$9,167
10	Striving Readers[a]	Title I-E (Section 1502)	$35,371	$0	$200,000
11	Close Up Fellowships	Title I-E (Section 1504)	$1,942	$0	$1,942
12	Comprehensive School Reform	Title I-F	$0	$0	$0
13	Advanced Placement	Title I-G	$43,540	$0	$45,840
14	High School Graduation Initiative	Title I-H	$0	$0	$50,000
15	Improving Teacher Quality	Title II-A	$2,947,749	$0	$2,947,749
16	School Leadership	Title II-A-5 (Section 2151(b))	$19,220	$0	$29,220
17	Advanced Credentialing	Title II-A-5 (Section 2151(c))	$10,649	$0	$10,649
18	Math and Science Partnerships	Title II-B	$178,978	$0	$180,478
19	Troops-to-Teachers	Title II-C-1-A	$14,389	$0	$14,389
20	Transition to Teaching	Title II-C-1-B	$43,707	$0	$43,707
21	National Writing Project	Title II-C-2	$24,291	$0	$25,646
22	We the People (Civic Education)	Title II-C-3 (Section 2344)	$20,076	$0	$21,617
23	Cooperative Education Exchange (Civic Education)	Title II-C-3 (Section 2345)	$13,383	$0	$13,383
24	Teaching of Traditional American History	Title II-C-4	$118,952	$0	$118,952
25	Educational Technology	Title II-D	$269,872	$650,000	$100,000

Count	Program/Activity	ESEA Citation	FY2009 Regular Appropriations	FY2009 ARRA Appropriations	FY2010 Appropriations
26	Ready to Learn Television	Title II-D-3	$25,416	$0	$27,300
27	English Language Acquisition	Title III-A	$730,000	$0	$750,000
28	Safe and Drug Free, State Grants	Title IV-A-1	$294,759	$0	$0
29	Safe and Drug Free, National Programs	Title IV-A-2	$139,912	$0	$191,341
30	Alcohol Abuse Reduction	Title IV-A-2 (Section 4129)	$33,348	$0	$32,712
31	Mentoring Programs	Title IV-A-2 (Section 4130)	$46,980	$0	$0
32	21st Century Community Learning Centers	Title IV-B	$1,131,166	$0	$1,166,166
33	Innovative Programs	Title V-A	$0	$0	$0
34	Charter School Grants	Title V-B-1	$216,031	$0	$256,031
35	Charter School Facilities Incentive Grants	Title V-B-1 (Section 5205(b))	(included in Charter School Grants)	$0	(included in Charter School Grants)
36	Credit Enhancement Initiatives to Assist Charter School Facility Acquisition, Construction, and Renovation	Title V-B-2	(included in Charter School Grants)	$0	(included in Charter School Grants)
37	Voluntary Public School Choice	Title V-B-3	$25,819	$0	$25,819
38	Magnet Schools Assistance	Title V-C	$104,829	$0	$100,000
39	Fund for the Improvement of Education, National Programs	Title V-D-1	$115,965	$0	$125,461
40	Teacher Incentive Fund[b]	Title V-D-1	$97,270	$200,000	$400,000
41	Academies for American History and Civics[c]	Title V-D-1	$1,945	$0	$1,815
42	Promise Neighborhoods[d]	Title V-D-1	$0	$0	$10,000
43	Elem/Sec School Counseling	Title V-D-2	$52,000	$0	$55,000
44	Character Education	Title V-D-3	$11,912	$0	$0
45	Smaller Learning Communities	Title V-D-4	$88,000	$0	$88,000
46	Reading is Fundamental	Title V-D-5	$24,803	$0	$24,803
47	Javits Gifted and Talented	Title V-D-6	$7,463	$0	$7,463
48	Star Schools Program	Title V-D-7	$0	$0	$0
49	Ready to Teach[e]	Title V-D-8	$10,700	$0	$0
50	Foreign Language Assistance	Title V-D-9	$26,328	$0	$26,928
51	Carol M. White Physical Education Program	Title V-D-10	$78,000	$0	$79,000
52	Community Technology Centers	Title V-D-11	$0	$0	$0
53	Exchanges with Historic Whaling and Trading Partners	Title V-D-12	$8,754	$0	$8,754
54	Excellence in Economic Education	Title V-D-13	$1,447	$0	$1,447

Table A1. (Continued)

Count	Program/Activity	ESEA Citation	FY2009 Regular Appropriations	FY2009 ARRA Appropriations	FY2010 Appropriations
55	Grants to Improve the Mental Health of Children, Mental Health Integration in Schools	Title V-D-14 (Section 5541)	$5,913	$0	$5,913
56	Grants to Improve the Mental Health of Children, Foundations for Learning	Title V-D-14 (Section 5542)	$1,000	$0	$1,000
57	Arts in Education	Title V-D-15	$38,166	$0	$40,000
58	Parental Assistance and Local Family Information Centers	Title V-D-16	$39,254	$0	$39,254
59	Combating Domestic Violence	Title V-D-17	$0	$0	$0
60	Healthy, High-Performance Schools	Title V-D-18	$0	$0	$0
61	Grants for Capital Expenses of Providing Equitable Services for Private School Students	Title V-D-19	$0	$0	$0
62	Additional Assistance for Certain Local Educational Agencies Impacted by Federal Property Acquisition	Title V-D-20	$0	$0	$0
63	Women's Educational Equity Act	Title V-D-21	$2,423	$0	$2,423
64	Grants for State Assessments	Title VI-A-1 (Section 6111)	$400,000	$0	$400,000
65	Grants for Enhanced Assessment Instruments	Title VI-A-1 (Section 6112)	$10,732	$0	$10,732
66	Funding Transferability for State and LEAs	Title VI-A-2	na	na	na
67	State and Local Flexibility Demonstration	Title VI-A-3	na	na	na
68	Small, Rural School Achievement Program	Title VI-B-1	$86,691	$0	$87,441
69	Rural and Low-Income School Program	Title VI-B-2	$86,691	$0	$87,441
70	Indian Education, Grants to LEAs	Title VII-A-1	$99,331	$0	$104,331
71	Special Programs and Projects to Improve Educational Opportunities for Indian Children	Title VII-A-2	$19,060	$0	$19,060
72	Indian Education, National Activities	Title VII-A-3	$3,891	$0	$3,891
73	Native Hawaiian Student Education	Title VII-B	$33,315	$0	$34,315
74	Alaska Native Student Education	Title VII-C	$33,315	$0	$33,315
75	Impact Aid, Payments Relating to Federal Acquisition of Real Property	Title VIII (Section 8002)	$66,208	$0	$67,208
76	Impact Aid, Payments for Eligible Federally Connected Children (Basic Support Payments)	Title VIII (Section 8003(b))	$1,128,535	$0	$1,138,000

Count	Program/Activity	ESEA Citation	FY2009 Regular Appropriations	FY2009 ARRA Appropriations	FY2010 Appropriations
77	Impact Aid, Payments for Eligible Federally Connected Children (Payments for Children with Disabilities)	Title VIII (Section 8003(d))	$48,602	$0	$48,602
78	Construction	Title VIII (Section 8007)	$17,509	$100,000	$17,509
79	Facilities Maintenance	Title VIII (Section 8008)	$4,864	$0	$4,864

Source: Table prepared by CRS based on CRS analysis of the ESEA. FY2009 and FY20 10 appropriations data provided by the U.S. Department of Education, Budget Service.

Notes: Attempts were made to be as comprehensive as possible when compiling this information.

na: not applicable. This indicates that this is not a program for which funding is applicable. This applies only to the Title VI-A-2 and 3 programs.

a. While still referred to as the Striving Readers program, the statutory requirements governing this program were modified and included in the Consolidated Appropriations Act, 2010 (P.L. 111-117). The authority for the program is provided under Section 1502 of the ESEA. The appropriation for the program for FY20 10 was originally $250 million. Of this, $50 million was rescinded due to the enactment of P.L. 111-226, authorizing the Education Jobs Fund.

b. The Teacher Incentive Fund was enacted through the Departments of Labor, Health and Human Services, and Education, and Related Agencies Appropriations Act, 2006 (P.L. 109-149), based on authority available under Title V-D- 1 of the ESEA.

c. The Academies for American History and Civics Program is authorized under the American History and Civics Education Act (P.L. 108-474), but funding for the program is provided based on authority available under Title V-D- 1 of the ESEA. The specific provision of funds for this purpose is detailed in the Conference Report accompanying P.L. 111-117 (H.Rept. 111-366).

d. The Promise Neighborhoods program was enacted through the Consolidated Appropriations Act, 2010, based on authority available under Title V-D- 1 of the ESEA. The specific provision of funds for this purpose is detailed in the Conference Report accompanying P.L. 111-117 (H.Rept. 111-366).

e. Originally, $10.7 million was appropriated for the Ready to Teach program for FY20 10. These funds were subsequently rescinded due to the enactment of P.L. 111-226, authorizing the Education Jobs Fund.

APPENDIX B. SELECTED ACRONYMS USED IN THIS REPORT

AMAO: Annual Measurable Achievement Objectives
AMO: Annual Measureable Objectives
AYP: Adequate Yearly Progress
ED: U.S. Department of Education
ESEA: Elementary and Secondary Education Act
HQT: Highly Qualified Teacher
IDEA: Individuals with Disabilities Education Act
LEA: Local Educational Agency
LEP: Limited English Proficient
NAEP: National Assessment of Educational Progress
NCLB: No Child Left Behind Act
SEA: State Educational Agency

End Notes

[1] For information on the Administration's FY20 11 budget request for ESEA programs, see CRS Report R41355, *Administration's Proposal to Reauthorize the Elementary and Secondary Education Act: Comparison to Current Law*, by Rebecca R. Skinner et al.

[2] For a current listing of these reports, see http://www.crs.gov/Pages/ subissue. aspx? cliid=2487&parentid=5.

[3] These changes complement changes made to the School Improvement Grant program by ED through Final Requirements (available online at http://www2.ed.gov/programs/sif/2010-27313.pdf). Based on these new requirements, each state is required to give priority in making competitive grants to LEAs that serve the lowest- performing schools. For the purposes of the School Improvement Grants program, ED has defined the lowest- performing schools using two tiers. A Tier I school is a Title I-A school that has been identified for improvement, corrective action, or restructuring and is among the lowest achieving 5% of all such schools or has a high school graduation rate that is less than 60%. A Tier II school is any secondary school that is eligible for, but does not receive, Title I-A funding and has been identified for improvement, corrective action, or restructuring and is among the lowest achieving 5% of all such schools or has a high school graduation rate that is less than 60%. LEAs using funds for a Tier I or Tier II school must select from four school intervention models prescribed by ED for each school. These models include the turnaround model, restart model, school closure, and transformation model. After making awards to LEAs serving Tier I or Tier II schools, grants may be awarded to LEAs that serve Tier III schools, which consist of schools identified for school improvement, corrective action, or restructuring that are not in the lowest achieving 5% of schools identified for improvement, corrective action, or restructuring. States may establish criteria for determining which Tier III schools to support (e.g., those in the lowest achieving 6%-10% of schools identified for improvement, corrective action, or restructuring). For more information, see http://www2.ed.gov/programs/sif/index.html.

[4] Although Title I-A funds are used to serve eligible private school pupils, funds remain under the control of public school authorities—i.e., they are not transferred to private schools.

[5] Currently, all states participate in ESEA Title I-A.

[6] A high-need LEA is defined as follows: an LEA with either a school-age child poverty rate of 20% or 10,000 school- age children in poor families, and a high percentage of teachers who are not fully certified or who are not teaching in fields or at grade levels for which they were trained.

[7] For example, the Teacher Incentive Fund and the Promise Neighborhoods programs are authorized under this broad authority.

[8] These schools and LEAs are now operated or funded by the Bureau of Indian Education (BIE).

[9] Other significant Impact Aid provisions include Section 8004, which details policies regarding children residing on Indian lands, and Section 8009, which prohibits states from considering Impact Aid payments in determining state aid to LEAs, unless the state has an approved program to equalize expenditures among LEAs.

[10] Since 1983, the Department of Defense (DOD) has assumed funding responsibility for other facilities owned by ED but located on domestic military bases that serve students whose parents are in the Armed Forces. These

were formerly known as Section 6 schools in reference to that section of P.L. 8 1-874. Currently, DOD has assumed financial responsibility for the maintenance and renovation of 32 facilities, while ED continues to be directly responsible for 24 facilities. (For more information, see ED, *FY2011 Budget Justifications*.)

[11] Several ESEA programs have relatively brief private school spupil or staff participation provisions that refer to Title IX-E for details, and there are separate, detailed private school participation provisions in Titles I-A and V-A.

In: Elementary and Secondary Education Act
Editors: D. M. Brown and A. Davies
ISBN: 978-1-61942-694-8

Chapter 5

A BLUEPRINT FOR REFORM: THE REAUTHORIZATION OF THE ELEMENTARY AND SECONDARY EDUCATION ACT

United States Department of Education

PRIORITIES IN A BLUEPRINT FOR REFORM

This blueprint builds on the significant reforms already made in response to the American Recovery and Reinvestment Act of 2009 around four areas: (1) Improving teacher and principal effectiveness to ensure that every classroom has a great teacher and every school has a great leader; (2) Providing information to families to help them evaluate and improve their children's schools, and to educators to help them improve their students' learning; (3) Implementing college- and career-ready standards and developing improved assessments aligned with those standards; and (4) Improving student learning and achievement in America's lowest-performing schools by providing intensive support and effective interventions.

Incorporating and extending this framework, this blueprint for a re-envisioned federal role builds on these key priorities:

1. College- and Career-Ready Students

Raising standards for all students. We will set a clear goal: Every student should graduate from high school ready for college and a career, regardless of their income, race, ethnic or language background, or disability status. Following the lead of the nation's governors, we're calling on all states to develop and adopt standards in English language arts and mathematics that build toward college- and career-readiness by the time students graduate from high school. States may choose to upgrade their existing standards or work together with other states to develop and adopt common, state- developed standards.

Better assessments. We will support the development and use of a new generation of assessments that are aligned with college- and career-ready standards, to better determine whether students have acquired the skills they need for success. New assessment systems will better capture higher-order skills, provide more accurate measures of student growth, and better inform classroom instruction to respond to academic needs.

A complete education. Students need a well-rounded education to contribute as citizens in our democracy and to thrive in a global economy – from literacy to mathematics, science, and technology to history, civics, foreign languages, the arts, financial literacy, and other subjects. We will support states, districts, school leaders, and teachers in implementing a more complete education through improved professional development and evidence-based instructional models and supports.

2. Great Teachers and Leaders in Every School

Effective teachers and principals. We will elevate the teaching profession to focus on recognizing, encouraging, and rewarding excellence. We are calling on states and districts to develop and implement systems of teacher and principal evaluation and support, and to identify effective and highly effective teachers and principals on the basis of student growth and other factors. These systems will inform professional development and help teachers and principals improve student learning. In addition, a new program will support ambitious efforts to recruit, place, reward, retain, and promote effective teachers and principals and enhance the profession of teaching.

Our best teachers and leaders where they are needed most. Our proposal will provide funds to states and districts to develop and support effective teachers and leaders, with a focus on improving the effectiveness of teachers and leaders in high-need schools. We will call on states and districts to track equitable access to effective teachers and principals, and where needed, take steps to improve access to effective educators for students in high-poverty, high-minority schools.

Strengthening teacher and leader preparation and recruitment. We need more effective pathways and practices for preparing, placing, and supporting beginning teachers and principals in high-need schools. States will monitor the effectiveness of their traditional and alternative preparation programs, and we will invest in programs whose graduates are succeeding in the classroom, based on student growth and other factors.

3. Equity and Opportunity for All Students

Rigorous and fair accountability for all levels. All students will be included in an accountability system that builds on college- and career-ready standards, rewards progress and success, and requires rigorous interventions in the lowest-performing schools. We will celebrate the Reward states, districts, and schools that do the most to improve outcomes for their students and to close achievement gaps, as well as those who are on the path to have all students graduating or on track to graduate ready for college and a career by 2020. All schools will be aiming to do their part to help us reach that ambitious goal, and for most schools, leaders at the state, district, and school level will enjoy broad flexibility to determine how to get there.

But in the lowest-performing schools that have not made progress over time, we will ask for dramatic change. To ensure that responsibility for improving student outcomes no longer falls solely at the door of schools, we will also promote accountability for states and districts that are not providing their schools, principals, and teachers with the support they need to succeed.

Meeting the needs of diverse learners. Schools must support all students, including by providing appropriate instruction and access to a challenging curriculum along with additional supports and attention where needed. From English Learners and students with disabilities to Native American students, homeless students, migrant students, rural students, and neglected or delinquent students, our proposal will continue to support and strengthen programs for these students and ensure that schools are helping them meet college- and career-ready standards.

Greater equity. To give every student a fair chance to succeed, and give principals and teachers the resources to support student success, we will call on school districts and states to take steps to ensure equity, by such means as moving toward comparability in resources between high- and low-poverty schools.

4. Raise the Bar and Reward Excellence

Fostering a Race to the Top. Race to the Top has provided incentives for excellence by encouraging state and local leaders to work together on ambitious reforms, make tough choices, and develop comprehensive plans that change policies and practices to improve outcomes for students. We will continue Race to the Top's incentives for systemic reforms at the state level and expand the program to school districts that are willing to take on bold, comprehensive reforms.

Supporting effective public school choice. We will support the expansion of high-performing public charter schools and other autonomous public schools, and support local communities as they expand public school choice options for students within and across school districts.

Promoting a culture of college readiness and success. Access to a challenging high school curriculum has a greater impact on whether a student will earn a 4-year college degree than his or her high school test scores, class rank, or grades. We will increase access to college-level, dual credit, and other accelerated courses in high-need schools and support college-going strategies and models that will help students succeed.

5. Promote Innovation and Continuous Improvement

Fostering innovation and accelerating success. The Investing in Innovation Fund will support local and nonprofit leaders as they develop and scale up programs that have demonstrated success, and discover the next generation of innovative solutions.

Supporting, recognizing, and rewarding local innovations. Our proposal will encourage and support local innovation by creating fewer, larger, more flexible funding streams around areas integral to student success, giving states and districts flexibility to focus on local needs. New competitive funding streams will provide greater flexibility, reward results, and ensure that federal funds are used wisely. At the same time, districts will have fewer restrictions on blending funds from different categories with less red tape.

Supporting student success. Tackling persistent achievement gaps requires public agencies, community organizations, and families to share responsibility for improving outcomes for students. We will prioritize programs that include a comprehensive redesign of the school day, week, or year, that promote schools as the center of their communities, or that partner with community organizations. Our proposal will invest in new models that keep students safe, supported, and healthy both in and out of school, and that support strategies to better engage families and community members in their children's education.

COLLEGE- AND CAREER-READY STUDENTS

The goal for America's educational system is clear: Every student should graduate from high school ready for college and a career. Every student should have meaningful opportunities to choose from upon graduation from high school. But while all states have developed and implemented standards as required under the Elementary and Secondary Education Act (ESEA), in many cases these standards do not reflect the knowledge and skills needed for success after high school, either in further education or in a job. Four of every 10 new college students, including half of those at 2-year institutions, take remedial courses, and many employers comment on the inadequate preparation of high school graduates. And while states have developed assessments aligned with their standards, in many cases these assessments do not adequately measure student growth or the knowledge and skills that students need, nor do they provide timely, useful information to teachers. We must follow the lead of the nation's governors and challenge students with state-developed, college- and career-ready standards, and more accurately measure what they are learning with better assessments. We must reward the success of schools that are making significant progress, ask for dramatic change in the lowest-performing schools, and address persistent gaps in student academic achievement and graduation rates.

A New Approach

- Supporting college- and career-ready standards, preparing college- and career-ready students.
- Rewarding progress and success.
- Turning around the lowest-performing schools.

Our proposal will maintain formula grants to high-poverty school districts, while making significant changes to better support states, districts, and schools, including middle and high schools, in improving achievement for all groups of students, including low-income and minority students, English Learners, and students with disabilities.

Rigorous College- and Career-Ready Standards. Following the lead of the nation's governors and state education leaders, we're calling on all states to adopt state-developed standards in English language arts and mathematics that build toward college- and career-readiness by the time students graduate from high school, and high-quality statewide assessments aligned with these standards. States may either choose to upgrade their existing standards, working with their 4-year public university system to certify that mastery of the standards ensures that a student will not need to take remedial coursework upon admission to a postsecondary institution in the system; or work with other states to create state-developed common standards that build toward college- and career- readiness. To ensure that all students are learning what they need to succeed, standards must be based on evidence regarding what students must know and be able to do at each grade level to be on track to graduate from high school college- and career-ready. Such standards will also give families and communities the information they need to determine whether their students are on track to college- and career-readiness and to evaluate their schools' effectiveness. States will continue to implement statewide science standards and aligned assessments in specific gradespans, and may include such assessments – as well as statewide assessments in other subjects, such as history – in their accountability system. Finally, states will develop and adopt statewide English language proficiency standards for English Learners, aligned so that they reflect the academic language necessary to master the state's content standards.

Rigorous and Fair Accountability and Support at Every Level. Building on these statewide standards and aligned assessments, every state will ensure that its statewide system of accountability rewards schools and districts for progress and success, requires rigorous interventions in the lowest-performing schools and districts, and allows local flexibility to determine the appropriate improvement and support strategies for most schools.

To foster public accountability for results and help focus improvement and support efforts, states must have data systems in place to gather information that is critical to determining how schools and districts are progressing in preparing students to graduate from high school college- and career-ready. States and districts will collect and make public data relating to student academic achievement and growth in English language arts and mathematics, student academic achievement in science, and if states choose, student academic achievement and growth in other subjects, such as history. At the high school level, this data will also include graduation rates, college enrollment rates, and rates of college enrollment without need for remediation. All of these data must be disaggregated by race, gender, ethnicity, disability status, English Learner status, and family income. States and districts also will collect other key information about teaching and learning conditions, including information on school climate such as student, teacher and school leader attendance; disciplinary incidents; or student, parent, or school staff surveys about their school experience.

Measuring and Supporting Schools, Districts, and States. State accountability systems will be asked to recognize progress and growth and reward success, rather than only identify failure. To ensure that accountability no longer falls solely at the doors of schools, districts and states will be held accountable for providing their schools, principals and teachers with the support they need to succeed. We will ask States to recognize and reward schools and districts making the most progress, provide flexibility for local improvement efforts, and focus the most rigorous support and interventions on the very lowest-performing schools and districts.

We will call on states, districts and schools to aim for the ambitious goal of all students graduating or on track to graduate from high school ready for college and a career by 2020. Performance targets, based on whole-school and subgroup achievement and growth, and graduation rates, will guide improvement toward that ambitious goal, and those that are meeting all of their performance targets will be recognized and rewarded. States, districts and schools will look not just at absolute performance and proficiency, but at individual student growth and school progress over time, and the additional data described above, to guide local improvement and support strategies for schools.

The schools, districts, and states that are successful in reaching performance targets, significantly increasing student performance for all students, closing achievement gaps, or turning around the lowest-performing schools (at the district and state level) will be recognized as Reward schools, districts and states. States will receive funds to design innovative programs to reward high-poverty Reward schools and Reward districts. Rewards may include financial rewards for the staff and students and development of and participation in "communities of practice" to share best practices and replicate successful strategies to assist lower-performing schools and districts. Rewards may also include flexibility in the use of ESEA funds and, as appropriate, competitive preference for Reward states, high-need Reward districts, and high-need Reward schools in some federal grant competitions. Reward districts will also be given flexibility in implementing interventions in their lowest-performing schools, described further below.

At the other end of the spectrum will be Challenge states, districts, and schools. States will identify Challenge schools that are in need of specific assistance. The first category of Challenge schools will be the lowest-performing five percent of schools in each state, based on student academic achievement, student growth, and graduation rates, that are not making progress to improve. In these schools, states and districts will be required to implement one of four school turnaround models, to support better outcomes for students. Reward districts will receive flexibility to implement a different research-based intervention model, beyond the scope of the four school turnaround models. The next five percent of low-performing schools will be identified in a warning category, and States and districts will implement research-based, locally-determined strategies to help them improve.

Schools that are not closing significant, persistent achievement gaps will constitute another category of Challenge schools. In these schools, districts will be required to implement data-driven interventions to support those students who are farthest behind and close the achievement gap. For all Challenge schools, districts may implement strategies such as expanded learning time, supplemental educational services, public school choice, or other strategies to help students succeed.

Challenge districts whose schools, principals and teachers are not receiving the support they need to succeed may also face significant governance or staffing changes, including replacement of the superintendent. Both Challenge districts and states will face additional restrictions on the use of ESEA funds and may be required to work with an outside organization to improve student academic achievement.

Building Capacity for Support at Every Level. As we ask more of each level of the system, we will also build state and district capacity to support schools, school leaders, teachers, and students. Our proposal will allow states and districts to reserve funds to carry out such activities as (i) supporting and complementing the adoption of rigorous standards and high-quality assessments, and supporting teachers in teaching to those standards; (ii) supporting the more effective use of data to identify local needs and improve student outcomes; (iii) improving capacity at the state and district levels to support the effective use of technology to improve instruction; (iv) coordinating with early learning programs to improve school readiness; or (v) carrying out effective family engagement strategies.

Districts will be required to set aside a portion of funds under this program to improve student performance in high-need schools, by implementing effective school improvement strategies and carrying out strategies to ensure the equitable distribution of effective teachers and school leaders. Reward districts will be allowed flexibility around this reservation.

Fostering Comparability and Equity. To give every student a fair chance to succeed and give principals and teachers the resources to support student success, we will encourage increased resource equity at every level of the system. Over time, districts will be required to ensure that their high-poverty schools receive state and local funding levels (for personnel and relevant nonpersonnel expenditures) comparable to those received by their low-poverty schools. In addition, districts that use their resources to provide strong support to disadvantaged students will be given additional flexibility to provide such support. States will be asked to measure and report on resource disparities and develop a plan to tackle them.

Assessing Achievement

Our proposal will maintain support for state efforts to improve the quality of their assessment systems, and to develop and implement the upgraded standards and assessments required by the College- and Career-Ready Students program. Improved assessments can be used to accurately measure student growth; to better measure how states, districts, schools, principals, and teachers are educating students; to help teachers adjust and focus their teaching; and to provide better information to students and their families.

States will receive formula grants to develop and implement high-quality assessments aligned with college- and career-ready standards in English language arts and mathematics that accurately measure student academic achievement and growth, provide feedback to support and improve teaching, and measure school success and progress. States may also use funds to develop or implement high-quality, rigorous statewide assessments in other academic or career and technical subjects, high school course assessments, English language proficiency assessments, and interim or formative assessments. Beginning in 2015, formula funds will be available only to states that are implementing assessments based on college- and career-ready standards that are common to a significant number of states. The program also will support competitive grants to consortia of states, and to other entities working in partnership with states, for research on, or development and improvement of, additional high-quality assessments to be used by multiple states in such areas as science, history, or foreign languages; high school course assessments in academic and career and technical subjects; universally designed assessments; and assessments for English Learners and students with disabilities.

School Turnaround Grants

Our proposal will make available significant grants to help states, districts, and schools implement the rigorous interventions required in each state's lowest-performing Challenge schools under the College- and Career-Ready Students program.

States will receive funds by formula and may reserve funds to build their capacity to improve low-performing schools, including developing and implementing effective school quality review teams to assist schools in identifying school needs and supporting school improvement. States will award the remainder of funds competitively to districts or partnerships of districts and nonprofit organizations to implement one of the following intervention models, to be selected locally, to ensure significant changes in the operation, governance, staffing, or instructional program of a school:

- *Transformation model:* Replace the principal, strengthen staffing, implement a research-based instructional program, provide extended learning time, and implement new governance and flexibility.
- *Turnaround model:* Replace the principal and rehire no more than 50 percent of the school staff, implement a research-based instructional program, provide extended learning time, and implement new governance structure.
- *Restart model:* Convert or close and reopen the school under the management of an effective charter operator, charter management organization, or education management organization.
- *School closure model:* Close the school and enroll students who attended it in other, higher-performing schools in the district.

Districts and their partners will receive 3-year awards to fully and effectively implement one of these intervention models, and will be eligible for two additional years of funding to support a school's ongoing improvement if the school is showing progress.

In addition, the Secretary will reserve a portion of School Turnaround Grants for additional activities designed to enhance state, district, and nonprofit capacity to improve schools, such as investing in model school quality review teams to identify school needs and support school improvement.

GREAT TEACHERS AND GREAT LEADERS

Of all the work that occurs at every level of our education system, the interaction between teacher and student is the primary determinant of student success. A great teacher can make the difference between a student who achieves at high levels and a student who slips through the cracks, and a great principal can help teachers succeed as part of a strong, well-supported instructional team. Research shows that top-performing teachers can make a dramatic difference in the achievement of their students, and suggests that the impact of being assigned to top-performing teachers year after year is enough to significantly narrow achievement gaps. We have to do more to ensure that every student has an effective teacher, every school has effective leaders, and every teacher and leader has access to the preparation, on-going support, recognition, and collaboration opportunities he or she need to succeed. Our proposals will ask states and districts to put in place the conditions that allow for teachers, principals, and leaders at all levels of the school system to get meaningful information about their practice, and support them in using this information to ensure that all students are getting the effective teaching they deserve.

A New Approach

- Elevating the profession and focusing on recruiting, preparing, developing, and rewarding effective teachers and leaders.
- Focusing on teacher and leader effectiveness in improving student outcomes.
- Supporting states and districts that are willing to take bold action to increase the number of effective teachers and leaders where they are needed most.
- Strengthening pathways into teaching and school leadership positions in high-need schools.

Effective Teachers and Leaders

Our proposal will continue and improve formula grants to states and school districts to improve the effectiveness of teachers and leaders, and ensure that students in high-need schools are being taught by effective teachers in schools led by effective principals. To help meet these goals, states and districts may choose how to spend funds to meet local needs, as long as they are improving teacher and principal effectiveness and ensuring the equitable distribution of effective teachers and principals. To measure, develop, and improve the effectiveness of their teachers, leaders, and preparation programs, states and districts will be required to put in place a few specific policies and systems, including:

- Statewide definitions of "effective teacher," "effective principal," "highly effective teacher," and "highly effective principal," developed in collaboration with teachers, principals, and other stakeholders, that are based in significant part on student growth and also include other measures, such as classroom observations of practice. As states transition to using these measures of effectiveness, we will maintain the provisions of current law relating to "Highly Qualified Teachers," but with additional flexibility.
- State-level data systems that link information on teacher and principal preparation programs to the job placement, student growth, and retention outcomes of their graduates.
- District-level evaluation systems that (i) meaningfully differentiate teachers and principals by effectiveness across at least three performance levels; (ii) are consistent with their state's definitions of "effective" and "highly effective" teacher and principal; (iii) provide meaningful feedback to teachers and principals to improve their practice and inform professional development; and (iv) are developed in collaboration with teachers, principals, and other education stakeholders.

Developing Effective Teachers and Leaders. Both states and school districts will carry out strategies to develop effective teachers and leaders that meet their local needs.

States may use funds to recruit and develop effective teachers and principals, support the creation of effective educator career ladders, and improve teacher and principal certification and retention policies to better reflect a candidate's ability to improve outcomes for students. Recognizing the importance of principal leadership in supporting teachers, states will work to improve the effectiveness of principals, through activities such as strengthening principal preparation programs and providing training and support to principals of high-need schools. States will also be required to develop meaningful plans to ensure the equitable distribution of teachers and principals that receive at least an "effective" rating. If states are unsuccessful in improving the equitable distribution of these teachers and principals, they will be required to develop and implement more rigorous plans and additional strategies more likely to improve equity.

School districts may use funds to develop and implement fair and meaningful teacher and principal evaluation systems, working in collaboration with teachers, principals, and other stakeholders; to foster and provide collaboration and development opportunities in schools and build instructional teams of teachers, leaders, and other school staff, including paraprofessionals; to support educators in improving their instructional practice through effective, ongoing, job-embedded, professional development that is targeted to student and school needs; and to carry out other activities to improve the effectiveness of teachers, principals, and other school staff, and ensure the equitable distribution of effective teachers and principals. Funds spent on strategies such as professional development and class size reduction must be aligned with evidence of improvements in student learning.

Districts that have put in place the required evaluation systems may generally spend funds flexibly, except that a district that is not improving equity in the distribution of effective teachers and principals will be required to submit a new plan to the state under which funds will be spent solely on ensuring its evaluation system meets the requirements described above and on specific activities aimed at improving the equitable distribution of effective teachers and principals.

Measuring Success. We will require transparency around the key indicators of whether students and schools have effective teachers and principals and whether teachers have the professional supports they need. Both states and districts must publish report cards at least every two years that provide information on key indicators, such as teacher qualifications and teacher and principal designations of effectiveness; teachers and principals hired from high-performing pathways; teacher survey data on levels of support and working conditions in schools; the novice status of teachers and principals; teacher and principal attendance; and retention rates of teachers by performance level. States will also be required to report on the performance of teacher and principal preparation programs by their graduates' impact on student growth and other measures, job placement, and retention.

Teacher and Leader Innovation Fund

Our proposal will continue competitive grants for states and school districts that are willing to implement ambitious reforms to better identify, recruit, prepare, develop, retain, reward, and advance effective teachers, principals, and school leadership teams in high-need schools. Grantees must be able to differentiate among teachers and principals on the basis of their students' growth and other measures, and must use this information to differentiate, as applicable, credentialing, professional development, and retention and advancement decisions, and to reward highly effective teachers and principals in high- need schools. School districts must also put in place policies to help ensure that principals are able to select and build a strong team of teachers with a shared vision and that teachers are choosing to be part of a school team.

Grantees may use funds to reform compensation systems to provide differentiated compensation and career advancement opportunities to educators who are effective in increasing student academic achievement, who take on additional roles and responsibilities in their schools, and who teach in high-need schools, subjects, areas, and fields. Grantees may also use funds to staff high-need schools more effectively, such as through the implementation or use of earlier hiring timelines. States and districts will be encouraged to use these funds to take on additional innovative reforms, such as improving teacher salary schedules so as to eliminate incentives for teachers to obtain credentials that have been shown not to be linked with student performance. Additionally, states must describe the extent to which high-performing pathways are in place. In all cases, applicants will be required to provide evidence of stakeholder involvement in the development of their proposal.

Teacher and Leader Pathways

Our proposal will continue competitive grants to improve and strengthen the recruitment and preparation of effective teachers, principals, and other school leaders by nonprofit organizations, colleges and universities, and school districts, through high- quality preparation programs that prepare educators for high-need districts, schools, subjects, areas, and fields.

Teacher Pathways. To strengthen traditional and alternative pathways into teaching, our proposal includes competitive grants for the recruitment, preparation, placement, and induction of promising teacher candidates for high-need schools, subjects, areas, and fields. Programs must be designed to meet the specific teacher needs of a district or districts, and must either have a record of preparing effective teachers or commit to tracking and measuring the effectiveness of their graduates in the classroom.

In making grants, the Secretary will take into account whether programs will prepare teachers to teach to college- and career-ready standards; the extent to which programs are designed to meet the needs of high-need areas, including rural areas, or high-need fields, such as teaching English Learners, students with disabilities, or other students with diverse learning needs; and the extent to which programs provide streamlined opportunities for applicants who can demonstrate competency in specific knowledge or skills. Priority may be given to programs that work to recruit and prepare high- performing college graduates or non-traditional candidates, such as military veterans or midcareer professionals. The Secretary also will carry out a teacher recruitment campaign, working with states, districts, and outside organizations to recruit talented candidates into the teaching profession.

Transformational Leaders. To strengthen traditional and alternative pathways into school leadership, our proposal includes competitive grants for the recruitment, preparation, and support of effective principals and leadership teams to turn around persistently low-performing schools.

Grantees must either have a record of preparing effective leaders or commit to tracking and measuring the effectiveness of their graduates, as well as provide a substantial residency or field-based component and induction support for new principals and other leaders to succeed. Priority will be given to programs that commit to put in place conditions that increase the likelihood that their graduates and other principals will succeed in improving low-performing schools, such as providing autonomy over staffing, budget, instructional program, and schedule; and those with a record of preparing principals who improve student academic achievement and other outcomes at low- performing schools. Finally, the Secretary will make grants to recruit, prepare, place, and support the retention of effective state and district leaders, such as superintendents, chief academic officers, and human resource directors, who are able to lead transformational change in their states and districts.

Meeting the Needs of English Learners and Other Diverse Learners

America's schools are responsible for meeting the educational needs of an increasingly diverse student population, and ESEA programs must provide a wide range of resources and support to ensure that all students have the opportunity to succeed in college and in a career. ESEA includes programs that help schools meet the special educational needs of children working to learn the English language, students with disabilities, Native American students, homeless students, the children of migrant workers, and neglected or delinquent students. In addition, the federal government has a responsibility to provide assistance to certain high-need regions and areas, including rural districts and districts that are affected by federal property and activities.

In each of these areas, the Administration's ESEA reauthorization proposal will continue and strengthen the federal commitment to serving all students, and improve each program to ensure that funds are used more effectively to meet the needs of the students they serve.

A Continued Commitment

- Improving programs for English Learners and encouraging innovative programs and practices to support English Learners' success and build the knowledge base about what works.
- Maintaining and strengthening formula grant programs for Native American students, homeless students, migrant students, and neglected or delinquent students; as well as for districts that are in rural areas or that are affected by federal property and activities.
- Meeting the needs of students with disabilities throughout ESEA and through the Individuals with Disabilities Education Act.

Students with Disabilities

While the primary funding for programs specifically focused on supporting students with disabilities is through the Individuals with Disabilities Education Act, our ESEA reauthorization proposal will increase support for the inclusion and improved outcomes of students with disabilities. Our proposal will help ensure that teachers and leaders are better prepared to meet the needs of diverse learners, that assessments more accurately and appropriately measure the performance of students with disabilities, and that more districts and schools implement high-quality, state- and locally-determined curricula and instructional supports that incorporate the principles of universal design for learning to meet all students' needs.

English Learner Education

Our proposal will continue to provide significant formula grants to help states and school districts implement high-quality language instruction educational programs to improve the education of English Learners. Grantees may provide dual-language programs, transitional bilingual education, sheltered English immersion, newcomer programs for late-entrant English Learners, or other language instruction educational programs. Grantees may also provide effective professional development for all teachers of English Learners, including teachers of academic content areas, that is responsive to demonstrated needs identified by evaluations. To ensure that formula grant assistance in these areas supports the conditions needed to foster English Learners' success, we will require states to:

- Establish new criteria to ensure consistent statewide identification of students as English Learners, and to determine eligibility, placement, and duration of programs and services, based on the state's valid and reliable English language proficiency assessment.
- Implement a system to evaluate the effectiveness of language instruction educational programs, and to provide information on the achievement of subgroups of English Learners, to drive better decisions by school districts for program improvement, and to support districts in selecting effective programs.

Districts that are not improving the performance of English Learners will lose flexibility around the use of funds under this program, and must work with the state to implement more effective strategies.

Our proposal will also provide new competitive grants to states, districts, and nonprofit partners to support the development of innovative programs, build the knowledge base about promising practices, and scale up effective practices to improve instruction for English Learners, including funding for graduate fellowships to support research and leadership in developing effective practices to improve English Learner outcomes, as well as state or district partnerships with colleges and universities for developing effective teachers.

In addition, under the College- and Career-Ready Students program, states will be required to adopt and implement statewide grade-by-grade English language proficiency standards that are linked to the state's college- and career-ready academic content standards.

Migrant Education

Our proposal will continue and strengthen formula grants to states, districts, and other providers to meet the educational needs of migrant students. To ensure that funds are most effectively targeted to the areas in which migrant students live, we will update the current funding formula to incorporate more accurate and timely data. We will also strengthen and facilitate interstate efforts to support the educational transition of migrant students into local schools and communities.

Homeless Children and Youths Education

Our proposal will continue and strengthen formula grants to help states and districts put in place systems and services to meet the educational needs of homeless students. First, we will better target funds to serve homeless students by allocating funds on the basis of counts of homeless students rather than by shares of Title I allocations. Second, we will remove barriers to effective services for homeless children. And third, we will clarify provisions of the current statute where ambiguity resulted in delays in services for homeless children and youths. Our proposal will also increase transparency by requiring grantees to report on the academic outcomes for students served by the program.

Neglected and Delinquent Children and Youths Education

Our proposal will continue and strengthen formula grants to states to improve educational services for students in state-operated institutions and community day programs for neglected or delinquent children and youths. To better direct funds to support students in locally-operated institutions, our proposal will ask districts to reserve funds received under the College- and Career-Ready Students program to support programs conducted by locally-operated institutions.

Indian, Native Hawaiian, and Alaska Native Education

Our proposal will continue strong support – through formula and competitive grants to states; districts; Indian tribes; Indian institutions of higher education; Indian, Native Hawaiian, and Alaska Native educational and community-based organizations; and nonprofit organizations, agencies, and institutions – to help meet the unique needs of Indian students, Native Hawaiian students, and Alaska Native students.

Grantees under the Indian education program will have greater flexibility to use funds to carry out programs that meet the needs of Indian students, including Native language immersion and Native language restoration programs, and develop tribal specific standards and assessments. Our proposal will improve access to funds for Indian tribes under other ESEA programs, and recognize and strengthen the role of tribal education departments in coordinating and implementing services and programs for Indian students within their jurisdiction. To ensure that programs reflect the academic, language, and cultural needs of Indian students, we will continue to require the participation of the parents of Indian children in the design of programs. To support effective programs, we will expand eligibility to school districts and public charter schools under the Native Hawaiian and Alaska Native programs.

Rural Education

Our proposal will continue formula grants to rural districts to address the specific needs of students in rural areas, through the Small, Rural School Achievement (SRSA) and the Rural and Low-Income School (RLIS) programs. In order to improve targeting of funds, we will update the method used to identify districts as rural. To allow additional districts needed flexibility, our proposal will also expand the current "REAP Flex" authority, which allows eligible small districts to use other federal education funds flexibly, to districts that are eligible to receive funds under RLIS. In addition, we will better align the accountability requirements of the College- and Career-Ready Students program with the rural education program, so that the rural education program supports school improvement efforts in persistently low-performing districts.

To help rural districts apply for competitive grants and determine effective strategies for improving student academic achievement, the Secretary may reserve funds for national activities such as technical assistance and research on innovative programs that are designed to help rural districts overcome common capacity constraints.

Impact Aid

Our reauthorization proposal will continue significant formula grant support designed to compensate districts for the expense of educating federally-connected children and for the presence in their districts of tax-exempt federal property or other property removed from the tax rolls by the federal government. Because these funds are compensatory, districts enjoy broad flexibility in the use of these funds.

A Complete Education

As we ask states to raise their standards to prepare their students for college and the workplace, we will also be asking more from students, families, teachers, principals, and every level of the educational system. To make higher standards meaningful, we must ensure that states, districts, schools, and teachers have the resources and assistance they need to help students reach these standards, such as instructional supports, high-quality professional development, and teaching and learning materials aligned with those standards. This means a new investment in improving teaching and learning in all content areas – from literacy to science, technology, engineering, and mathematics to history, civics, foreign languages, the arts, financial literacy, environmental education, and other subjects – and in providing accelerated learning opportunities to more students to make postsecondary success more attainable.

A New Approach

- Strengthening instruction in literacy and in science, technology, engineering, and mathematics, aligned with improved standards that build toward college- and career-readiness.
- Supporting teachers and students in teaching and learning to more rigorousstandards that prepare students for college and a career.
- Improving access to a well-rounded education for students in high-need schools.
- Expanding access to college coursework and other accelerated learningopportunities for students in high-need schools.

Literacy

Our proposal will provide competitive grants to support the transition to higher standards by assisting states in strengthening their literacy programs and by providing substantial support to high-need districts in implementing high-quality literacy instruction. States will be required to develop comprehensive, evidence-based, preK–12 literacy plans and to align federal, state, and local funds to provide high-quality literacy instruction. States may carry out strategies to improve literacy instruction statewide, such as supporting districts in identifying effective instructional materials and improving teachers' knowledge and skills in effective literacy instruction for all students, including English Learners and students with disabilities.

Priority will be given to states that have adopted common, state-developed, college- and career-ready standards. Priority may also be given to states that use technology to address student learning challenges, which may include the principles of universal design for learning.

States will provide competitive subgrants to high-need districts to support comprehensive literacy programs in the grades and schools with the greatest local need. Programs must provide effective professional development for teachers and school leaders; high- quality state- or locally-determined curricula, instructional materials, and assessments; interventions that ensure that all students are served appropriately; and language- and text-rich classroom environments that engage and motivate students. Literacy programs may also include activities related to family literacy, improving library services, and other efforts to improve literacy.

Priority will be given to districts that propose to align other local, state, and federal resources with their plan to improve literacy instruction; propose to implement programs that have the strongest available evidence; propose to implement activities in the schools with the greatest need; or have a plan for sustaining the strategy.

Science, Technology, Engineering, and Mathematics (STEM)

Our proposal will provide competitive grants to support the transition to higher standards by assisting states in strengthening their STEM programs and by providing substantial support to high-need districts in implementing high-quality instruction in at least mathematics or science and may also include technology or engineering. States will be required to develop comprehensive, evidence-based plans and to align federal, state, and local funds to provide high-quality STEM instruction. States may carry out strategies to improve STEM instruction statewide, such as partnering with statewide Race to the Top partnerships, supporting districts in identifying effective instructional materials, and improving teachers' knowledge and skills in effective STEM instruction for all students, including English Learners and students with disabilities.

Priority will be given to states that have adopted common, state-developed, college- and career-ready standards. Priority may also be given to states that use technology to address student learning challenges, which may include the principles of universal design for learning; cooperate with outside partners with STEM expertise; or propose to prepare more students, including students from underrepresented groups, for advanced study and careers in STEM.

States will award competitive subgrants to high-need districts to support comprehensive STEM instruction in the grades and schools with the greatest local need. Programs must provide effective professional development for teachers and school leaders; high-quality state- or locally-determined curricula, instructional materials, and assessments; and interventions that ensure that all students are served appropriately. Subgrantees may use program funds to integrate evidence-based, effective mathematics or science programs into the teaching of other core academic subjects and for technology-based strategies to improve STEM education.

Priority will be given to districts that propose to align other local, state, and federal resources with their plan to improve instruction in STEM subjects; propose to implement programs that have the strongest available evidence; propose to implement activities in the schools with the greatest need; or have a plan for sustaining the strategy.

Ensuring a Well-Rounded Education

To help more students in high-need schools receive a well-rounded education, our proposal will provide competitive grants to states, high-need districts, and nonprofit partners to strengthen the teaching and learning of arts, foreign languages, history and civics, financial literacy, environmental education, and other subjects.

Grants may support either the development of new, promising instructional practices or the expansion of instructional practices for which there is evidence of improving student performance in one or more of these subjects. Such practices, which should be aimed at improving instruction for all students, including English Learners and students with disabilities, may include high-quality professional development, better assessments, high-quality state- or locally-determined curricula aligned with state standards, or innovative uses of technology.

Priority will be given to applicants proposing to integrate teaching and learning across academic subjects; to use technology to address student learning challenges; and at the high school level, to work with colleges or universities to ensure that coursework is truly aligned with those institutions' expectations.

College Pathways and Accelerated Learning

Our proposal will provide competitive grants to states, districts, and nonprofit partners to increase access to accelerated learning opportunities for students. At the high school level, these opportunities will include college-level work. At the elementary and middle school levels, these opportunities will include access to gifted and talented education programs.

Grantees will carry out activities that help students prepare for, or directly provide, college-level work (including early-college or dual-enrollment programs, Advanced Placement (AP) programs, and International Baccalaureate programs), other accelerated learning programs, and gifted and talented programs in elementary or middle schools. Applicants may propose additional activities, such as allowing credit based on successful demonstration of competency via examination or other valid means, or providing counseling, mentoring, or programs to develop study skills. Priority will be given to applicants that propose to serve high schools with low graduation rates and that partner with state higher education offices and institutions of higher education in a program that allows higher education credits to be portable beyond the individual partner institution or institutions. Our proposal will continue to provide support to states to improve access to AP tests for low-income students.

Activities to Strengthen a Complete Education

Under our proposal, the Secretary will set aside funds to carry out additional activities to improve teaching and learning in academic subjects, such as grants for the creation of high-quality educational digital content; grants to states to develop and improve their capacity to use technology to improve instruction; or grants to nonprofits to develop and implement innovative and effective strategies to improve the teaching and learning of specific subjects.

SUCCESSFUL, SAFE, AND HEALTHY STUDENTS

Supporting student success requires deploying every tool at our disposal. The students most at risk for academic failure too often attend schools and live in communities with insufficient capacity to address the full range of their needs. The result is that students cannot always focus on learning and teachers cannot always focus on teaching.

Preparing students for success requires taking innovative, comprehensive approaches to meeting students' needs, such as rethinking the length and structure of the school day and year, so that students have the time they need to succeed and teachers have the time they need to collaborate and improve their practice. It means supporting innovative models that provide the services that students need; time for teachers to collaborate to meet academic challenges; environments that help all students be safe, healthy, and supported in their classrooms, schools, and communities; and greater opportunities to engage families in their children's education and strengthen the role of schools as centers of communities.

A New Approach

- Providing a cradle through college and career continuum in high-poverty communities that provides effective schools, comprehensive services, and family supports.
- Supporting programs that redesign and expand the school schedule, provide high-quality afterschool programs, and provide comprehensive supports to students.
- Using data to improve students' safety, health, and well-being, and increasing the capacity of states, districts, and schools to create safe, healthy, and drug-free environments.

Promise Neighborhoods

Our proposal will provide new, competitive grants to support the development and implementation of a continuum of effective community services, strong family supports, and comprehensive education reforms to improve the educational and life outcomes for children and youths in high-need communities, from birth through college and into careers. Programs must be designed to improve academic and developmental outcomes for children and youths through effective public schools, community-based organizations, and other local agencies.

Programs will be encouraged to take a comprehensive approach to meeting student needs, drawing on the contributions of community-based organizations, local agencies, and family and community members. Grantees will conduct a needs assessment of all children in the community in order to establish baseline data against which the grantee will aim to improve outcomes, and will promote and coordinate community involvement, support, and buy-in, including securing and leveraging resources from the public and private sectors.

21st Century Community Learning Centers

Our proposal will provide competitive grants for states, school districts, nonprofit organizations, and partnerships to implement in school and out of school strategies that provide students and, where appropriate, teachers and family members, with additional time and supports to succeed.

Competitive grants will be awarded to states, school districts, and community-based organizations to leverage models that comprehensively redesign and expand the school day or year, provide full-service community schools, or provide services before school, after school, or during the summer. All programs will focus on improving student academic achievement in core academic subjects, ranging from English language arts, mathematics, and science, to history, the arts, and financial literacy, as part of a well- rounded education, and providing enrichment activities, which may include activities that improve mental and physical health, opportunities for experiential learning, and greater opportunities for families to actively and meaningfully engage in their children's education.

Priority will be given to applicants that propose to carry out programs to support the improvement of Challenge schools identified under the College- and Career-Ready Students program, and those that propose to implement comprehensive and coordinated programs, including comprehensively redesigning and expanding the school schedule for all students, providing comprehensive supports to students and families through full- service community school models, or establishing partnerships between school districts and nonprofit organizations for in school or out of school strategies.

Successful, Safe, and Healthy Students

Our proposal will provide competitive grants to support states, school districts, and their partners in providing learning environments that ensure that students are successful, safe, and healthy. To better measure school climate and identify local needs, grantees will be required to develop and implement a state- or district-wide school climate needs assessment to evaluate school engagement, school safety (addressing drug, alcohol, and violence issues), and school environment, and publicly report this information. This assessment must include surveys of student, school staff, and family experiences with respect to individual schools, and additional data such as suspensions and disciplinary actions. States will use this data to identify local needs and provide competitive subgrants to school districts and their partners to address the needs of students, schools, and communities.

Grantees will use funds under the Successful, Safe, and Healthy Students program to carry out strategies designed to improve school safety and to promote students' physical and mental health and well-being, nutrition education, healthy eating, and physical fitness. Grantees may support activities to prevent and reduce substance use, school violence (including teen dating violence), harassment, and bullying, as well as to strengthen family and community engagement in order to ensure a healthy and supportive school environment.

Priority will be given to applicants that propose to support partnerships between districts and nonprofit organizations, including community-based organizations. Priority will also be given to grantees willing to direct funds to schools with the greatest need, including Challenge schools, as identified under the College- and Career-Ready Students program, or schools with the greatest needs as identified through the school climate needs assessment.

FOSTERING INNOVATION AND EXCELLENCE

For all students to thrive in the classroom, in college, and in a career, our educational system must continuously develop and embrace the very best practices, policies, and ideas. Innovative practices are constantly emerging to help more students graduate ready for college and a career. We will ask policymakers and educators at all levels to carefully analyze the impact of their policies, practices, and systems on student outcomes. We will provide students and families with increased high-quality public school educational options, and empower them with improved information about the options available to them. And across programs, we will focus less on compliance and more on enabling effective local strategies to flourish.

A New Approach

- Providing incentives for a Race to the Top among states and districts willing to take on ambitious, comprehensive reforms.
- Developing, validating, and scaling up promising and proven educational strategies to improve student outcomes.
- Expanding educational options to increase choice within the public school system through high-performing new schools and meaningful public school choice.

Race to the Top

Modeled after the Race to the Top program authorized by the American Recovery and Reinvestment Act of 2009, our proposal will provide competitive grants to states and school districts to take on ambitious and comprehensive reforms, and to encourage the broad identification, dissemination, adoption, and use of effective policies and practices. State and school district grantees will be required to develop and implement comprehensive plans, in collaboration with other stakeholders, to dramatically improve student outcomes, including focusing on rigorous college- and career-ready standards and high-quality assessments; providing better information to families to help them evaluate and improve their children's schools, and to educators to help them improve their students' learning; supporting effective teachers and school leaders; turning around persistently low-performing schools; and supporting innovative models for reform.

States and school districts that receive grants may spend funds flexibly in a manner aligned with their plans, but states must award at least 50 percent of their grant funds to school districts that participate in the state plan. Grantees will be required to meet specific annual performance targets related to the implementation of their plan and to improving measurable outcomes for students and schools, and will receive continuation funding only if they implement their proposed plans effectively and meet their performance targets. Grantees must invest in rigorous evaluation of their ongoing performance and reform efforts.

Investing in Innovation (i3)

This program builds on the i3 program launched through the American Recovery and Reinvestment Act of 2009, and will provide additional competitive grants to expand the implementation of, and investment in, innovative and evidence-based practices, programs, and strategies that significantly improve student outcomes. The Secretary will use a rigorous, three-tiered evidence framework that directs the highest levels of funding to programs with the strongest evidence, and also provides significant support for promising programs that are willing to undergo rigorous evaluation. Grantees will use funds to scale up practices, strategies, or programs for which there is strong evidence of success in significantly closing achievement gaps between groups of students and in significantly increasing student academic achievement for all groups of students; validate and expand practices, strategies, or programs for which there is moderate evidence of success; or develop and test promising practices, strategies, or programs for which there is potential and some research-based support. Each grantee will be required to conduct or participate in an independent evaluation of its project. Grantees will be required to form partnerships with the private sector to secure matching funds.

Applicants will be required to propose projects that develop or expand innovations in critical areas of education reform. The Secretary may also give preference to applicants that propose to develop or expand innovations around specific pressing needs, such as improving the teaching and learning of STEM subjects, improving early learning outcomes, addressing the learning needs of English Learners and students with disabilities, and serving schools in rural areas. The Secretary will also reserve funds for inducement prizes to drive breakthrough inventions in education or for dramatic and innovative approaches to improving educational outcomes.

Expanding Educational Options

In addition to broad-based comprehensive state and local reforms and the expansion of evidence-based practices and innovations, the Administration's ESEA reauthorization proposal will encourage educational entrepreneurship by expanding competitive grants aimed at increasing the supply of high-quality public educational options available to students.

Supporting Effective Charter Schools. Our proposal will provide competitive grants to states, charter school authorizers, charter management organizations, districts, and nonprofit organizations, to start or expand high-performing public charter schools and other high-performing autonomous public schools, with a priority for applicants proposing to start or expand high-performing public charter schools. Autonomous schools are public schools that, as much or even more than charter schools, have ongoing autonomy over key operational elements, including staffing, budget, schedule, and program. Both charter schools and other autonomous schools funded under this program must be subject to the same accountability systems as traditional public schools, as well as increased accountability for improving student academic achievement.

To ensure that funds are used to start or expand high-performing schools that improve outcomes for all subgroups of students, applicants will be evaluated based on their record of past success in funding, supporting, authorizing, managing, or operating (as relevant) high-performing public charter schools or other high-performing public autonomous schools; their record of cutting off funding to or closing low-performing charter schools or other low-performing autonomous schools; and their commitment to improving the quality of their schools in the future. Grantees will be required to develop plans to appropriately serve all students in charter or other autonomous schools, including English Learners and students with disabilities, and to provide information to ensure students and families are aware of and able to apply to these schools. The Secretary may reserve a portion of funds to improve charter schools' access to facilities or to facilities financing.

To build greater capacity to support and hold schools accountable under this program, grantees at all levels will be allowed to set aside funds to improve their capacity to oversee and support schools funded under this program. Additionally, charter management organizations that commit to work with districts to support the districts in implementing effective strategies in district schools may be eligible for larger grants.

Promoting Public School Choice. Our proposal will continue to provide competitive grants to districts, consortia of districts, and states in partnership with districts to expand high-quality public school educational options for students, especially students in low-performing schools, and ensure that students and families are aware of these options. Grantees will use funds to implement programs that increase high-quality public school options for students, especially students in low-performing schools, through creating or expanding inter- and intradistrict choice programs, theme-based schools, high- quality online learning programs, or academic pathways. Grantees must also carry out activities to provide students, families, and the community with information about how to identify, evaluate, and access high-quality educational options. Priority will be given to interdistrict choice programs and programs that provide comprehensive choices to every student in a district. Priority will also be given to programs that increase diversity in the schools served by the program.

Magnet Schools Assistance Program. Our proposal will continue to provide competitive grants to districts to support magnet schools under a desegregation plan ordered by a federal court, state court, or other authorized state agency or official, or approved by the Secretary. The reauthorized program will expand and improve options for students and increase diversity by placing a greater emphasis on funding whole- school magnet school programs or models that have a record of success in raising student academic achievement and reducing minority group isolation.

ADDITIONAL CROSS-CUTTING PRIORITIES

Throughout this proposal, we have sought to redefine the federal role in education: shifting from a focus merely on compliance to allowing state and local innovation to flourish, rewarding success, and fostering supportive and collaborative relationships with states, districts, and nonprofit partners. There are several cross-cutting changes we are proposing in order to allow local innovations to lead the way and to support the development, identification, and scaling-up of strategies that are working.

A New Approach

- Increasing flexibility in return for improved outcomes.
- Expanding programs, projects, and strategies that show results.
- Focusing on key priorities across programs.

Flexibility for Success

A re-envisioned federal role means giving states and districts additional flexibility in how they spend federal dollars as long as they are continuing to focus on what matters most – improving outcomes for students. States and districts will be allowed to use most federal administrative funds and reservations flexibly to build their own capacity to support reform and improvement. Most districts will also be allowed to spend more ESEA program funds flexibly, as long as they continue to comply with the conditions associated with those funds and are improving student outcomes.

Growing Success

Where grantees are successfully improving outcomes for students, we should not only reward them, but replicate their successful practices. For each competitive program in this proposal, grantees that are significantly improving outcomes will be eligible for both continuation funds and additional funds to expand their strategies to additional students, schools, districts, or states. This will ensure that federal funds flow to projects that are successfully serving students.

Evaluation and Building the Knowledge Base

To foster ongoing improvement of ESEA programs and to advance knowledge in the field, investments are needed in data analysis and evaluation at the federal, state, and local levels. Consequently, this proposal encourages federal, state, and local levels to work together to use data for continuous improvement, test innovative ideas, evaluate and replicate promising approaches, and scale up what strong research evidence suggests works across all ESEA programs. In addition, a new evaluation authority will authorize rigorous, objective evaluations of ESEA programs, policies, and practices and support performance measurement of those programs. The Secretary will submit to Congress a biennial plan on ESEA evaluation and performance measurement and will establish an independent panel that advises on the plan.

Cross-Cutting Priorities

There are some priorities that are relevant in numerous areas of education reform. We may apply specific priorities across programs, as appropriate, including priorities for:

(1) **Technology.** Technology, effectively and thoughtfully deployed, can improve how schools work, how teachers teach, and how students learn. Priority may be given to programs, projects, or strategies that leverage digital information or communications technology to accomplish the stated goals of the grant.

(2) **Evidence.** As evidence develops in new areas, funding should be devoted to the areas with the most evidence of effectiveness in improving outcomes for students. Priority may be given to programs, projects, or strategies on the strength of their evidentiary base.

(3) **Efficiency.** Particularly in the current economic situation, it is important to do more with fewer resources. Priority may be given to programs, projects, or strategies that are designed to significantly increase efficiency in the use of resources to improve student outcomes.

(4) **Supporting English Learners and Students With Disabilities.** Schools, districts, and states must be held responsible for educating all students, including English Learners and students with disabilities, to high standards, but more work could be done to develop and scale up effective strategies for these students. Priority may be given to programs, projects, or strategies that are designed to specifically improve the performance of English Learners or students with disabilities.

(5) **Supporting Rural and Other High-Need Areas.** In new competitive programs, we will be putting in place appropriate strategies to ensure that rural districts and other high-need districts are not disadvantaged and are able to receive the funding they need to help students succeed. Priority may be given to programs or projects designed to serve rural and other high-need areas.

CHAPTER SOURCES

The following chapters have been previously published:

Chapter 1 - This is an edited, reformatted and augmented version of a Congressional Research Service publication, report R41533, dated February 7, 2011.

Chapter 2 - This is an edited, reformatted and augmented version of a Congressional Research Service publication, report R41267, dated November 18, 2010.

Chapter 3 - This is an edited, reformatted and augmented version of a Congressional Research Service publication, report R40576, dated January 3, 2011.

Chapter 4 - This is an edited, reformatted and augmented version of a Congressional Research Service publication, report RL33960, dated January 5, 2011.

Chapter 5 - This is an edited, reformatted and augmented version of a United States Department of Education publication dated March 2010.

INDEX

D

E

F

G

M

N

O

P

Q

R

S

V

W

Y